WILDERNESS FEVER

A Family's Adventures Homesteading
In Early Jackson Hole, 1914-1924

Linda and Harold (Mac) McKinstry in 1915 or 1916.

WILDERNESS FEVER

A Family's Adventures Homesteading
In Early Jackson Hole, 1914-1924

with a foreword by

SHERRY L. SMITH, PH.D.

University Distinguished Professor of History

Linda Preston McKinstry

with Harold Cole McKinstry

HIGH PLAINS PRESS

Front cover illustration: Oxbow Bend near Moran, Wyoming (Shutterstock)
Linda and Harold McKinstry (McKinstry Family Collection)

LIBRARY OF CONGRESS CATALOGING-IN-PUBLICATION DATA

Names: McKinstry, Linda Preston, author. | McKinstry, Harold Cole, author.
Title: Wilderness fever : a family's adventures homesteading in early Jackson
    Hole, 1914-1924 / Linda Preston McKinstry with Harold Cole Mc-
    Kinstry; with a foreword by Sherry L. Smith, Ph.d., University Distin-
    guished Professor of History.
Description: Glendo, WY : High Plains Press, 2016. | Includes index.
Identifiers: LCCN 2016033142 | ISBN 9781937147112 (trade paper : alk.
    paper)
Subjects: LCSH: McKinstry, Linda Preston. | McKinstry, Harold Cole. | Jack-
    son Hole Region (Wyo.)--Description and travel.
Classification: LCC F767.T28 M395 2016 | DDC 978.7/55--dc23
LC record available at https://lccn.loc.gov/2016033142

FIRST PRINTING
10 9 8 7 6 5 4 3 2 1
Manufactured in the United States of America

HIGH PLAINS PRESS
403 CASSA ROAD, GLENDO, WY 82213
WWW.HIGHPLAINSPRESS.COM
ORDERS & CATALOGS: 1-800-552-7819

~ℰ CONTENTS ℰ~

Wrestling for Wilderness

For most Americans, the word "homesteader" evokes an image of a nine-teenth-century man striding into the West leading a sun-bonneted wife, a clutch of tow-headed children, and a pair of oxen or stocky horses hauling a wagon of supplies. Their destination: a sod hut on the wide open prairie. Part of the inspiration for this picture is undoubtedly movies and television shows or novels such as Laura Ingalls Wilder's *Little House on the Prairie* or Willa Cather's *My Antonia*. Of course, there is some historical justification for this impression. The Homestead Act which provided people the oppor-tunity to gain a free slice of the nation's public lands dates to the Civil War era. It was, initially, a nineteenth-century phenomenon and certainly helped greatly accelerate the peopling of the Plains.

Yet, much of Wyoming, with its arid high plains and mountains, did not attract significant numbers of homesteaders until the turn of the twen-tieth century. Several factors explain this. The greater attraction of more suitable farm and ranch land and better access to transportation and markets elsewhere was certainly crucial in explaining Wyoming's tardy involvement. Jackson Hole, ringed by mountain ranges, was particularly isolated and its altitude and rocky soil posed impediments, too. However, as prices for agricultural products increased and a "back to the land" movement (in re-sponse to the more distressing consequences of urbanization and industri-alization) emerged among the educated middle class, Wyoming's high, dry grasslands and its remote northwest mountain region beckoned.

Linda and Harold McKinstry, then, were among those who started anew in homesteading's later phase, staking their claim to a patch of countryside near Moran in 1915. The very earliest Jackson Hole home-steaders had arrived thirty years before, in 1884, when John Holland and

[1] John Daugherty, *A Place Called Jackson Hole: The Historic Resource Study of Grand Teton National Park* (Moose, Wyoming: Grand Teton National Park, 1999), 109; Michael Cassity, *Wyoming Will Be Your New Home...Ranching, Farming, and Homesteading in Wyoming, 1860-1960* (Cheyenne: Wyoming State Historic Preservation Office, 2011), 104-5.

[2] Cassity, 11.

John Carnes selected their homestead lands in the Flat Creek area (near the present day town of Jackson). The following year a handful of Mormon families, the Wilsons and Cheneys, settled along Fish Creek and South Park, having migrated over Teton Pass from Idaho. But the real surge in homesteading came decades later, peaking between 1908 and 1919. It unfolded in a south to north trajectory, eventually spreading to the Gros Ventre River, Spring Gulch, Moose, Jackson Lake, and finally to the Moran/Pacific Creek areas.[1]

So, what propelled the McKinstrys west and were they typical Jackson Hole homesteaders? From their own accounts, their motive seemed straightforward and commonplace. Harold McKinstry, tiring of his bureaucratic job in Washington, D.C., longed to be a rancher. He and his bride were ripe for adventure and their government was offering free land. They may have shared the century-old Jeffersonian vision of the public domain as a resource which, as historian Michael Cassity aptly described it, would create a nation of "independent producers" who would "subsist in freedom, and ...prosper morally and politically, if not always financially."[2] Many homesteaders embraced this prospect, so why not the McKinstrys?

Yet, this couple had certain qualities which set them apart from other Wyoming homesteaders. Both were college educated, young professionals living and working in an urban setting—Linda as a home economics teacher and Harold as an employee of the Department of Agriculture. Neither had experience with ranching or living in the arid and mountainous west. Linda grew up in Massachusetts. Harold hailed from North Dakota where he had studied dryland farming at North Dakota State University. So Harold, at least, had some background in agriculture. Still, they both faced steep learning curves when they arrived at their homestead on Pacific Creek.

Interestingly, it was a *Saturday Evening Post* article about Jackson Hole's potential for cattle ranching that initially brought the valley to Harold's attention. Consequently, he included it in his itinerary during a whirlwind tour of Montana, Idaho and Wyoming in the summer of 1914 in search of just the right spot for his homestead. Once in Jackson Hole, he became convinced the Teton area was the place for him. Although he did not say so in his fragmentary memoir, it seems quite possible the aesthetic appeal of Jackson Hole played some role in the choice. Who can resist the pleasures of Rocky Mountain summer days? The beauty of the Tetons had certainly attracted an influential cluster of other Jackson Hole homesteaders whose educational and economic profile resembled that of the McKinstrys. Princeton-educated Struthers Burt and his wife novelist Katherine Burt took up land along the Snake River to develop their famous Bar BC Dude Ranch.

Geraldine Lucas, an Oberlin College graduate and retired teacher from New York City, planted herself at the base of the Grand Teton in 1913 primarily because of its stunning view of the mountains.[3]

The Burts, Lucas and the McKinstrys all shared one other thing. They brought capital. They had means. They were not a hardscrabble bunch. If the homestead venture did not pan out, they had other options. Yet the McKinstrys were more "typical" homesteaders in one respect: they came to establish a working cattle ranch. They hoped to earn their living from the land, not from dudes. In their struggle to get the enterprise off the ground —even with the railroad boxcar load of machinery, tools, and the impressive, top-of-the-line Majestic Range (kitchen stove) they brought with them— they replicated the experience of many Wyoming homesteaders. They endured incredibly hard physical labor and the loneliness of long winter months with short days and deep snows. They relied upon neighbors for help. They took joy in community social events and shared the sorrow of other families' losses. Linda longed for women's companionship and in their ultimate failure to actually achieve their original dreams, their experience was "classic."

Among the McKinstry neighbors on the terraces along Pacific Creek were Elmer Arthur, the Bramans and the Snells. William Thompson filed on 160 acres at the outlet of Two Ocean Lake and Samuel Wilson homesteaded along Pilgrim Creek. All arrived around the same time, hoping to graze their cattle on National Forest Service lands during the summer and grow sufficient hay on their homesteads to feed their livestock through the winter.[4] Weather, altitude, isolation, and the short growing season posed near impossible challenges.

They soon realized, however, they shared additional concerns and possible obstacles to their success—issues particular to their corner of the state. Northwest Wyoming, for all its isolation, was not unknown. Other people with other interests competed with the homesteaders for the power to ultimately decide the future of its lands and waters. Would it sustain small ranches? Would its water snake around the Teton range and irrigate Idaho farms? Or would it become parkland, either as part of Yellowstone National Park or perhaps a distinctive park in its own right?

Farmers and ranchers in Idaho, for instance, hoped to control the clear, cold water, planning to dam lakes and transport water to the west side of the Tetons for irrigation. Their first success came with the erection of Jackson Lake Dam in 1906 (replaced by today's concrete version in 1911). This Bureau of Reclamation Project elicited no protest whatsoever.[5] Then the irrigators set their sights on Jenny, Two Ocean and Emma Matilda Lakes. This time some of the federal government employees balked. Congress

[3] Daugherty, 115; Sherry L. Smith, "A Woman's Life in the Teton Country: Geraldine L. Lucas," *Montana: The Magazine of Western History*, 44 (Summer 1994): 18-33.

[4] Daugherty, 115.

[5] Robert W. Righter, *Crucible for Conservation The Struggle for Grand Teton National Park* (Moose: Grand Teton Natural History Association, 1982, reprinted 2000), 9-10.

had created Yellowstone National Park in 1872 to protect that vast expanse from development. It consequently closed parklands to settlement. By the turn of the century, some began to lobby to expand its boundaries to incorporate the startling beauty of Jackson Hole and close it all to homesteading and additional water diversion projects. Further, the realization that the wasteful dispersal of public lands and resources during the nineteenth century was no longer sustainable led Congress to pass the Forest Reserve Act in 1891. This remarkable piece of legislation allowed Presidents to set aside land as national forests with the power to regulate the resources and withdraw these lands from homesteading, as well. The consequences for northwest Wyoming were dramatic.

President Benjamin Harrison was the first to exercise these powers, creating Yellowstone Park Timber Reserve in 1891 that included the northern reaches of Jackson Hole. Six years later President Grover Cleveland effectively closed most of the valley, north of the forty-second parallel, to homesteading when he established the 829,440 acre Teton Forest Reserve. In 1908, President Theodore Roosevelt expanded that reserve to 1,991,200 acres but simultaneously reopened the valley lands to settlement. This helped set off a "small-scale land rush" in Jackson Hole.[6] In short, the federal presence in the area was considerable and actually preceded most homesteaders. Importantly, neither the National Forest Service, created in 1908, nor the National Park Service, established in 1916, considered homesteaders' interests as necessarily pre-eminent. In fact, it is fair to say national parks and homesteads had antithetical goals.

For the McKinstrys and their neighbors, the greater concern came from those with ambitions to expand Yellowstone National Park. As early as 1897, Colonel S.B.M. Young, the park's Superintendent, suggested the park's southern boundary be extended into Jackson Hole. The following year Director of the United States Geological Survey Charles D. Walcott concurred; or, if that proved politically difficult, he recommended Congress create a separate national park. Interestingly, his greatest concern was protecting the elk herd rather than the scenic values of the Teton Range or the valley at its base. Congress, however, failed to respond to either option.[7]

The next push came when Stephen Mather and Horace Albright, Interior Department employees in charge of the national parks, came through the Teton Country in 1915. They immediately hoped to incorporate the spectacular country into the park system. Once they secured the more formal bureaucratic power of the National Park Service in 1916, they enlisted the aid of Wyoming Congressman Frank Mondell to renew the park extension effort. Two years later he introduced a bill attaching the Tetons, the gorgeous lakes at its feet, and the country down to the Buffalo

[6] *Daugherty, 120.*

[7] *Righter, 22-3.*

Fork to Yellowstone National Park. This plan included the McKinstry "neighborhood." A slightly modified bill passed the House but failed in the Senate when an Idahoan, on behalf of constituents who feared (wrongly) they would lose grazing rights, killed it.[8]

The homesteaders of Pacific Creek and vicinity certainly followed these events. In fact, as Linda and Harold noted in their memoirs, representatives of the National Park Service including Yellowstone Superintendent Horace Albright, occasionally came through to talk with the settlers about park extension. The prospect of such an outcome undermined homesteaders' sense of security and raised doubts about whether investment in their properties would be worthwhile. Would they be allowed to remain as in-holders or would they be forced to sell out? Things looked particularly ominous when President Wilson issued a 1918 Executive Order that prevented all future forms of entry onto the Teton National Forest and allowed NPS veto power over any proposed developments, including water and irrigation projects, pending resolution of the Yellowstone extension issue. In fact, the NPS effectively used this power to stop a plan to dam Jenny Lake.[9]

Meanwhile, the McKinstrys and some of their neighbors filed for water rights to Emma Matilda and Two Ocean Lakes. Albright could have blocked these plans, as well. Instead he allowed them, supporting a right of way for their ditches. In return, Harold and a handful of others informed Albright they wanted to go on "record as being in favor" of the extension. He had calmed their fears, although one of the men later indicated people still worried that park jurisdiction would effect their right to carry firearms and exterminate wolves and coyotes. Other interests were less easily appeased, however. The National Forest Service, the livestock interests who opposed further federal controls, and the dude ranchers who also disliked rules, regulations, and roads, all continued to oppose extension. So the issue died, at least for another decade.[10]

In the thick of these competing interests, Harold McKinstry had the wherewithal to back up his dream to become a rancher with acquisition of an additional skill. He became a surveyor. This proved to be an important source of income for the family, as their ranching prospects were not flourishing. Local homesteaders hired him but so too did the Osgood Land and Livestock Company, a group of Idaho ranchers, who coveted northwest Wyoming waters. In 1920 they purchased one homestead below Two Ocean Lake and the water rights of six additional Pacific Creek area homesteads before constructing headgates at Two Ocean and Emma Matilda. By the early 1920s they began diverting water to Idaho. The following year the Utah-Idaho Sugar Company purchased these water rights. The state of Wyoming and the National Forest Service approved the plan but the NPS

[8] Ibid., 27-31.

[9] Daugherty, 174; Righter, 32-3.

[10] Daugherty, 308; Righter, 32-3.

did not, setting the stage for a legal showdown. In the meantime, McKinstry benefited from a steady income in the company's employ.[11]

Of course, Horace Albright opposed water diversion to Idaho, hoping to protect the Tetons from further development or what he may have seen as desecration. Finally, in 1928, Congress added the Teton range to Yellowstone. The following year President Calvin Coolidge signed a bill that established the area as the new, separate Grand Teton National Park. This, however, left the valley to the east open to potential exploitation. Not yet satisfied, Albright introduced John D. Rockefeller, Jr. to Jackson Hole, showing him the breath-taking landscape while educating him about the threats to it. He inspired the wealthy philanthropist to purchase the valley lands. Starting in 1928, Rockefeller eventually purchased, under the auspices of the Snake River Land Company, 33,562 acres and deeded them to the NPS in 1949.[12] Among the parcels he bought was the McKinstry homestead.

By the mid to late 1920s, the McKinstrys and many other homesteaders in Jackson Hole were ready to call it quits. As early as 1920, one rancher informed Albright that making a living on these properties was impossible. The "climate was too cold, the soil too barren, and . . . people were destroying the lives of themselves and their families by trying to ranch in this country."[13] An agricultural economic depression that hit rural America a full decade before the Great Depression slammed the rest of the country, only underscored the difficulties. True, once people learned it was John D. Rockefeller, Jr. who was buying up property, they were resentful. The idea of a wealthy Easterner coming in and determining the fate of Jackson Hole disturbed many. Complaints arose that the Snake River Land Company did not pay fair market prices. But historians have concluded such rumors were unfounded. The prices were fair and most homesteaders, though not all, were eager to sell.[14]

The Snake River Land Company also prevailed over the Idaho irrigators. Challenging the legality of separating water rights from the land, they claimed the Idaho Sugar Company did not control the waters they had purchased, after all. Rather, the Snake River Land Company, in buying up the homesteads, was the legal owner. The two sides fought this out in the courts between 1938 and 1942 with the Wyoming State Supreme Court finally siding with the Snake River Land Company and effectively ending Idaho's efforts to secure northern Jackson Hole water.[15]

By the 1940s it was clear the NPS had won the contest for control of Jackson Hole, peeling back National Forest Service jurisdiction as Grand Teton National Park expanded its boundaries and receiving the generous gift of homesteads and water rights from the Rockefeller's Snake River Land Company. Conservation trumped cattle; tourists trumped water for

[11] Daugherty, 174.

[12] Righter, 40. For more extensive discussion on the Rockefeller involvement in Grand Teton National Park see Righter, *Crucible*, and Robert W. Righter, *Peaks, Politics and Passion: Grand Teton National Park Comes of Age* (Moose: Grand Teton Natural History Association, 1914).

[13] Quoted in Daugherty, p. 208.

[14] Daugherty, 310; Righter, *Crucible*, 64.

[15] Daugherty, 174.

Idaho potatoes and sheep. The McKinstrys by this time had moved on, leaving Wyoming for another new start—this time in Colorado. But they departed with some additions to their family, three children all born in Jackson, and the rich trove of memories both Linda and Harold preserved over the years regarding their experiences among the last homesteaders of Jackson Hole.

Clearly, for all the hardship they endured during their years on Pacific Creek they felt enriched by their time there. Happily for us, they recorded their daily lives in letters to Linda's mother and in the memoirs they crafted years later. Although Linda meant these pages for her own family, I think it very likely she would enjoy knowing others find them interesting, as well. One hundred years after their arrival in Wyoming, you now hold those memories in your hands.

Sherry L. Smith, Ph.D
Southern Methodist University
and Moose, Wyoming

The Jackson Hole Historical Society and Museum is truly honored to be able to offer Linda and Harold "Mac" McKinstry's memoirs of homesteading in the Moran area of Jackson Hole in the early twentieth century. We were fortunate indeed that Stella McKinstry of Pinedale, Wyoming—Mac and Linda's youngest daughter—generously offered to share her parents' memoirs with us. And we are grateful to Stella's friend Herb Pownall of Laramie for drawing our attention to this manuscript and for suggesting that we get in touch with Stella. It isn't often that a manuscript lands in a museum's lap that excites all who have the opportunity to take a quick look at it but such was the case with the McKinstrys' joint memoirs.

The words that describe their wilderness adventures, starting in 1915, are Linda's and Mac's, taken directly from their memoirs with very few alterations or editing. We wanted to convey the young couple's excitement and joy in their venture, even in the face of the many challenges they faced in homesteading on Pacific Creek—so we left both to speak freely in their own unique idiom. The words within brackets are editorial clarifications.

Located on the far reaches of the Jackson Hole Valley, just outside the boundaries of what was to become Yellowstone National Park, the McKinstry ranch was at the center of the competing interests that played out in one of the last chapters of homesteading in the American West. According to Stella, her parents always remembered their time in Jackson Hole with great fondness and felt no regrets at having followed their dreams into the wilderness. Looking back on her parents' experiences, however, Stella confided that she often "wondered what they could have been thinking"—raising a young family miles from town with no telephone and roads that drifted shut for months on end. Yet, despite the many close calls that are revealed more fully in the details recounted in Mac's memoir (hair-raising details deliberately kept from his wife until much later, when safely down in the Denver area), they felt lucky to have played a part in shaping the history of Jackson Hole and clearly relished being members of the close-knit community of settlers who claimed the valley as their home.

We are grateful to Stella and her family for sharing the historical photographs of the McKinstrys' homesteading years. While the majority of the photographs are from Mac and Linda's albums, we added some from the museum's collection and from other collections to help give a sense of what their lives and that of their neighbors were like "back then." Excerpts from the McKinstry memoirs, along with the photographs were used by the JHHSM to mount their award-winning exhibit, "The Last Homestead" which won an Award of Merit from the American Association of State and Local History in 2015.

Our thanks especially to Stella's niece, Kathy Nelson, for copying and scanning the family photos and for checking the book's proof for errors.

Our thanks, too, to Nancy Curtis without whose High Plains Press many of the most fascinating stories of Wyoming would never have seen the light of day!

SHARON KAHIN, PH.D.
Executive Director
JACKSON HOLE HISTORICAL SOCIETY AND MUSEUM
JULY 2016

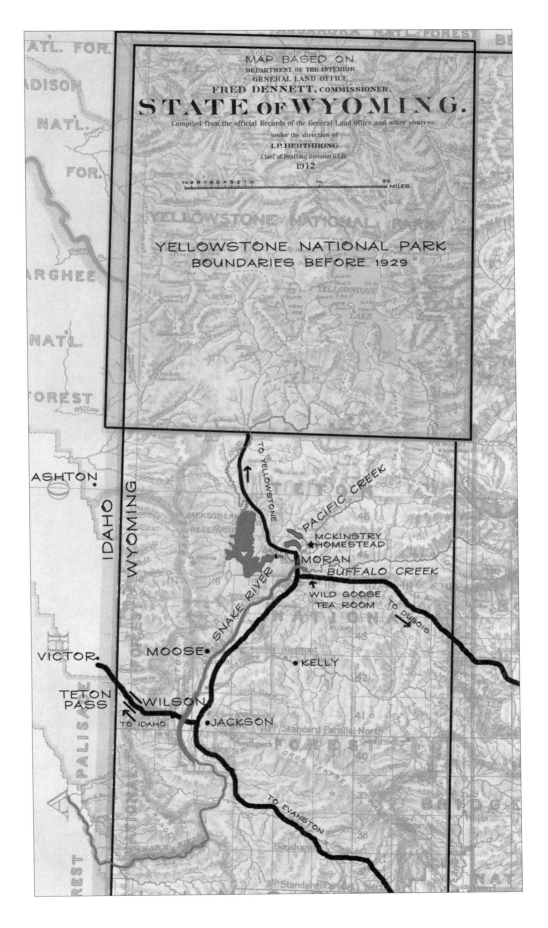

Linda Preston McKinstry
February 6, 1886 –
April 2, 1980
(McKinstry)

Harold Cole McKinstry
February 23, 1889 –
July 29, 1978
(McKinstry)

CHAPTER ONE

Wilderness Fever Ran High

Linda Preston McKinstry:

With my New England heritage and background, I was hardly prepared for homesteading in Jackson Hole, Wyoming in 1915. My home had been in Springfield, Massachusetts until I attended college near Boston and then [went] to Washington D.C. to teach cooking (Home Economics).

My husband, Harold Cole McKinstry, had had a little more western experience, his home having been in Fargo, North Dakota, until [his graduation] from North Dakota Agricultural College, now North Dakota State University. He had gone to Washington to work in the USDA, more specifically the U.S. Office of Dry Land Agriculture. His winters were spent in Washington and his summers on an experimental station at Hettinger, North Dakota. He had always wanted to go into ranching, and during his vacation the year preceding our marriage had visited areas in Montana, Idaho, and Wyoming, searching for what seemed the most desirable location. He had decided on Jackson Hole, and we were to start out a week after our New England honeymoon. Needless to say, relatives and friends were skeptical about the venture but refrained from saying too much to us.

As Mother was breaking up her home in Washington, we were welcome to whatever furniture and household equipment we wanted. The furniture was crated, and all dishes, utensils, books, wedding gifts, and many much-needed household articles packed in barrels or boxes. Mother was a wonderful packer, and hardly a dish was broken even though all were sent by freight and endured a seventy-mile wagon trip over unbelievably rough roads of Teton Pass and Jackson Hole.

Mac and I took the train to Fargo. En route we stopped at the Twin Cities, Minneapolis and St. Paul, where we purchased leather goods, including

The McKinstry home in Fargo, North Dakota, in the 1880s and 1890s. (McKinstry)

two saddles, harness, tools, and a beautiful bearskin carriage robe. We considered that a gift from Dr. Jay T. Stocking, who had performed our marriage ceremony in Washington and who had insisted on returning much of the wedding gratuity. Otherwise we would not have afforded that luxury, although something of the kind was an absolute necessity.

Reaching Fargo, I stayed with Mac's sister and family while he went on ahead to Wyoming. Later I learned of his experience en route.

He first went to Hettinger [North Dakota]. While stationed there [during] the preceding summer months, he had purchased considerable farm machinery and two mares, one a young black Percheron named Jet, not too well broken, the other a white part Percheron called Ginger, gentle and dependable. In order to transport all this to Wyoming, he had made arrangement for an immigrant car, a boxcar available at a special rate.

Into this went the mares, hay, grain, and a fifty-gallon barrel of water for use on the trip. The equipment included a Studebaker wagon, sulky plow, mower, hay rake, and the necessary tools for building and for getting out logs. Among these were a crosscut saw, ax, log chains, peavey,[†] and a draw knife for peeling logs.

† *A peavey in a hand tool with a shovel-like handle and prong and hook on the end, used in logging and in fire-fighting.*

Also there was the Majestic range, which Mac had purchased at an auction. Probably this means only mountain scenery to the present generation, but to that of fifty-five years ago that meant a kitchen stove, probably

the best ever made. A cook stove was an absolute necessity for both cooking and heating, and this model had a generous sized reservoir at the right hand end for heating water, a much appreciated convenience. Also loaded into the car were 1200 or 1500 pounds of potatoes. These were attainable at a price much below the market and in demand in Wyoming.

In due time the boxcar was added to a passing freight, and he was en route to Victor, Idaho, the nearest railroad station. During the long, slow trip he kept busy caring for the horses, watching the scenery, visiting with the train crew and preparing meals, simple and cold; canned salmon sandwiches (salmon was ten cents a can then), cheese, graham crackers, and fruit. His only hot meal was at Butte where the train made a stopover. Blankets over the hay made a comfortable bed.

Arriving in Victor, the car was unloaded and the less urgently needed articles stored with the freight, which had already arrived from Washington.

The next day the most necessary equipment, including logging and building tools, the Majestic range, and a supply of staple groceries and sacks of potatoes for our own use were loaded in the wagon. Sugar and flour were purchased in hundred-pound sacks, dried fruit in twenty-five-pound boxes, lard in a fifty-pound pail, and bacon by the slab. Jet and Ginger were harnessed to the wagon, and a man [was] hired in Victor with a lead team as four horses were required for the trip over Teton Pass.

Harold McKinstry unloaded the machinery and household goods at Victor, Idaho, the nearest train station to the Jackson Hole area. (JHHS&M)

This photograph shows a sleigh pulled by one team of horses on Teton Pass. The sleigh Mac McKinstry borrowed was fully loaded and was pulled by four horses.
(JHHS&M)

At first the roads were dry but soon became muddy from melting snow, and as they neared the mountain they ran into snow. This became deeper as they started to climb.

Soon they reached the west side roadhouse, a stopping point where food and lodging could be obtained, so the wagonload had to be transferred to a sleigh borrowed at the roadhouse.

After eating dinner and [feeding the] horses, [they continued] the trip through the snow over Teton Pass to the roadhouse on the eastern side. The return trip was made to the first roadhouse for the wagon, which had to be taken apart and loaded on the sleigh. By the time they reached the east side roadhouse, it was dark and they remained there overnight. The next morning the wagon was put together and reloaded as that could be used the rest of the way. Upon reaching Snake River, [they] had to ford [it] as there was no bridge. It was fortunate that Ruf [Rufus] Eynon, the Victor man, was with Mac as the river was treacherous and fording places changed constantly. As it was, they barely made it across safely, and from there to Jackson was uneventful. Ruf returned to Victor the next day, taking the sleigh back to the west side roadhouse.

Today this road over the pass is a beautiful, blacktopped highway, but even yet some tourists become panicky because of the sharp hairpin turns and steep drop-offs. In 1915 it followed the contour of the mountain, seemingly hung where it seemed there should be no road. Some of the pitches were unbelievably steep, and with spring breakup the mud [was] hub deep. Through the winter some places became so sliding that the stage passengers had to ride the upper runners to keep the sleigh from rolling into the canyon, thousands of feet below.

After staying in Jackson overnight, Mac spent the following day there, allowing the horses to rest and attending to business matters. The next day he started on the forty-mile trip north to Pacific Creek where our homestead was located. This was a gradual uphill pull, and although the roads were rough and Spread Creek had to be forded, it was an easier trip than over the pass. The last few miles were only a trail.

Three days later, he was back in Victor as he had sent word for me to meet him there on April 17.

April 1915

Mac's brother, Will, just out of high school, made the trip from Fargo with me. He wanted to see the country and find summer work on a Wyoming ranch.

Train service was not very good in those days, and although we left Tuesday evening we did not reach Victor, Idaho, until late Saturday P.M. We stopped off in Hettinger for several hours but otherwise were always traveling or waiting for trains. At Butte we were met by Mac's cousin and a friend of his as they, too, had decided they wanted to spend the summer working in Jackson Hole. It was after one o'clock in the morning when we arrived in Idaho Falls on Friday night. Our train for Wyoming did not leave until 8:45 in the morning so Will and I took some rooms at a hotel. After traveling three days and two nights on dirty, dusty trains, with no sleeping accommodations, a bath and comfortable bed were most appreciated even at that time of night. The other two boys spent the night in the railroad station.

In the morning we took the train for Ashton, a two-hour trip for a distance of some fifty-three miles, where we had to change again for the train to Victor. That distance was only forty-six miles, and although we left at 12:30 P.M., we were not due in Victor until 5:30. The train was passenger, baggage, freight, and mail but in order to consume time had to stop and wait at stations and even ranches along the way. Finally we reached Driggs, only eight miles from Victor, but an hour was allowed for that distance. As no stops were required along the route that day, the trip was made in half an hour, so we arrived at 5:00 instead of 5:30.

For me, that part of the journey seemed endless for I was so anxious to arrive and see Mac. Even the mountain scenery went almost unnoticed. Finally we reached Victor and I saw Mac waiting on the platform, so tanned and brown he seemed almost a stranger.

All the group stayed at the little frame hotel in Victor that night. It bore no resemblance to the one in Idaho Falls, but we were reaching frontier country. Lack of conveniences [was] not important for Mac and I were together again. Little else mattered.

Harold Cole McKinstry:

Back in 1914 there appeared in the *Saturday Evening Post* an article lauding the virtues of the Jackson Hole country of Wyoming for the cattle business. Already being afflicted with that ranching fever for which there is no cure, I penetrated that gloriously scenic area in September and filed on a homestead.

Being young and inexperienced in that kind of country precluded any feeling of futility as to my ability to select a good homestead site. A beautiful flat, lying between Pacific Creek and the foot of the mountain, was my choice. Down the mountainside, just opposite the proposed building site, a beautiful little mountain stream tumbled and cascaded. Spring water, clear and cold, was abundant. At that time the distance from nowhere meant nothing. The wilderness fever ran high.

The following March 3, Linda and I were married. She had, the previous fall, quit her job as teacher of Home Economics in Washington D.C. I resigned my government job to become effective March 15. As jobs went, it had paid fair wages, but to me its future was filled only with futility. It consisted basically of experimental work in Dry Land Farming. During the summer I was located in western North Dakota, during the winter in Washington. The lure of the frontier was in our blood.

Linda stayed with my sister in Fargo while I went ahead to make advance preparations. I had accumulated a fine young team of horses, a little haying machinery, and household goods. With the help of two of my very good friends, I loaded them into an immigrant car at Hettinger and was on my way. The trip was long and slow. The route led through Butte, Montana, then south through Idaho over the O.S.L. [Oregon Short Line railroad] with its termination in Victor. It was not only the end of the rails. It was the beginning of frontier life.

Linda stayed with my sister in Fargo while I went ahead to make advance preparation for our little grey home in the west. During the previous summer I had patronized a few auction sales and thus had come into possession of a Majestic wood range, but little did I realize then how valuable and cherished it was to become. I had purchased a new Studebaker wagon, a few pieces of farm machinery, and a fine young team of mares, Jet and Ginger. Jet was a bronc, green broke, and not to be trusted, Ginger, a faithful six year old, adding a stabilization influence.

The town of Victor was very small. Everyone knew everyone else. Friendliness pervaded the atmosphere.

The proprietors of the road-house on Teton Pass were helpful in loaning Mac a sleigh to use on the way over the pass. (JHHS&M)

"Where can I find a man with a team to help me over the pass?" I asked the station agent.

"Ruf Eynon can do the job if he isn't busy. That's him plowing that garden over there."

So it was that Ruf helped me unload the car, storing everything in his barn. Then before night fell, we had my wagon loaded to capacity, ready for an early morning start.

He had a fine team of mares, broke for the mountains, so we put them on the lead and my team on the wheel. The going was pretty good for the first few miles, but that was all. As soon as the road really began to climb up the west side of Teton Pass, the mud and the chuckholes became hub deep. Water from the melting snows above ran down the ruts, washing out holes on the lower side, making a loblolly on the upper side or clear across.

The wagon dropped into a hole behind a plugged log culvert, and we had to chop out the whole culvert before we could move another inch.

By ten o'clock we reached a roadhouse and the snow. From there on there was no chance to use a wagon, but luck was with us for the roadhouse man had a sleigh, which we were able to rent.

"There's no use trying to pile it too high," Ruf advised. "She won't stay right side up."

So we took what seemed enough, leaving the rest piled beside the road, and began inching our way over the crumbling snow road. The higher we climbed, the worse it became. Ruf's horses, wise to the mountains and the treacherous snow roads, kept their feet. Mine, prairie-bred and unaccustomed to anything of the kind, could never have made it without the help of those experienced leaders.

Although the load was not heavy, the grade was so steep and the going so bad that only a few rods could be gained between breathers.

From the top it appeared that no team could get down the east side. The snow road, through snow thirty feet deep, hung on the side of the mountain. The upper track crowded the cliffs. The lower track, at a dangerously

lower level, hung on the edge of the canyon, which dropped away hundreds of feet below.

"We'll have to rough lock," said Ruf. "With enough luck we might make it."

So we rough locked, wrapping a log chain underneath a hind runner.[†] Then we took off the leaders, letting them follow behind, and down we went. In some miraculous way the horses kept their balance, we swinging hard on the upper runners to keep the load from rolling into the canyon. The roadhouse on the east side was a welcome sight.

Early the next morning, we returned for the wagon and the rest of the goods. The snow had frozen during the night, and although rough and precipitous, was less of a horse killer. But by the time we had taken the wheels off the wagon and loaded it on the sleigh, along with the rest, the road was again softening. "Only by the Grace of God," as Ruf said, did we arrive right side up.

The following morning, with the wagon loaded again, we started down the road for Jackson. Gradually the road became better until we reached Snake River. It was not yet the season for high water but it looked high to me.

Jackson, looking east on Broadway, circa 1910-1920. (JHHS&M)

[†] To "rough lock" is to fasten a chain or rope around a sled runner or wagon wheel to retard its movement down hill. With a sleigh, the direction the vehicle slides can be controlled by which runner is rough locked and how much chain is used.

"Let's watch that thing a while," Ruf said. "I hit a deep hole that last time I crossed."

So we watched, he studying the surfaces of the water where it riffled over the shallower places.

"I believe we're safe in following the curve of that big riffle," he finally decided and spoke to the team.

They went in, belly deep, the water lapping the bottom of the wagon box. At times we bounced over boulders; again we seemed to be settling into the gravel. But it was old business for Ruf. He knew the river, guiding the team in a long rainbow around the upper edge of the riffle. Only once did we hit dangerously deep water and that was just below the far bank where the water was starting to cut a deep channel. But the leaders were through before the wheelers hit it[†], and the wagon box was tight enough to protect the load against the quick dunking.

As the team stood once again on dry land, puffing after the pull, Ruf looked down at the channel.

"That's the kind that scares me," he said. "In another thirty minutes it can be cut deep enough to take this whole outfit downstream."

I spent the next day in Jackson, getting the team shod and letting them rest. But early the following morning I headed north for the homestead on which I had filed. The road was still heavy, spongy from the melting snows. The going was slow, but there were no canyon walls to creep around or crumbling snow roads to fight. Forty miles was a long way, when all uphill, with a loaded wagon. But on the evening of the second day I arrived.

[When I turned] the horses loose, they immediately picked a nice sandy spot and rolled, relieving the itching of the dried perspiration in their hair. Watching them, I marveled at their stamina. Ginger was a fine work animal but never had experienced an ordeal as tough as that of the last three days. Jet, a bronc when we started, had become a quiet and dependable teammate.

About all I could do at the time was to build temporary shelter for the equipment brought. The real job of building was to come later. The important thing was to get back to Victor and meet Linda. She was due to arrive there on April 17, and I had been counting the days. So I left the team in the livery barn in Jackson and with two rented saddle horses again crossed the divide.

† *The "wheelers" are the pair of horses closest to the wagon. The "leaders" are all the animals in front of the wheelers.*

CHAPTER TWO

Beginning Pioneer Life

Linda Preston McKinstry:

April 1915

The next morning we all started for Jackson. The three boys hiked over the pass, but Mac and I rode horseback. I had thought that would be far more fun than going by stage, so Mac had hired two saddle horses. That is where I made a dreadful mistake. My horseback riding experience had been limited to an occasional, summer trip of ten or twelve miles, but those had been so much enjoyed, I was really anticipating this trip. I did not realize that thirty miles would be quite different, especially since I had not ridden for months.

That morning I happily dressed in one of my new riding outfits, one which was made of brown velvet corduroy (another, khaki). This featured a divided skirt, each half of which was almost a skirt by itself, and came down to my ankles. Underneath I wore sturdy, brown flannelette bloomers, reaching well below the knees—one was really modest in those days. My tan and brown silkaline blouse was handmade with numerous buttons down the front. I always felt well dressed in that outfit and really was.

Mac hardly looked familiar wearing cowboy chaps. Chaps were standard equipment for men in that country at that time. His own plain leather ones were left at the homestead, and these, which had been loaned to him in Jackson, had angora fur down the sides. He did not care for that variety but they proved really useful later.

It was a beautiful spring morning, warm and sunny. Being with Mac again made everything perfect and it was such fun to be riding again. The whole country was delightful. Early wild flowers were blooming everywhere and on ahead [were] spectacular snow covered peaks. We started out wearing sweaters but they were soon discarded as the sun was so warm.

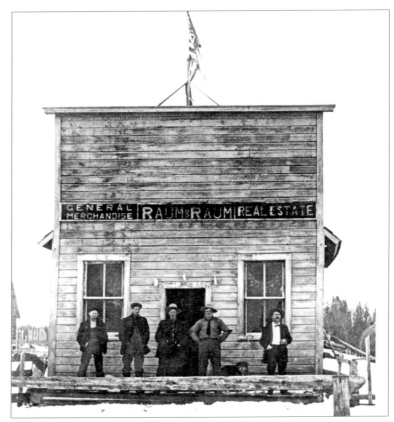

When Linda and Mac rode into Wilson, it was a wide spot in the road and they were still eight miles from Jackson. The Wilson General Store was built by Nick Wilson and also served as the post office, barber shop, pool hall, real estate office, and a garage.
(JHHS&M)

It was all too perfect to last. After about ten miles, my unused muscles began to rebel. Also we had begun climbing the mountain, and instead of patches of snow, we found ourselves in a snow covered country. Our sweaters were most welcome then. The road was muddy and slippery under the snow, which made footing uncertain for the horses. I was thankful when we reached the west side roadhouse where we were to stop for dinner. It was a relief to get off the horse and walk.

The boys, who had started out much earlier than we, were already there so we ate dinner[†] together. It was served in rough and ready style, but I was hungry and everything tasted so good, especially the meat. I made a remark about the delicious beef, which was received with a laugh.

"Beef? That's elk, lady," volunteered one of the men. So I had my first taste of elk, not realizing then that elk would be our main meat supply for some years to come.

After dinner, feeling quite refreshed, we continued on. The snow on the pass had been deep and the road was now "breaking up," so called. This meant the packed snow was softening and would no longer hold the weight of the horse. At each step one foot or another would chug down through the snow [to a] depth of one to two feet or even more. Not only

† Like many people of the period, especially rural people, Linda refers to the noon meal as "dinner" and the evening meal as "supper."

was this hard on the horse but also on the rider, and a novice would receive a terrific jolt. After this continued for a few miles, I was lame, sore, and very tired. There was nothing to do but go on, remembering it was my bright idea to come over horseback.

Upon reaching the eastern roadhouse, we were well over Teton Pass, and the snow depth had greatly lessened. Soon the roads were bare again so it was much easier riding, but I was exhausted by then.

A little farther on we reached Wilson and found the boys there preparing to camp out for the night. Mac asked if I would not rather stay there than ride the eight miles more into Jackson. He said he was sure we could get a room at a house. Looking around I [couldn't] remember even seeing a house. Wilson seemed to be only a wide place in the road and hardly that. So I said, "Let's go on." I was sure the Jackson hotel would be preferable and had visions of a hot bath and comfortable bed. But we did stop and rest a while, and then [I] appreciated Mac's chaps. [After he slipped] them off, they made a nice fur robe on which to sit.

After our brief rest we went on, but those were the longest eight miles I ever rode. It was then late afternoon and soon began to grow dark. But finally we saw a light [and] some buildings and were ultimately at the hotel, a bare unpainted wooden structure, most uninviting.

I was so tired and lame, I simply fell off the horse when I was helped down. I refused supper for all I wanted was a hot bath and bed. The hot bath proved to be from a washbowl with a lard pail full of hot water, which Mac brought up from the kitchen. I wondered why I had ever come out to this awful place.

But youth recuperates quickly and the next morning, though still frightfully lame and sore, I was feeling much better.

Perhaps it was well that we had arrived in Jackson after dark for I fear the drabness of the town would have been too much for me. Even in the morning it looked hopeless. There was an occasional log building, otherwise [it consisted of] unpainted frame structures, rather few and far between. A typical, early frontier town. The big open square around which the buildings were placed is now beautifully landscaped with towering evergreens. Then it was a flat, pebbly waste with hardly a weed growing on it.

But we did not remain in Jackson long. After eating breakfast we were ready to start on the forty-mile trip to Pacific Creek. Mac had planned to take the big wagon and another load of goods, but I was still so lame that he decided to hire a team and buggy instead, so that I might travel more comfortably.

Some homesteaders had a place about four miles below where we were to locate, and I was to stay with them until something was available on our place. We arrived at Thompsons' about 6:30 that evening, and although they were not expecting us until the next day, they made us welcome.

Harold Cole McKinstry:

She arrived on schedule, my brother, Will, my cousin Don and a friend of his, accompanying her. That was a great day. We put up at the hotel that night and early the next morning again headed east over the pass. The boys started early, hiking. Linda and I, riding the saddle horses, got started by 9:00. Spring was in the air. Flowers bloomed on all sides. Trees were donning their spring garb. Birds filled the air with their songs. The going was good for the first few miles. The horses, headed for home, traveled freely.

But after the first five miles we began to hit muddy roads. At ten miles we hit snow, soft, crumbling, treacherous. The horses picked their way cautiously, and they were wise to such going, but the warm weather had so softened the snow that it let the horses down just as they put their weight it. Down they'd go to the bottom, jolting us unmercifully.

Linda had not ridden very much before. Had the going all been good and the horse as easy riding as a cradle, the thirty-mile trip would still have been an ordeal for her. But she was game. When we finally reached the roadhouse on the east side of the pass, again below the snow, I suggested staying there overnight.

"No," she said wearily, "if it's only twelve miles farther let's go on. I won't be able to move in the morning."

So I took off my angora chaps, spread them on the ground for a blanket, and we stretched out to rest a few minutes before taking the last lap. The snow covered mountains over which we had just come towered above us. The lush valley lay below. The sun poured down so warm and radiant that the existence of snow so near seemed unreal. Those last ten or twelve miles proved long. Linda's endurance had nearly reached its limit. I was too dumb, inexperienced—call it what your will—to realize her limitations.

At 7:30 in the evening we reached Jackson.

The solicitation of Mrs. Jack Eynon (Ruf's sister-in-law) at the Jackson Hotel for Linda's welfare was comforting, or at least appreciated. The good supper offered had no appeal. Bed was the only thing that seemed inviting. I managed to get a small pail of hot water from the kitchen, and with that in a hand basin she tried to take a bath before rolling in. In looking back over the years now, I often wonder how she survived the trip at all.

With the dawn of another day we were anxious to get on to the homestead, but objection loomed up to change our plans. In the first place Linda was so lame as a result of her rough trip over the pass that she was in no condition, mentally or physically, so start out on a two-day trip over

rocky roads in a lumber wagon. In the second place, the team just had to have time to rest and recuperate after their punishment. We finally compromised by renting a livery team and buggy, thus making possible the forty-mile trip in one day. Thus we arrived one day ahead of schedule at the homestead of Billie and Emily Thompson with whom I had previously arranged for lodging while Billie and I might cut logs and erect a one room cabin.

Linda Preston McKinstry:

"Come in, folks," Mrs. Thompson greeted. "We'll have some supper pretty quick."

She was a sturdy woman, medium height, but gave the impression of being big and strong. She moved with efficiency in the small area that served as a kitchen, hampered but little by the severe limp, which she said later was the result of a childhood injury. With her big, capable hands she lifted a loin of elk from a spike in the log wall to the table and sliced off steaks with the skill of professional meat cutter.

The hotel in Wilson, built in 1899, provided a resting spot for Linda, who then climbed back in the saddle for the trip to Jackson.

Shown are proprietors Abraham Ward, Edna Jane Wilson Ward, and Irene Edna Ward. Note the pool hall and barber shop next door. (JHHS&M)

As she fed the fire in the wood burning range she said, "I like to split this wood as I need it. This way it's always dry. When Billie splits a pile ahead it gets rained on and don't burn so good."

Billie was of medium height but with powerful shoulders. His black hair and deep tan gave him the complexion of an Indian. He was quiet and congenial. That meeting was the beginning of long and genuine neighborly relations.

Their cabin, made of logs, was about eighteen feet square, with a new small room built on one side. This eighteen-foot room was their original building in which they had been living. Just now were they completing their new room. We were to have the small room in which they had been putting new paper over the logs and fixing up the floor covering. Everything was damp and smelled of paste but clean.

Thompsons slept in the large room, which was a bedroom, living room, dining room, and kitchen. In that room was a double bed, large kitchen stove, wood box, sacks of flour and sugar, cooking utensils, canned goods and cereals on the shelves, a table and some straight back chairs. A bench with basin and a pail of water and the towel above was near the door. On the other side of the room beyond the bed, their clothing was hung covered by a curtain, and some bureau drawers held other necessities.

Although it was crowded indoors, there was unlimited space outside. The quietness and beauty were an inspiration. To the west were the majestic Tetons with their ever changing color and cloud effects. Nearer were evergreens and aspens with open meadowland between and the little streams coming down from Two Ocean Lake.

Mac returned to Jackson the next day to return the team and buggy and bring the wagonload of goods. I had hoped he could return [to Pacific Creek] the following day, but it was late afternoon two days later when he arrived. His brother, Will, was with him. Our suitcases were the most welcome part of the load as they had not arrived in Jackson before we left.

Although [it was] snowing, I rode with them up to the Pacific Creek crossing leading to our homestead, a distance of some three miles. [As it was] so late and stormy, we did not cross, but the rest of the goods were unloaded on the creek bank and covered. It was a wet ride but fun. Coming back to Thompsons', we all stood up in the wagon as that kept us more dry than sitting in the wet seat in the wagon. Snow laden branches met overhead and showered down upon us, but it was beautiful.

The next day Will returned to Jackson with the lead team, as the load had required four horses. Mac and Mr. Thompson went up to our homestead to put up a tent and start work on a cabin.

First, the lodgepole pines had to be found that were suitable for logs. They must be straight and of uniform size and long enough to furnish sixteen-foot or eighteen-foot logs as the cabin was to be that size. Some trees

that looked straight at a distance had to be rejected. Standing close and sighting up the trunk, [the men] found [the trees] to be bowed, too tapered or too knotty. But there were many nearly perfect trees and it took but a few days to find them. They were cut down, the branches lopped off, after which they were skidded to the camp site. Here they were peeled, a drawknife being used. Logs should be allowed to dry for two or three months, at least, before going into a building, but there was no time for that, so they had to be used while green and extremely heavy.

After only two days' start it was Sunday so the men decided not to work on that day. Mac and I decided to go to our homestead, which was my first opportunity to see it. I did not wonder [why] Mac had selected that particular 160-acre site, with acres of beautiful grassy meadows, many huge green spruce near the creek, a clear spring close by the building site. Elk were plentiful and feeding in the meadow. On my first trip up from Jackson, I had seen many elk grazing in the meadows and on the hillsides. Since then I had seen them practically every day and they had remained a thrilling sight. It was fascinating to watch them, after grazing, go single file up the hill, then [they] might be silhouetted against the sky as they stood on the top.

Moose, too, were frequently seen among the willows and in the beaver ponds, often crossing our meadows. [As they are] such huge creatures I was somewhat frightened of them.

Grouse were plentiful and seemed not to be much disturbed by people. Once I almost stepped on one. The baby grouse were adorable. We enjoyed

The homesteaders had plenty of pine trees to choose from, but only the straight, solid timber was suitable for house logs. It could be a slow process to find the right trees. (JHHS&M)

our day ever so much. After eating lunch we took a hike up the creek, and I had my first lesson in shooting. I used the revolver which Mac had gotten before leaving Hettinger. I didn't particularly enjoy the lesson as handling the revolver frightened me. About seven o'clock we left the homestead and drove some eight miles to Elk for mail. It was a beautiful moonlight night but plenty cold. Our fur robe had been brought to the Elk Post Office, and we were very glad to have it driving back for it was nearly eleven o'clock when we arrived back at Thompsons'.

The next morning Mac and Mr. Thompson, better known as Billie, returned to the homestead to continue work. This time they planned to camp out there rather than drive the four miles every morning and night. The horses would have more time to rest and graze, and they had a good supply of staple groceries stored in the tent. Bread and eggs could be taken from Thompsons'.

Mrs. Thompson was better known as Emily, but I never called her by that name. My eastern heritage was still too much with me. When she was busy I spent the time writing, hiking or napping out-of-doors. The change of altitude made me sleepy, and even long daytime naps did not interfere with sleeping at night. It was fun to explore the nearby country and enjoy the abundance of wildlife.

From Emily I also learned about housekeeping with no conveniences and how to milk a cow. Fortunately their cow was a gentle, patient creature, and I met with some success even in my first attempt. It was sometimes difficult to find the cow and bring her home, and if she was across the creek we had to cross on the fence. As the days ended the sunsets over the Tetons were just too beautiful to be described.

When the men returned home on Friday night they brought a porcupine Mac had killed en route. It was a real task to dress it out and we were glad to have the meat the next day.

As it snowed the next morning, the men decided not to go back to work, so Mac and I decided we would go up in the afternoon and camp in the tent over Sunday. But when we arrived, the ridgepole of the tent was so weighted with snow that Mac would not let me go in until it was cleared off. This was the first day of May. Of course it was cold inside but a fire in the range warmed things very quickly, and we were comfortable as could be. The porcupine was put on to parboil, and when browned in the frying pan the next day was delicious.

Harold Cole McKinstry:

It didn't take us long to get the job started. Beautiful lodgepole timber was at hand. Billie was a good timber man, and I had a lot to learn. But it was pleasant work and within a few days the job was far enough along so we could move in with a roof overhead.

But we soon found there was too much time being consumed in traveling back and forth from Thompsons', a distance of about four miles. To avoid some of that, we set up a tent on the homestead and Linda and I moved in. The tent was a 10 x 12 with low side walls, too low for me to stand in erectly. Our wonderful Majestic range was placed in one end, our blankets on a pile of hay along the side, what few dishes we had were piled on and in boxes along the other side. A packing box was our table.

The next morning the tent was weighted down with snow, fourteen inches, wet and heavy, sagging the canvas nearly down to our faces as we lay in bed. That was May 1. I rolled out and started bouncing the snow off the tent. The sun came out with a blinding glare, so bright we could hardly see without using colored glasses. But within less than two days the ground was again bare, with spring in all its beauty struggling to remain.

Linda Preston McKinstry:

Since priority in goods brought from Victor had to be given to necessary tools, building equipment, staple groceries and two trunks, we had no furniture and all household equipment [was] very limited. My cooking utensils consisted of one double boiler, one frying pan (it was called a spider then), one large round enamel pan, one baking pan, a coffee pot, and two round layer cake tins. Also a couple of large tin cans brought from Thompsons', a small dishpan, a water pail, and a long handled dipper.

For serving, the two layer cake pans plus the cover from the big lard pail served as plates. There were four tin cups and a good supply of eating utensils, three wooden handled knives and forks, four teaspoons, two tablespoons, and six silver-plated forks I found in my trunk.

Our sleeping accommodations were horse blankets over hay piled in one corner of the tent. But we did have good pillows as Will's trunk had been brought and stored in the tent. In that were two big pillows stuffed with goose feathers that Mac's sister had sent. Since we had no pillowcases, these were put under the blankets where they were protected.

When we awoke the next morning, the ridgepole was again weighted down and sagging. Looking out we discovered the snow was fourteen inches deep. Down in the meadows the horses and elk were pawing the snow and grazing together. A little later we saw a bear ambling across.

In the tent it was warm and comfortable. I stayed inside until after noon when we went out for a walk. Even following in Mac's tracks it was difficult walking but worth the effort as [the] snow-covered trees were so beautiful.

The snow was so deep we did not try to return to Thompsons' the next day. Mac continued to work on the cabin although it was difficult to do much in the deep snow.

By Tuesday the snow was melting so we returned to Thompsons' that evening, though we had to break trail all the way. They were not at home but cabins were always left unlocked in those days. After building the fire, we enjoyed hot cocoa and read the mail [that] was awaiting us. It was midnight when [the] Thompsons arrived.

As Billie was to start work at Moran the next day, he could not help with our cabin, so Mac and I went back to the homestead. By using a pulley and a horse, he was able to continue building, although it was difficult working alone as the logs were so very heavy. When it [was] high enough for roof logs, help was essential, so he started laying the floor. With that completed the next job was chinking. This consisted of tacking small poles between the logs on the inside to prevent the mud daubing, which later would be put on the outside, from pushing through.

One day when we were both busy chinking and shortly before noon, two forest rangers arrived. They had come to survey the homestead, so Mac went out with them.

I knew they would be back for dinner later, and probably would be there for supper, so I had plenty to do. With such limited equipment it was necessary to plan ahead. When they returned for a very late dinner, there was mashed potato, gravy, bacon, tomatoes with rice, cornbread, coffee, applesauce, and donuts, the last were already on hand as they had been made before. Everything cooked, except the bacon, was served in the cooking dishes, but as I needed the frying pan for gravy, the bacon was served in the dishpan.

Since the men were so late in returning, I went ahead and ate my dinner, and thus there were three plates as such for the men to use. At supper I used the dishpan for my plate, that being the only unused utensil, and Mac, the lard pail cover. The rangers were given the cake pans. The supper menu was varied a little as we had potato cakes, hot biscuits instead of cornbread, and tea.

The next afternoon the rangers returned to finish surveying. For supper we had our usual Saturday night New England baked beans and brown bread with stewed prunes instead of applesauce. They seemed to enjoy the meals anyway and not mind the table service.

Harold Cole McKinstry:

We were just ready to move into the cabin, although the log walls were not chinked or daubed and we could look out between the logs on all sides.

Together Linda and I chinked them by using small peeled poles, nailing them snugly between the logs on the inside. Then, with gumbo mixed to a stiff plaster consistency, I daubed the cracks on the outside. The method was standard for the country and produced a wall of remarkable warmth.

Then company arrived, two forest rangers, to survey and establish our lines. We were glad to see them, but it was meal time. We had two tin plates and the dishpan. The rest of our dishes were still in Victor or somewhere along the line. But in some way, plagued with more inconveniences than any city girl ever imagined, Linda soon had a good meal ready.

We had unpacked the tin plates and a few cooking utensils. Hence by suppertime, the dishpan was pressed into service for one plate, and the other ranger ate from a kettle cover.

"This is luxury," one said. "In camp we're lucky to have grub some times."

Linda brought the sizzling bacon from the stove, along with perfectly baked potatoes.

The head ranger looked at the bacon and hesitated before helping himself. "How come you don't have fresh meat?" he asked.

"At this time of year?" I asked.

"You can't make it in this country unless you take what the country offers, and keep still," he announced.

Soon after that I shot an elk, and from that time on we were seldom without fresh meat.

The McKinstry homestead on Pacific Creek, 1915. (McKinstry)

The next day the rangers came again to finish their surveying and to give us some advice.

"You ought to be located closer to the mail road," they told us. "This soil is too gravelly. Too hard to water. You can pick some pretty good agricultural land three miles down the creek. You'll get ten feet of snow up here. Never get out in the winter."

CHAPTER THREE

Learning the Lay of the Land

Linda Preston McKinstry:

Wonderful as our location was, we began to realize the serious disadvantages. During the preceding winter, there had been very little snow; yet, there were times when Pacific Creek could not be crossed. Under normal winter conditions, the spring runoff would last two or three weeks, during which time we would have no possible means of crossing, so [we] would be completely isolated. So when the rangers told us of land some three miles down the creek and on the opposite side, which might be available, we decided to consider a possible change. They also told us the snow would be ten feet deep where we were and much less at the lower location. After looking over the land, [we thought] it seemed advisable to apply for it.

May 1915

If the application was accepted, it would mean taking down the cabin and rebuilding, but the advantages would be many. We would not have to ford Pacific Creek [and] would be within a mile or so from Thompsons' ranch and only three miles [from] the highway. Also, over one mile of road building would be eliminated.

It was not such a beautiful location, but a good spring was available, there was open meadow with groups of lodgepole and spruce and [a] marvelous view of the Tetons. Mac would probably have selected that site in the first place but understood it was not available. Mr. Miller, the forest supervisor in Jackson, suggested that, without withdrawing our original claim, we make application for the change and gave us the necessary papers to do so.

Since we were in need of so much household and farm equipment, Mac started on another trip to Victor. I returned to the Thompson ranch to await his return.

The trip to Victor to bring in supplies was a regular challenge for the residents of Jackson Hole. Shown here is Harry R. Scott, who besides hauling freight, was one of the first mail stage drivers. (JHHS&M, Evelyn Cherry)

With horses the seventy-mile trip to Victor would take at least two days each way. With loading and business matters to attend to, a minimum of five days would be required for the trip. On reaching Jackson, he learned the pass was almost impassable and it would be impossible to take a wagon over the trail. Leaving the wagon in Jackson, he decided to ride over to Victor on Ginger [leading Jet] and bring back a pack load on Jet. He was not at all sure Jet would cooperate, for she still was not too well broken, but she did all right. With a mattress, blankets, slicker, my .22 rifle, and our tent wrapped over the top, she started out with the ungainly load. Wagons and buggies were stuck in the mud all along the way, but some way she managed to wallow through and up the steep pitches, though falling several times. It was a hard trip but ultimately all arrived safely in Jackson.

The next day, six days after the start of the trip, they returned [to Thompsons' place] and there was quite a procession. Two different horses were pulling the wagon, for Jet and Ginger were so worn out when still fifteen miles from home, they could not be driven farther. Mac had stopped at Nelson's and hired a fresh team. In the wagon were the Victor supplies, some machinery [that] had been stored in Jackson, and a month-old calf. Behind the wagon was tied a cow, and behind her came Almer Nelson riding Nellie, a little buckskin pony that Mac had purchased for me in Jackson, and Almer was leading Jet and Ginger.

Although it had begun to rain, we all left Thompsons' for our place, Almer helped Mac put up the tent he had brought. We had been using Billie's and now Billie needed it back.

Our tent was smaller than the one borrowed, and Mac could not stand upright in it. We either had to build side walls for that or finish the cabin sufficiently to make it livable, even though we might have to tear it down later. He decided to work on the cabin. Tar paper, as far as it went, was put over the roof boards and dirt on top of that. The chinking was completed and the outside was daubed with mud. We moved in May 21, just about a month after arriving in Jackson Hole.

Harold Cole McKinstry:

Still we had only a part of our belongings from Victor. The rest were still stored in Ruf Eynon's barn. The snow road over the pass was still breaking up and travel too difficult to be undertaken lightly. But there were things we needed badly, so we decided to bring what we could on a packhorse.

I took the team and wagon to the roadhouse on the east side of the pass. From there I rode one horse, leading the other. The things most needed made an ungainly load, hard to pack on and hard to load. Ruf again helped me get the pack on, for in that too he'd had years of practice. It rode well so long as we were on a good trail, but once on the crumbling snow road, trouble began. First, a treacherous ridge of snow gave way and dropped Jet into a hole with water halfway up her sides. The bottom and sides was slick and by the time she had struggled to the top, her pack had slipped. It took a half hour to adjust that, balancing it to prevent injury to Jet's back. Time after time she went down as did my saddle horse. Before going far, I found myself walking, leading both horses but even then wondering whether we were ever going to make it over the top.

Back at the roadhouse on the east side, we spent the night. There, with some things the stage driver had brought over from time to time as roads permitted, I loaded my pack into the wagon. After a good night's rest, I headed for Jackson.

There I purchased a cow and a calf, for we had no milk and neither Linda nor I liked the condensed variety. I rearranged the load, leaving enough room in the back end for the calf. The next morning, [after] tying the calf in this little stall and the cow and Linda's pony Nellie behind the wagon, we again started up country.[†]

The first day we made only a little over twenty miles and camped. The team was dead tired and I wondered about their ability to finish the trip the next day. When morning came, I did not have the nerve to hook them onto the wagon. A neighbor [Almer], not far from my camp, had a strong, fresh

---

[†] *"Up country" and "down country" are regional expressions that refer to land higher and lower in elevation. Thus "going up country" usually means going higher into the mountains and "going down country" means going deeper into the valley.*

A freight area was established at the top of Teton Pass to allow freighters to make adjustments. Shown here are Harry Scott (bending over) and Rufus Eynon tending to the bobs while other men and horses are stopped for dinner. Circa 1930. (JHHS&M)

team. I hired him to haul my load through, and it was well that I did. Rains again softened the road and my tired team could not have made the trip.

As we approached the Thompson house, Linda came out to meet us. She threw up her hands and laughed at the sight. Almer was driving his big grey team hooked to the wagon, which was loaded with everything from farm machinery to china, the calf in the back, the cow tied behind. I followed on Nellie, leading my team.

Taking Linda aboard, we continued the remaining four miles to our homestead, and the further we went, the harder it rained. In a downpour of rain and slushy snow, we set up the tent and turned my horses loose. Hardly had we got under cover than the rain stopped with almost miraculous deadness, and in the rays of the setting sun [that] peaked through a cloud bank over the Tetons, a glorious rainbow framed the mountain to our east.

We thought much about this advice of the rangers. The road was proving itself very long, even in the valley where there was no longer any mud or snow to fight. So our next job of importance became that of relocating. As the ranger had said, we were able to select land in such a shape as to include some fair agricultural land, some good timber, and excellent springs.

Linda Preston McKinstry:

Some two weeks later we received a letter from Ogden Land Office saying our new application was not accepted as the land had already been applied

June–July 1915

for. We could not understand it as the ranger had said it was available. Mac decided to go and see Rosencrans at his ranger station several miles up Buffalo Creek. He started out after an early lunch, expecting to be back in time for supper, though perhaps a late one.

It was a beautiful day and the ride rather anticipated but weather could change quickly. Clouds came up, evening came but no Mac although I had expected him much earlier. Then a terrific electrical storm broke and the drenching rain lasted seemingly for hours. Nine o'clock, ten o'clock, and on to midnight. Utter blackness outside except when the lightning flashed, and that was followed by deafening thunder. Alone in the cabin, no one else within miles, my fears increased with the hours. I knew no trail could be found in the darkness unless the horse could find the way, but the country was new to her.

The hands on the clock were at 1:30 when I heard someone outside. I flung open the door and there stood Mac and Ginger. Both were dripping wet but safe. How thankful I was to see them!

"How could you ever find your way in this blackness?"

"I couldn't, but Ginger did. Knowing how worried you'd be, I just kept coming. Except when the lightning flashed, I couldn't see a thing, not even the horse, but [I] knew she was there because sparks kept flying from her ears."

"But what took so long?"

"It was a far longer trip than I expected. I must have ridden forty miles. Be in as soon as I take care of Ginger."

[When Mac had] dry clothing, a warm fire, and a much needed supper, things were normal again. Then I inquired about what he had learned.

"At first Rosencrans said he could not understand the rejection. Papers he had sent in told of the availability of the land, but as we kept talking, he was rummaging through his desk. Suddenly he exclaimed, 'I made a &*#!@ mistake. I forgot to send these in. I'll make a new application and am sure it will go through.'"

Harold Cole McKinstry:

True to the ranger's description, there was open land among the pines. He had told us where to look for one of the section corners, and from that we were able to describe the land that looked good to us, fairly open and with excellent springs, one on the east side and one on the west. So we sent in the new application and awaited confirmation of its approval. Instead came notice of its rejection on the grounds that the land selected was not classified as agricultural. Again we tried, this time with the assistance of the ranger and his OK. Two weeks passed without hearing from the Land Office, and upon inquiry we were told, "No application received."

It was mid-afternoon of June 7 when this word came. We decided the thing to do was immediately contact the ranger at the Blackrock station. Never having been there, we did not realize its distance by trail or how much time the trip could consume. Nevertheless, I started right after lunch and did not arrive until after dark. The ranger was in bed and did not appreciate being routed out. At first he was loath even to get up, but [he] finally did roll out and read the letter I handed him.

"I can't help that," he said. "You can't hurry those guys." Then pausing, he pulled from a pigeon hole in his desk my application. "A damned bad mistake," he began. "I made it."

"The summer's getting away fast," I reminded him. "There's a lot of work to be done."

"I'll get it in the mail in the morning," he promised.

Rain was falling as I turned toward home. The night was black and I could see no sign of a trail. I gave old Ginger her head and just sat in the saddle, trusting to her keen sense of memory and homing instinct. The distant thunder began to roll as a violent electric storm approached. I could feel the electricity in the air. A lightning bolt crashed into a crag and I could smell the brimstone. Sparks flashed from the point of the horse's ears intermittently. Still she walked on with a strong, sure stride. Finally she began to twist and turn. I felt her sink into a bog, climb out, trip over downed timber and resume her steady stride. I knew that we had passed the soap holes where many a luckless elk, weakened by starvation through a long winter, had mired down for keeps. I could hear the roar of the water in Pacific Creek, see its turbulent surface glisten in the lightning. The feeling of that water on my legs as the mare plowed through, belly deep, was wonderful. It meant that we were nearly home.

The light in the cabin window never looked better. Linda was waiting, wondering why so late, worrying. It was 1:30 A.M.

Linda Preston McKinstry:

The next day, to add to our difficulties, our cow and calf ran off. I saw them start down the flat but thought Mac would meet them on his return from the mailbox. When he arrived, he said he had not seen them so immediately [he] started out on Nellie to hunt them. We thought they had probably started back to Jackson, but after an all-day search no trace of them was found. Not only did we miss the milk but [we] were more concerned about the cow. Unless milked she would be spoiled, and as the calf was muzzled he could not do the job. It was late the following day before we learned that a fine looking cow and calf had been seen in the lane near Moran. We never could understand why she had gone in that direction,

but there she was. Evidently the calf had succeeded in getting some milk, fortunate for him and the cow, too.

The days passed quickly. There were many interesting happenings as well as plenty of problems. The day the cow was found and brought home, Mac was greeted with, "Jet is missing now."

The horses had the whole country as range as we had no fences. Finding them often took many hours although one always wore a bell. Usually Jet and Ginger stayed together, but that day Ginger came for salt but alone. If the horses could not be located when needed, we just had to wait until they were sufficiently salt hungry or lonesome [and] they came of their own accord.

I enjoyed many rides on Nellie. Mr. Sheffield, dude rancher and postmaster at Moran, said this was the safest place in the world for a woman, but it was often lonesome riding alone. Mac could seldom go with me because there was so much to do at home. Mr. Sheffield also said that I probably followed elk trails where no white woman had ever been before.

In the spring it was fun to see the baby elk. They were supposedly hidden in the brush by their mothers but often very visible. The beautiful little creatures instinctively lay motionless. If I stopped to pet one, he would lie perfectly still and utterly ignore me, even though his soft brown eyes might be watching.

It was not unusual to see a coyote lope across an open flat. Elk were plentiful but quickly ran away. I worried about meeting a moose, and although I occasionally saw one in the willow swamps, we each kept our distance.

Ben Sheffield, both the postmaster of Moran and a prominent dude rancher, thought that the valley was the safest place in the world for a woman.

The photograph shows dudes in front of the Moran post office and some of Sheffield's hunters on the right.

The wild flowers were of many varieties, profuse and beautiful, some familiar, others entirely new to me. The birds, some of which were gaily colored, seemed to wait to be admired.

Our weather was unpredictable. A snowstorm in the middle of June, and once a Fourth of July picnic was nearly ruined because of snow, three or four inches deep. Fortunately it did not last long, so the celebration, along with the good eats, was thoroughly enjoyed.

Some Sundays we would go over the divide to Buffalo Creek to the little one room log schoolhouse where ranchers held a community Sunday school. The attendance varied, but the first Sunday we attended there were about thirty-five men, women, and children, to say nothing of innumerable dogs, present. Occasionally we would take our lunch, or supper, eating on the grassy hillside, but often we were invited to dinner with some of the Buffalo ranchers.

At home we struggled along with inconveniences. No real furniture, as that was still stored in Victor. Mac borrowed a table of sorts from an unused cabin, and we used nail kegs and boxes for chairs. He made a frame for the single mattress brought over on Jet's back. We tried to make it into a double bed but that was not successful, and he made a bed of blankets on the floor. Eating and cooking utensils remained a problem, but it was surprising how much could be done with so little. Our butter churn was a lard pail with a homemade wooden paddle. Through a hole in the center of the tin cover for the handle of the paddle it was chugged up and down in the cream. Washing equipment was still the tin wash boiler plus a washboard brought in by parcel post. Since all white clothes were boiled in those days, this had to be done in relays in the little dishpan. All water had to be brought by the pailful from the spring several rods distant. It was amazing how many times the water could be used and reused. Our flat irons were borrowed from Emily Thompson until some Buffalo Creek friends insisted on loaning us two of theirs.

They also loaned us four china plates although they had few enough for their own use. Ranchers, riding for cattle, frequently stopped by and meals had to be offered to everyone regardless of the time of day. Occasionally a whole family would arrive and in some way, we always managed to have plenty of food on hand or could prepare something. Acquaintances were welcome, but I resented preparing meals for utter strangers who would stop by only for a handout. Mac's brother would come for a few days at a time, and cooking daily for three people, or more, complicated matters, but he accepted all inconveniences cheerfully.

Since our [application for a] permanent location was still unsettled, Mac could not go ahead with any permanent building but continued

getting out logs for a house, barn, and chicken coop [while] also making bucks.[†] As over two miles of fencing would be required, an enormous number would be needed. A temporary chicken coop was made by placing several bucks together, covering them with a canvas wagon cover and using a horse blanket for the door.

Some ten days after Mac's trip to see Rosencrans, another letter was received from the Ogden office saying the land applied for was Forest Service Reserve, therefore non-agricultural. The enclosed sheets showed the land classified as agricultural was still open and unapplied for. In studying the maps, Mac realized they must be incorrect. Open land was marked Forest Reserve and parts of Pacific Creek designated as agricultural land. Since Rosencrans, who really knew the land, had made out the application, we thought it must be correct and should be accepted, but would it be? At best there would be more delay and uncertainty.

One morning several days later we started for Moran on horseback. Stopping at Thompsons' we learned that some official from the Ogden Land Offices had arrived at Moran the day before. He had come in to check land classification. Just then an auto drove in, bringing Mr. Hoyt, the Ogden official, Rosencrans, and Ohl. They said they were en route to recheck the area. Finding Mac there, [they] invited [him] to go with them and he was very glad to do so.

It was after noon before Mac arrived home, but [he] brought good news. "Mr. Hoyt agreed the present maps are incorrect. We are to make another application and he assured me it will be approved."

The "buck and rail" method of fencing (shown above) was commonly used by Jackson Hole homesteaders both because of the availability of timber and because the rocky, shallow soil made digging post holes difficult. (Shutterstock)

A photograph of Moran in 1912 shows Sheffield's living quarters and dude dining hall (the long building). To the right is the Lambert homestead cabin. The Lamberts were of the family which produced Listerine mouthwash. Note the square water tower on the left. (JHHS&M)

"Am I glad," I replied. "Is it really settled now?"

"Looks like it."

So, some three months after our arrival in Jackson Hole, we thought we could make definite plans, permanent plans.

Another trip to Victor seemed to be of the greatest urgency. The roads were now reasonably good, and all our crated furniture, boxes and barrels of household supplies, and some ranch equipment and tools were still stored there.

Since the horses had to be shod before making the trip, we started for Moran the next morning. A blacksmith was located there doing government work needed in the building of Jackson Lake Dam. He also did work for the ranchers as time permitted.

About six miles down the road, we found several Buffalo Creek families who had come to Pacific Creek for a Fourth of July picnic. They insisted we have dinner with them and we did not need much urging. Besides all the good eats they had brought, there was fresh trout they had just caught in Pacific Creek. The picnic dinner was far better than our sandwiches would have been.

All too soon we had to go on to Moran and upon arriving were fortunate in finding that the blacksmith could do the work immediately. Putting on eight horseshoes takes considerable time, so as usual it was late when we reached home again.

Two days later, while Will was staying with me, Mac started for Victor. This proved to be a six-day trip. He took time to get most of our freight over the pass and as far as Wilson and [then] brought home one load. The trip to Wilson and back could usually be made in two days, so it helped to have the freight there rather than Victor. A few days later, we found a Buffalo homesteader who was willing to haul our goods from there. He was to take our wagon, so Mac made a large, flat frame to use instead of the wagon box. The crated furniture and farm machinery were bulky and required much space. Bob, the homesteader, was taking four horses so felt he could bring an extra big load.

Mac was glad to be able to continue work at home. It was time to cut the wild hay, and we would have to have that for winter feed. With only two work horses it would be a slow job. Then Ginger's colt arrived, so little Nellie had to be worked with big Jet for a few days. In late July we had more difficulties. Mice or some other rodents were eating on our bacon and cheese. Since the ground under the cabin was the coolest place, Mac had made a sort of trap door in the floor and stored perishable food underneath. One night Mac had awakened from his bed on the floor to find a mouse perched on [his] ear chewing his hair. That was funny, but a night or two later he was awakened to find a weasel running across his face. That was not funny at all for weasels are vicious little creatures.

On the following morning, when [it was] barely daylight, he heard the chickens making an uproar. Dashing out in the semi-darkness, he found a weasel raiding the chicken coop. Fortunately he arrived before any chickens had been killed, but the weasel easily escaped out the back of the coop. We had no traps and did not know how we could possibly catch him. The chickens were left out that night and most roosted in the trees, afraid to go back in the coop. But a terrible squawking the next morning [had] Mac rushing out again. This time the weasel had the rooster by one leg but let loose when Mac arrived.

This was getting serious, for the little weasel seemed to know he had the upper hand. He began to run about in daylight and even in the cabin. He could always escape between the floorboards and the lower log. I wondered if I could possibly hit him with my little .22 but knew it was doubtful. Once I tried when he ran out behind the cabin but I missed, of course. He was not even worried, soon returned, and came into the cabin and calmly started chewing on a bone under my bed. As he moved back into the corner, I thought maybe there was a chance of hitting him so tried again. As usual he disappeared between the floor and log. However, to our surprise he did not show up again. A couple of days later Mac decided to take up the floorboard where he had disappeared. Sure enough there lay the little creature with a bullet hole through his head.

It was then we finally succeeded in getting some kittens. The weasel had been taking care of the mice, which helped, and though the kittens were still small, we thought they might be of some use. Squeals was most appropriately named, the other was called Rats, but they never proved very efficient. A few days later I nearly choked my pony to death. I had tied her too near the creek bank and she had gone over but fortunately [was] discovered in time.

Laddie, a Collie dog, soon became a family member. He was a stray, unusual in that country, and very timid. It took several attempts to get him to come to the cabin, but I finally succeeded, and then he was willing to stay. He was a friendly, gentle dog but never would chase or round up cattle or horses. He retreated from spitting kittens and trembled when coyotes howled. Yet, some months later probably saved Mac's life by his bravery.

Harold Cole McKinstry:

It was not long before we received another letter from the Land Office, again rejecting our application on the grounds that we were still applying for Forest Land. About that time one of the inspectors from the Land Office arrived and personally inspected the land. He found their maps to be wrong, assured us that our application would be approved and that we could count on a letter of approval as soon as he returned to Ogden.

I had hoped to get in some crop and raise a little feed for winter use. With all this uncertainty there was nothing that could be done in this line other than mow such small patches of wild hay as could be found. Thus I was able to put up a few loads of hay but at a tremendous expenditure of time and effort. I did cut timber and make fence bucks and fence poles, for I knew they could be hauled to any chosen spot.

I stacked about a dozen of these fence bucks together near the cabin and piled enough hay on top to make a rather cozy, although thoroughly unscientific, chicken coop. Our dozen chickens roosted there quite comfortably. One night they set up a terrible clamor. I ran out, barefooted and in my PJs. In the bright moonlight I spotted a chicken flopping wildly on the ground, squawking bloody murder. As I reached for him a weasel loosed his hold on the rooster's leg and disappeared. Hardly had I gotten back to sleep when the racket again aroused me, and the weasel had a death grip on a hen. As the weasel darted off into the night, I threw a block of wood after him. It must have hit close for he did not return to bother the chickens that night.

The sun had just come up when I suddenly awoke again. I could feel the sharp claws of some animal as he ran across my throat. I opened my eyes to see the weasel on my pillow, not six inches from my face. I grabbed for him but missed.

As usual I left soon after breakfast to cut timber. Linda was busy baking when she noticed something run across the floor. Watching, she saw the weasel appear, scamper under the bed and through a hole in the floor in the far corner. She was ready when he stuck his head up again and shot him dead center. It was the first thing she had ever killed, almost the first time to use her new rifle or any other for that matter.

On the third of August we had a substantial increase in livestock. I had gone to Elk for mail, and while [I was] there, one of the neighbors came in and asked, "Anybody want some kittens?"

"Sure," I said. "We need some to keep the mice down."

So I put the kittens in the gunny sack I had tied behind the saddle to hold the mail and started home. Before reaching the house, I circled around through the willows where I had seen Ginger early in the morning. Sure enough, she had foaled. A fine little sorrel colt with a star on his face stood beside her, nursing. He tried to play but stepped in a hole and fell down. Jumping up, he stood while I stroked his neck and face, paying no heed to Ginger's nervous coaxing.

That event entitled Ginger to a rest, so that afternoon I hitched Jet and Nelly together to rake hay. Jet was one-third larger than Nelly. I had difficulty taking the harness in enough to keep it from falling off the little nag. They really made a "side-hill" team, but raking hay was a light job and Nelly really didn't have to do much but hold up her end of the neck yoke. So we got the hay raked and shocked,[†] in shape to leave until Ginger could again start working. So, little by little, we accumulated a stack of hay. It looked like plenty, but little did we realize then the demands that a long Jackson Hole winter can put upon the feed supply.

On August 14 we further increased our livestock. When Linda rode to the post office for mail, the postmistress asked her if we did not want a dog, saying there was a shepherd dog that someone had lost, intentionally or otherwise, and she wanted to get rid of it. So Linda put a rope around the dog's neck and led him home beside her pony. The little pooch convinced us that he was the most timid thing that ever lived. We couldn't make him chase a cow, not even a rabbit. If the kittens spit at him, he retreated. If the coyotes howled near at hand, he crowded the door, trembling. But he was an affectionate pet and apparently intelligent in some ways, so he became a member of the household.

Linda Preston McKinstry:

All summer we enjoyed wonderful vegetables. We had not been able to plant a garden, but our Buffalo friends supplied us generously. The mountain-grown peas, lettuce, onions, carrots, and turnips were wonderful. Everything they had was shared with all neighbors who could use them and we surely could.

[†] To "shock" hay is to put it into small, often conical, piles in the field while it awaits removal to a large stack or barn.

August–September 1915

In August, we attended our first schoolhouse dance. It was quite typical of the one described by Owen Wister in *The Virginian*. However, the Buffalo school had only one room so the little youngsters slept on benches around the sides. Most of the time, Bob Coolidge, the man who had brought our freight from Wilson, played the fiddle. He was sometimes seconded by someone playing the little portable organ [that] had been brought in for the occasion. Later in the evening, Ben Taylor played the harmonica for dances, and he could play and dance at the same time.

There were several square dances at which Ben or Beaver Tooth Charlie would call the numbers. Both were efficient. We enjoyed round dances, the waltz or the two-step, and I was surprised to find how well the ranchers and cowboys could dance. Dancing with them was really a pleasure.

Since this was Saturday night, they quit dancing around midnight. A table was brought in and all the eats spread out, sandwiches, fried chicken, and lots of cake. After enjoying the supper and friendships, we started our six-mile trip back over the hill. It was so cold though after mid-August that riding horseback, my toes ached miserably before we reached home. Mac walked all those miles because Jet and Ginger were working so hard during the day he would not use either one at night. He said he kept warmer anyway. By the time we reached home and warmed up it was daylight, and most of Sunday was spent sleeping.

The next day Rosencrans and the man from Ogden arrived to make new surveys and reclassify the land for which we had applied. Then on the following day, the twenty-third of August, we were stunned to receive another letter from Ogden saying, "Applications not being considered now." Did we have a homestead or didn't we?

Mac had already been stacking hay on the supposed new site, hauling down bucks, and building logs as opportunity offered. We had decided on the location for our house, cabin, barn, and chicken coop, for after meeting Mr. Hoyt in July felt the matter was definitely settled. Mr. Miller, the Forest Supervisor, had told us that Mr. Hoyt would have the final say about it.

Mac immediately wrote to Mr. Hoyt and had the letter ready to mail in the morning. At 6:30 that morning Billie Thompson arrived much perturbed. They would have to leave the next day for Idaho Falls. The expected baby was due to arrive and Emily would require a Caesarean operation. Dr. Huff, though a qualified physician, could not take the case because there was no hospital or needed equipment.

Since they must leave at once, they asked if we would move into their cabin and care for their livestock until they returned. As always, the unexpected. Of course we agreed to help them though moving there meant more delay. They said they would be gone for two months. There really

Ginger (white) and Jet (black) served the McKinstry's well, as riding horses, work horses, and by pulling all types of wagons, buggies, and sleighs. (McKinstry)

were some advantages for us as their cabin was only a mile instead of four from our new location—if it was ours. Also they had a corral and barn of sorts.

We started packing things needed, stored our crated furniture, boxes, barrels, etc., in our cabin. Two days later we moved to the Thompson place.

It was 9:30 in the evening when we arrived. Mac had had a long hunt for the horses, which caused considerable delay. By the time we finished packing, gathered the cow, calf, Ginger's colt, chickens, and dog, it was late before we were ready to start. After arriving, it was much later before we ate supper, for the Thompson stove was not like our Majestic. It even upset Mac's calm disposition and mine was nearly ruined as the days passed. But we settled down and made the best of things. Incidentally, [it] was at that time that our long expected wash tubs arrived from Jackson, now that I had Emily's to use.

On every mail we looked for a letter from Mr. Hoyt, but none arrived until more than two weeks later. It was then September 6. First he apologized for the delay because of having been out of town, and then came the good news. Since he had seen the land and listed it as agricultural, he was sure the application would go through. In the meantime, he would have Mr. Miller give us a Special Use Permit. So again we believed the matter settled, and this time it really was, nearly five months after our arrival. Even then our official application could not be filed, pending the public opening of the land.

Mac continued hauling logs and bucks and started building a barn. With winter coming, the horses must have protection and that had priority. The house logs could continue drying.

Harold Cole McKinstry:

The next day Linda went over the hill to the little school house on the Buffalo where Sunday school was held. I stayed at home rather than ride one of the horses I had been working so hard all the week. Toward evening storm clouds blackened the sky and made it seem much later than it actually was. But Linda had not come and she was long overdue. The wind had been blowing a gale all day, and I thought of the many trees along her trail, long since killed by fire, but still standing like huge flagpoles, but ready to topple in the right kind of wind. Under one of those both horse and rider could be crushed.

The team was out on the range, somewhere. I ran a mile to find them. Jumping on Jet I started over the hill on the trail over which I hoped Linda might come. But there were several [routes]. We could pass within calling distance and not know it. I called. The "yip-yip" of coyotes from all sides was the only answer. For the first time in my life I hated the sound of them. It was growing too dark to see far. Then the horse threw up her head and nickered. Nelly's answering nicker came, and I saw Linda come into sight.

Behind her saddle she carried a sack full of fresh vegetables. Germanns, on the Buffalo, had a wonderful garden and had insisted that she wait for a supply of the fresh stuff. They looked inviting, all right, but not half so much as did Linda as she came riding out of the timber in the gathering darkness.

She brought word of dance plans, scheduled for the following Wednesday evening at the Buffalo schoolhouse. Even though [I was] putting in long hours in the timber, such an event was not to be passed up. On the day set, we started right after supper. Again I preferred to let the team rest, so Linda rode Nelly and I walked. It was about four or five miles over the hill. We never did know exactly, but it took a big hour to make the trip.

Everyone was there. Babies were stacked on the table and under the table. For the latecomers there was no room inside so they parked their babies in the wagon from which the horses had been unhitched. Beavertooth Charlie was there in all his glory—some might have another name for it—and called some of the dances. We still hear him as he was then, slouched on a bench against the log wall, "Not too fast and not too slow–," his protruding yellow teeth flashing in the light of the kerosene lanterns, his sing-song nasal voice for some indefinable reason adding zest to the party.

It was midnight when we stopped to eat. The coffee in the big camp pot on the box stove was boiling. Mountain appetites were sharp. The babies asleep on the table were moved to the floor and in their place came covered dishes brought from the wagons. There was fried chicken, elk steak, potato salad, sandwiches, cake, pie, two big freezers of homemade ice cream and no end of coffee.

Before one o'clock, we [were] dancing again and did not quit until the brilliant red across the eastern sky heralded the new day. The party broke up. Linda rode and I walked. The August night was chilly, a slight touch of frost in the air. I was glad to be walking. It was warmer that way. We reached home just in time to get the morning chores done on time, eat breakfast and get into the timber for a full day's work.

But no timber work was done. Early in the day the rangers came again to reclassify the land for which we had applied. Working with them used up the day. Then, the following day, came word from Ogden informing us that our application could not be considered, that additional information was needed. That meant another S.O.S. letter to Ogden and another special trip to the post office.

About that time, Billie and Emily Thompson had both [gotten] jobs at Moran, he on construction, she in the kitchen. They wanted to move up there through September and asked if we would not move over to their place to care for it and their livestock. We jumped at this opportunity, for with our own plans so indefinite we were glad to quit camping for a while. With our livestock, some loaded, some trailing, we moved over there, still awaiting the necessary permit, still optimistic. On September 6 our long hoped for answer came. The Ogden office would approve the issuance of a Special Permit for the land, and appropriate instructions were being sent to the U.S. Forestry office in Jackson. Thus we were ready to start our permanent buildings.

But when we rolled out the next morning the ground was white with snow, and the storm continued through the day. The logs were too wet and slippery to handle so I went to the post office for mail. The stage driver had brought our sewing machine, it having been in storage all summer in Victor. For Linda that was a real event, for she had long awaited its arrival.

By night of the next day, the sky had cleared so we could see the stars. As much for the joy of setting stakes on our own place as for necessity, we went over at night followed by two kittens and the dog, and by the aid of the North Star, set stakes due north and south in the approximate area of our planned house. The uncertainty up to this time had prevented even this much definite planning.

Immediately I started tearing down the cabin built on the upper place, preparatory to hauling it down for reassembly on the new land, ours to be. I did not relish the idea of having to refit every log, and the only way to avoid that seemed to require the identification for replacing in its same relative position. So, with lumber crayon, I numbered the logs from the ground up, prefixing the number with N for north, E for east, etc. Taking off the roof was not too difficult. It was only pine boards covered with tar paper. Nor was the removal of the floor a big job. But the logs had to be pried loose with a crowbar. The 20D spikes had been put in to stay, and the corners could not be split if the logs were to retain their usefulness. So I set skid poles against the wall at each end in such a way as to prevent either end of the log from falling until both ends were free. Thus, one by one, I tore them from the building we had worked so hard to construct, hauled them to the new site and laid them out in proper order.

CHAPTER FOUR

The Logs Go Up Again

Linda Preston McKinstry:

It was the first of October. I had taken hot soup over to Mac to add to his lunch and stayed to eat with him. Returning to Thompsons', I was surprised to see a team and wagon in the yard and several people moving about. I was more surprised to find that the Thompsons had returned with the new baby, and Almer Nelson, Emily's brother, was with them. We had heard nothing from them and [they] were not expected for another two weeks.

Since Billie was to help move down our cabin upon his return, that was still on the upper place piled full of the crated furniture and freight. So we all had to live in the two-room Thompson cabin until ours could be moved. (As usual, the unexpected.) The most unfortunate part was that the Thompsons had returned with severe colds, and under such crowded conditions we knew we could not escape. We didn't.

Mac and Billie, as soon as he was able, started moving down the cabin. Mac brought the roof and flooring first, and then the men started tearing down the logs, marking them so they could be more easily reassembled. Several days later we moved in, even though the cabin still had to be chinked and daubed. It seemed good to be in our own little place again and once again settled until our house could be built.[†]

In early October the moose were becoming belligerent. One day when Mac was up in the woods for a load of logs and bucks, he had a most unpleasant encounter. Usually, even at this time of year, the moose do not look for trouble, but this was a young bull wanting to show his authority. As Mac was busy loading, the horses suddenly snorted and then started to run. Looking up, Mac saw a moose, bristles up, running across the nearby opening and heading directly for the team. He had barely time to jump

October–December 1915

[†] *The McKinstrys decide to live in the reconstructed cabin made of moved logs only temporarily while they build a bigger house. From here on Linda and Mac refer to the small temporary home as "the cabin" and the bigger home being constructed as "the house."*

onto the wagon and reach for the reins. The moose continued to come, apparently to charge on Jet's side. So Mac turned the team directly toward the moose, hoping he would stop. He did stop but stood his ground and did not leave. [Mac tried] to load a few more logs, but as soon as he would get off the wagon on the opposite side from the moose, the bull would dash around after him. He had to give up. Then, too, the horses were getting so restless, they would not stand, and with half a load he started home. The moose tagged along for some distance but finally stopped. The next time Mac went to the woods he carried his rifle.

By mid-October Mac had the barn pretty well along. Putting up the logs seemed to be accomplished quite rapidly, although I never could understand how he accomplished the work alone. The [barn] logs were twenty-eight feet long, the lower logs over fourteen inches in diameter at the larger end, and twelve or thirteen inches at the smaller. The upper logs averaged nine or ten inches in diameter, but green logs of that size are frightfully heavy, each weighing several hundred pounds. He used a pulley, rolling them up on skids, which he said was easy, although Jet and Ginger had to pull hard to get them up. Occasionally, a dry log from a dead tree could be found, but seldom was one of the right length in good condition. Fencing was not yet started, but some 4000 poles and 1000 bucks would be needed for both fences and corrals.

The last of October we had to make a trip to Jackson. A dentist was there and both of us needed some work done. Then, too, I had continued to feel half sick since my severe cold and needed to see the doctor. More groceries and equipment were also needed, including windows and doors for our house. That meant a three-day trip, at least, allowing only one day in town. It took a whole day each way to drive the forty miles between Jackson and the ranch. As Ginger could not make the trip with her colt, we borrowed a second horse from Joe Chapline, a young man who had come to Elk to teach school there.

At the ranch, Ginger, her colt and Nellie were turned loose, also the cow. But all could go into the barn for protection. The calf was left in the corral, the poles of which were sufficiently far apart allowed him to reach through for milk. Two chickens were put in a box in the barn, but the others were roosting in the trees and we could not catch them. Mac had made one wonderful coop for them, using bucks well covered with hay. Then the cow ate the hay and the chickens could get out as they wished.

The kittens were left out and we hoped they would learn to hunt. Although mice and chipmunks were everywhere, the kittens spent their days yowling for feed. There were very few coyotes around so we were not worried about them, although the biological survey man told Mac there

would be plenty down after the first winter storm arrived, wolves, too. We were glad no bad storm had yet come although we had many light snows.

I had a wonderful time in Jackson, even with dentistry work to be done and still not feeling too well. We had timed the trip so I could attend the meeting of the Pure Food Club there. A University of Wyoming nutritionist had told me of the club, and when I had made inquiries, I was warmly welcomed. It seemed so good to be back with people with whom I had so many interests in common. Mrs. Huff, wife of the doctor, Mrs. Wagner, wife of the banker, Mrs. Miller, wife of the forest supervisor, and Mrs. Van Vleck, whose husband owned the Mercantile business, were all members. With these people we had many pleasant contacts over the years. It was a treat to again be using lovely china and silver and to enjoy luscious, dainty refreshments. It was on this trip, too, that the doctor informed us that we would have another member in the family in early June.

Back at the ranch the days passed quickly. Mac was more than busy with the barn to finish, chicken coop and house to be built, and roadways to make. But first of all a path through the woods to the spring was needed. All our water had to be brought from there, and to go around the grove of trees was quite a walk. The pathway had to be cut through the pines and the windfalls removed, thus shortening the distance by several hundred feet.

The Pure Food Club thrived from the nineteen teens until the 1960s. Linda's reference to the club in 1915 is one of the earliest mentions of its existence.

This photograph taken around 1930 shows in the back row (l to r): Amy Dallis, Christobel Kent, Mrs. Susie Loyd, Lucy Miner, Georgia (Ely) Crail, Etta Leek, and Grandma Deloney. In the front (l to r) Grace Loyd, Phoebe Beagle, Francis Deloney (Clark), Calvin Beagle, Mrs. Ely and Mrs. Hoagland and son. (American Heritage Center, University of Wyoming, S.N. Leek Collection, Box 49)

A later photo of the Pure Food Club at the Mercill home. Bottom row (l to r) Eva Boyle, Ella McClain Mercill, Mrs. A.C. McCain, Clara Murie, Gretchen Huff. Middle row (l to r) Margaret Steed, Mrs. Harry Weston, Mrs. Billy Owen. Top row: Mabel Eynon, Jennie Kelly, Mrs. Charles Huff, Mardy Murie, Mrs. Roy Van Vleck, and Grace Miller. (JHHS&M)

I kept busy with indoor work. Baking, especially bread, for we ate so much, cake, cookies, donuts, pies, and regular meal preparation took much time. For several weeks during the winter we had no eggs but were happily surprised that good cakes and cookies could be made without them. A friend had given me a bread mixer for a wedding present and it was a big help. Since I would use some five quarts of flour at a time, Mac would often help turn the mixing crank as the mixture had to be very stiff at that altitude.

We had begun to unpack some of our barrels and boxes but had room for only needed utensils. It was good to have even a little more cooking equipment and china. We had feared the latter, after the seventy-mile freight haul from Victor over the rough roads, would be broken to bits, but practically everything came through in perfect shape. All the credit goes to my mother for her wonderfully efficient packing.

In early November we finally received our bed springs, en route since last March. Why they were so long in arriving we never knew. Was it nice for both of us to have real beds! To save space Mac made upper and lower bunk beds in one corner of the cabin.

Our first Thanksgiving was approaching and we expected Will up from Jackson. Without traditional turkey, celery, and cranberry sauce, I wondered how we could have a very good dinner, but we did. Hot bouillon made from bouillon cubes found in one of the barrels, roast duck, which we did not even have when I planned the dinner, but Mac got some in time, dressing, mashed potatoes, boiled onions, and scalloped tomatoes completed the main part. Dessert was apple and peach pies made from dried fruit, cheese, and stuffed prunes.

It snowed all day on Wednesday and as Will had not arrived by nightfall, [we] thought he might have lost the way. Mac started out later in the evening and found him at Thompsons' abed and asleep. He had come horseback, had evidently gotten on our land, but finding no road in the knee-deep snow had gone back to Thompsons'. So he came over Thursday morning.

Mac had gotten our [new] house well started and the side logs in place in order to have Will help him with the rafters, as that work was most difficult for one man alone. By working Thursday afternoon and Friday, [they] succeeded in getting them in place.

Our house was square and built of twenty-eight-foot logs and was to have a hip roof. Therefore the rafters went from each corner to a point in the center. After those were in place, Mac could more easily continue the roof work alone. Many ranchers, I am sure, thought we were out of our minds to think of building a house right away, but we wanted an attractive home as soon as possible. Building could be done while the snow was too deep for outside ranch work. There was to be a kitchen and bedroom, each thirteen feet square, a living room thirteen by sixteen, a pantry, and another room each about six by nine and a half. The latter could be used as a bedroom although we thought some time it could be made into a bathroom — it never was. Will left a couple of days after Thanksgiving as he was working in Jackson.

While putting up logs, Mac sprained his back. We tried to doctor that with antiphlogistine[†] and that not being successful, tried a mustard plaster. Unfortunately, I did not remember that flour must be mixed with the mustard, and the hope for cure, which was worse than the sprain, was never forgotten.

In early December we had a nice surprise visit when a young ranch couple from Buffalo Creek arrived. They, the McClures, had come over the hill horseback. Although the snow was up to the horses' knees, it was light and fluffy so they had no special difficulty. Their children had been left with their grandmother and the trip was in celebration of their fourth wedding anniversary. These were the people who had loaned us plates and flat irons when those articles were so badly needed. We had a wonderful two-day visit and hated to see them leave.

[†] *An anti-inflammatory medicine.*

[dagger] *"Outside" was a regional shorthand expression which meant out of the valley into the wider world. Thus, "going outside" meant leaving the Jackson Hole area.*

Work on the house had to be stopped long enough to get a bridge built where the beaver were flooding a place on our road. This was necessary in order to reach the main road or even over to Thompsons'. In the deep snow, this proved a far more difficult task than expected. It was a wet, stormy day when [Mac] started out. Driving Jet through the snow to haul logs, cutting them and working in heavy, wet clothes and overshoes proved almost too much for Mac. He was so tired when he arrived home, he could not even eat his supper. He said he did not realize how tired he was until he stopped working and had the bridge completed. I was really worried for I had never seen him quite so exhausted. However, a night's rest and a late breakfast the next morning made him feel better, though still overtired.

Another trip outside[dagger] must be made as we had to have a sleigh for winter use. I could not stay on the place alone and decided to accept McClures' invitation to go there. They had only a one-room cabin for a family of four, but Mr. McClure went to his mother's at night as she had a cabin nearby. She, too, had a houseful, as a married daughter and children were there while her husband was on a trip outside. On Sunday Grandma McClure invited us all over for a late dinner after Sunday school. There were nine of us, but these one-room cabins never seemed overcrowded.

According to present day living standards, we would all have been classed as sub-standard and poverty stricken. It was the usual thing for families of four or more to be living in a one-room cabin. But none of those pioneers felt abused, only lucky. Even overnight strangers, as well as guests, would always be accommodated some way.

Mac and I sometimes wondered why more of the ranchers, after getting a good start, did not build better homes more quickly. One little extra room, or place for cooking, might be added but frequently that was all. All available money was used to buy more livestock, extra hay, grain for feed, needed farm equipment, etc. We, too, soon learned that these things took more cash than anticipated. But we continued to plan [and began to construct] a real house as soon as possible.[dagger]

To return to Mac's trip outside and my visit with McClures: He had arranged with Billie to look after our livestock and was to bring back a sled for him as well as for ourselves. Mac rode one horse of the team, the second horse carrying the harnesses. It proved to be a seven-day trip, as roads were not good, sleds needed in some places, wagons in others. Snowstorms caused complications, but ultimately he arrived back, although there were such big drifts by Grovont that he could travel only about fifteen miles farther and had to stay at Ferrins' that night. Although only twelve miles from home, the team had to rest. He arrived home about noon the next day then came after me.

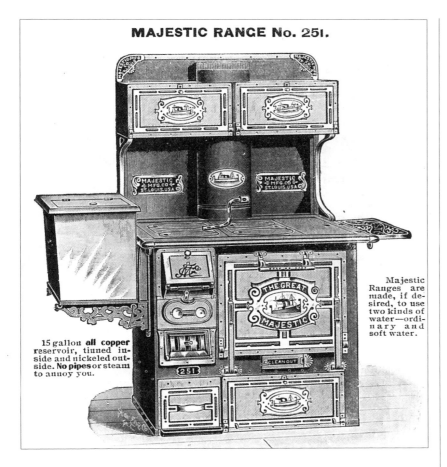

MAJESTIC RANGE No. 251.

Majestic
Ranges are
made, if de-
sired, to use
two kinds of
water—ordi-
nary and
soft water.

15 gallon **all copper**
reservoir, tinned in-
side and nickeled out-
side. **No pipes** or steam
to annoy you.

That was about ten days before Christmas and had been candy-making day at McClures'. Pounds and pounds of it had been made. With plenty of cream and butter, the quality was outstanding. After supper we started for home, and descriptions in my letter to Mother tells how much the trip was enjoyed:

"It was glorious riding home from McClures the other night, and although cold we managed to keep warm. There was a full moon but so cold that our collars, front of our caps and the fur robe were white with frost. And so were Mac's eyebrows. My hair gets white with frost where it slips out from under my cap. We keep the lighted lantern under the fur robe at our feet, and that makes quite a foot warmer."

Harold Cole McKinstry:
The Thompsons returned October 1, [although they were] not due for two weeks, but by that time winter was threatening. The nights were cold. So it was agreed that we should live with them until we could get our cabin rebuilt. Another snowstorm hit October 3, temporarily slowing the work,

but with some occasional help from Billie, we had the job far enough along so that we could move in October 9. He came over to help me move the good old Majestic range. By night we had moved in, although there was much chinking and daubing yet to be done to make the walls really tight.

From one of the soap holes across the creek I hauled some gumbo clay, already mixed to the consistency of heavy putty. During the warm part of the day, I troweled it into the cracks between the logs, and at night it froze dry, staying put far better than if it had dried in the sun. On the roof I spread tar paper and covered it with clay dug from a nearby bank. No cold could hurt us in that cabin.

The next job was fencing. I had many fence bucks piled in the woods. They needed to be hauled in for fences and corrals. I drove to the pile and started loading. The horses snorted and moved restlessly. Down the flat, not 100 yards away, came a young moose at a fast trot. His bristles were up. There was blood in his eye.

I jumped for the reins, stopping the team almost before they had got started to run. He made a sashay as though to attack from the side. To avoid that I headed the team straight for him, hoping he'd hit the neck yoke. But just as he was about to hit, he sidestepped, strutting stiff legged around the wagon. He seemed to have decided the horses were not his enemy but had his eye on me. I circled the team around, again pulling up to the pile of bucks. Thinking the brute might leave, I climbed out to continue loading. Hardly had I hit the ground before the moose was there. I gained the safety of the wagon just in time. The moose stood there, shaking his great antlers, pawing the ground. I lifted a big seven-foot buck and tried to drop it over his head, but he was too fast. I could not get hold of a thing that I could swing as a club. The team was getting restless and ready to take off, so I guided them into the trail and headed off for home to get a rifle. When I returned a half hour later, the moose was gone.

Little by little we got groceries via P.P. [parcel post]. After long delay we got a sack of flour and Linda baked bread. What a treat! We had had only hot bread up to that time.[†] We intended to go to the R.R. [railroad] for our winter's grocery supplies as soon as time permitted. But news came that a dentist would be in Jackson for a few days late in October, and we needed some work done. So we borrowed a horse to use in Ginger's place, a spring wagon in the place of our big one, and left the morning of the twenty-eighth.

We were able to get our dental work done on the morning of the twenty-ninth, and in the afternoon Linda had the opportunity of meeting some of the women of the town, attending their Pure Food Club, etc. Other than our brief stay when we came over the pass, she had not been in Jackson.

On the last day of October a neighbor from Mormon Row arrived with a load of oats I had purchased for horse feed. With that on hand we felt pretty secure, still not realizing the tremendous demands of the long winter. My brother Will came with him, and together we got lots of work done. But on November 7 the snow started, daily increasing in depth. Wild ducks lit on our ponds occasionally, and I shot some preparatory to a celebration on Thanksgiving. I also killed a fine young bull elk. Our larder was full of meat.

Still our grocery supply was short for the six months of winter ahead. Will left just after Thanksgiving to work for a rancher down country. Again we were alone and I had to make the trip to Victor. So we arranged for Linda to stay with some neighbors over on the Buffalo and for Billie Thompson to care for our livestock.

It was December 10 when I left, riding one horse, leading the other, which carried both harnesses. At the foot of the pass, I bought a secondhand sleigh and proceeded on to Victor, arriving the night of the eleventh. I spent the next day shopping, and on the morning of the thirteenth started back over the pass. At the roadhouse on the west side, I hired a lead team to help pull the load to the top.

"Turn 'em loose when you get to the top," said the owner. "They'll come home. They do it right along."

[†] *In the margin is written "Flour all the time, made bread. Just ran out." Perhaps Linda was rationing the remaining flour and making only one or two loaves at a time occasionally, rather than making bread ahead.*

Weather had been fine that far, but when I got down into the valley again I struck a storm. Snow was drifting badly and the temperature dropped to minus twenty-five. The sleigh pulled hard in the intense cold and the drifts became steadily deeper. I did not reach home until the night of the sixteenth. The next day I went to get Linda on the Buffalo.

Christmas 1915

Linda Preston McKinstry:

On Christmas Eve, a program, tree, and social evening was planned at Buffalo school and we planned to attend. We were just ready to start for the affair when Will arrived, and as this caused some delay in starting, the program was about over when we reached the school. The gifts were then distributed and there was a little bag of candy for each youngster. A social time followed and although over seventy were present in that little one-room school, no one felt overcrowded and all had a good time.

It was long after midnight before we arrived home and got into bed, so [we] were weary for Christmas day, but after our noon dinner [we] brought in our Christmas tree and decorated it. Mac had tried to bring some special treats for Christmas dinner when he came from Victor, but the celery had frozen stiff, the squash, onions, and cabbage [were] partly frozen, though some was still usable. With night temperatures averaging twenty to thirty below and daytime temperature near zero, there was no chance to keep things from freezing in an open sleigh. The tree decorations were mainly strings of popcorn and paper chains, although a few more were added when we opened Mother's box and found decorations in there.

We all enjoyed our gifts and had been most generously remembered. Mother's boxes were always filled with surprises and treats. My sister had sent a lamp with an attractive shade she had made, and to enjoy a soft light in place of the regular kerosene lamp was much appreciated. So were my fur-lined gloves from Mac. For him I had ordered a rifle scabbard from a leather goods company in Thermopolis. I knew I would have more peace of mind knowing he had a safe way of carrying his rifle when riding horseback. I had gotten *The Virginian* (by Owen Wister) as we wanted to read that book together since the locale was in Wyoming and Jackson Hole.

Mother had sent material for drapes for our living-room-to-be, which we liked very much. As the necessary chinking on the inside of the log buildings is not attractive, we planned to cover our living room walls and ceiling with two tones of brown burlap and already had it ordered. It was March before we could finally move into our house, but when we did, and our living room was ultimately completed, it proved to be a most attractive place. We were delighted.

Will stayed for three days before having to return to his job in Jackson. The day after Christmas was Sunday and we all drove over to Sunday school.

Even arrived on time which was something of a record. It was a frightfully cold day and we should have remained at home, for we were all thoroughly chilled before we arrived back at 6:30. On Monday Will helped Mac [with] boarding the [new] roof and had time to put on some of the tar paper.

The snow was getting deeper and deeper, and it had snowed all Christmas day. In order to keep our road open at all, Mac had to travel it almost daily to the junction with the Thompson road. He would drive, standing on the doubletrees to help drag down the center of the road. From there to the main highway, he and Billie tried to keep the road open but had to give up in early January. One of Billie's horses lost a colt trying to wallow through the snow, and trying to keep the road open proved too much for all the horses. Since our extra heavy storm on November 7, we continued to have snow every day for the next sixty.

The only way one could get about was on skis or webs. I had my snowshoes, or webs, and could enjoy short walks on them, but since they were not large enough for Mac, he was helpless. Roy Lozier said he would make skis for us, or help Mac, but had been too busy to do it.

So Mac had to make his own from what information he had gathered, as it was impossible to get to Loziers' for assistance. Mac had brought the

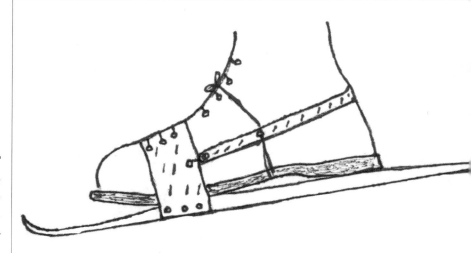

Mac made his own skis after it snowed for 60 days in a row. The illustration was drawn by either Mac or Linda.

lumber, fir boards eight feet long, four inches wide, and one and a half inches thick on his last trip outside. These had to be planed down from the center to both ends, then one end had to be steamed in order to bend the curve for the front. They were put over the wash boiler, and the water had to boil for hours and hours in order to soften the wood sufficiently. From here on Mac can describe the procedure:

"The actual bending was accomplished by inserting the points down between two parallel eight-foot logs and weighting down the skis just behind the logs to force the right degree of curve as the wood dried. After three days they were removed, and to our great satisfaction the job was a success.

"Then came the sanding, polishing, and waxing. It took a lot of arm-strong, the only power we had. With a good old flat iron, heated on the stove, candles were then melted and the hot wax ironed into the wood. This produced a beautiful, slick finish to which no snow would stick.

"For the bindings I cut three-inch wide strips from an old high-top leather boot, looped them over the center of each ski, countersinking them on the sides, leaving room for the toe of the shoe to slide under, and fastened on the edge of the ski with small screws. Then I cut out the leather up the center and punched eyelets for laces by which the size could be regulated.

"A hole in each side of this toe piece permitted the use of thongs for attaching the heel straps, and a hole on each side of this provided the way to hold it in place with a thong around the instep.

"To facilitate hill climbing, I chiseled out a furrow in the bottom, 1½ inches wide, 24 inches long, and ⅛ inch deep. In this I laid a strip of dry elk hide taken from the shin, pointing the hair to the rear, then fastening it firmly in place with small tacks. This did not impede forward travel as the hair was as slick as the polished ski, but when rubbed the wrong way by a backward slide, the bristles dug into the snow. Shiny tin tacked on the ski where the foot rested prevented snow from balling up under the foot.

"We used a single ski pole, six feet long, usually lodgepole, peeled and straight. In running thickly timbered hills or mountainsides, we needed lots of braking power, and the only way we could get it was by holding the pole in both hands, extending it back between the legs and sitting on it hard enough to gouge the end into the snow with whatever force necessary.

"The whole outfit was not fancy but extremely durable and very serviceable."

I tried them but found them too heavy for me to handle and never could use them. But they were really serviceable and lasted Mac the ten years we were in the country. He must have traveled thousands of miles through all kinds of weather and snow conditions. Had I known then of some of the dangers encountered, I would have worried even more than I did. Although he had never skied before, he must have learned well for he won a first when a ski meet was held at Moran.

Harold Cole McKinstry:

With the grub box full, we settled down to the job of the winter, cutting firewood and building a house. It seemed impossible to ever get enough wood ahead to last long. The minus thirty-degree weather demanded lots of fuel. Fortunately the house logs were cut and piled at hand. Every morning I had to shovel snow from them and shovel a place to work. For sixty days, starting November 7, there had been snow every day. With the flat rocks previously hauled, I laid up a dry foundation, twenty-seven feet square. Beneath the snow the ground was not frozen, but after being uncovered, it froze in a hurry, so I had to work fast.

The first few rounds of logs went into place with surprising ease. There was no high lift. I could keep my feet on the ground. One end of the twenty-seven-foot log could be skidded approximately into place and tied there while the other end was moved up. But it was all time consuming. The end of each log had to be flattened on the top and bottom and inside in order to make a square, well-fitted corner. This done, the log was put into place for trial, but always there were humps and irregularities that had to be hewn off the bottom of that log or top of the one below in order to let the corners fit down tight. Sometimes I found it necessary to try three or four times before getting the right fit.

Skis were not only necessary for travel, but they became a source of entertainment also. Here young people hitch a ride on the back of Ernest Van Leuwen's milk delivery sleigh.
(JHHS&M)

The partitions had to be notched in at the same time, and because of the bows in the logs, these notches could only be marked by trial. But little by little the walls took form. As they rose, it became necessary to skid them to the top with a horse. That was where the trouble began. The logs were so frosty and slick that when once started moving, they kept going. Only by slowly moving one end to the top on a skid, then tying it securely in place before starting the other end up the skid, could any headway be made. The intense cold kept everything covered with frost constantly and the heavy logs about as unruly as great icicles.

Each log weighed hundreds of pounds. Lady Luck must have been riding with us all through the winter for we finally finished the walls without an accident.

For the roof, I set a pole on end, six feet high on top of the partition wall and directly in the center of the house. The corner rafters were placed from the corners of the house to the top of this pole, thus establishing the shape of the roof. Since all the rafters were poles, none perfectly straight, each had to be hewed to fit, and the tops hewed to make a reasonably even foundation for the roof sheathing.

Once the rough pine sheathing was on, the whole was covered with tar paper. Snow on top of that made good insulation. The doors and windows and the chinking and daubing still remained to be done, and on those I could work, weather or no weather.

CHAPTER FIVE

Spring, Struggling for Birth

Linda Preston McKinstry:

January–March 1916

The days passed quickly and Mac spent all the time possible working on the house. Activities around the ranch, both bad and good, added to the work and interest. The calf got sick and Mac spent much time trying to doctor him. He seemed in great pain but medicine and heat did little good, although Mac got up in the middle of the night to apply the heat. We were glad when his suffering ended. After an autopsy Mac wished he had put him out of his misery sooner as there had been no chance of recovery.

The good news at this time was that our milk cow had another calf, this time a little heifer. We named her Betty from Beta. At that rate, the first calf should have been Alpha, but since the cow's name was Buttercup we had named that calf Cutterbup. It was surely good to have milk and cream again. One of our favorite desserts was whipped cream and chocolate sauce, and at this time of year, the flavored whipped cream became mousse by setting it outside.

When the snow would let up for a while, Mac and Billie would sometimes try to get a trail, at least, to the highway, but it was hopeless. The snow on the flat was six feet deep then and drifts were far deeper. Fences were completely covered. Usually the nights were very cold, and on one or two nights the thermometer would go to fifty below. However, if the days were sunny, the temperature might get above freezing for a short time, otherwise always below.

In January, after our sixty days of snow, we had the so-called January thaw. It warmed up so much that for a few days we had rain instead of snow. We were much concerned for fear our frozen elk [meat] would start to thaw, but fortunately it soon turned cold and no damage to the meat

Hauling out logs in December 1915. The horse rounds the corner between walls of deep snow accumulation as the teamster (possibly Mac) walks on top. (McKinstry)

[occurred]. The rain did cause considerable discomfort. Our cabin roof was made of poles, boards over these and dirt on top. In winter, [the snow cover] helped keep the cabin warm and comfortable, but when it rained and melted the snow, muddy water came raining through. We tried to catch it in pots and pans but never knew where it might come next, beds, kitchen table or chairs, so there were many small catastrophes.

Caring for and doctoring animals really took considerable of Mac's time. Fortunately, he had had a short, but practical, vet course while at college and that proved invaluable. Ginger was growing thinner and thinner, rubbed her chest on poles until raw, whereupon it became infected and abscessed. Twice that had to be cut open, which gave relief, but still she stayed thin. Although she seemed ravenously hungry, she ate very little. Finally Mac decided her teeth might be to blame, and an examination showed some had grown long and pointed on one side. With Billie's help, he got them filed down and she was able to eat again and began gaining.

Her colt was always rather sub-normal and continually getting into trouble. He got a stick in his eye, injured a leg, and walked on three so long that one never did grow to proper length. Something seemed always wrong with him. He was always trying to get milk, even when much too old for that, from any animal around. The horses would kick him and the cow would butt him but with little effect on the colt. Once, shortly after the cow had her Betty calf, the colt crowded into her stall ahead of her. That was too much [for the cow] and she butted him right over the bars into the manger. He landed flat on his back, legs up in the air. Fortunately Mac was in the barn, heard the thud and suspected what had happened then had to tear out the poles in front of the manger to get him out. That poor colt seemed never able to learn anything and finally just passed out of the picture.

Our mail was the only contact with the outside world, but the snows and storms caused much delay. Loziers, at the main road, told us the train did not get into Victor for sixteen days, and the road over the pass was impassable for days at a time. Mail was brought from Jackson only, and that at most irregular times. Once, the weekly *Jackson Courier* was printed on brown wrapping paper, that being the only kind available in town. Our outside mail was two or three weeks in arriving.

In February, Dr. Huff was called to the Nelson ranch about twenty-seven miles from Jackson. The Nelsons were Emily's parents, and she reported that Dr. Huff had had to ski the last seven miles to reach the house. That was nothing unusual for him to do and he never thought about himself if called. An interesting sidelight is that Dr. Huff had left a wonderfully promising career at Johns Hopkins University and come to this little frontier town because of a lung or throat condition which had been discovered. Not only was he an outstanding physician but also an outstanding leader in all community affairs and improvements. Jackson was a most fortunate town because of him.

My birthday arrived in early February, and we celebrated in the only way we could—an extra supper. The weather was typical of many I remember, snow and storm all day.

Valentine's Day [was] another special celebration, even with place cards, little special cookies frosted with a red layer and red paper hearts for decorations.

Our first wedding anniversary came in early March, and this called for a really special supper. Mother had sent a can of chicken so we had chicken sandwiches, potato salad, [and] cocoa and whipped cream. The sandwiches were garnished with tiny green plants Mac found in the spring. Dessert was vanilla ice cream with chocolate sauce, anniversary cake, and salted peanuts. Our wedding cake had had a lovely cream colored rose in the center, but this one had one white tissue paper rose holding a white candle. The centerpiece [was] a cotton snow scene, mirror lake, bits of pine for trees, and a brown paper tent and sled. Mac had tied green pine branches on the table legs so the general effect resembled a huge, green porcupine. But it was pretty anyway. There was a big, pink bow for Laddie, which he did not appreciate until we told him how pretty he looked. Also, a bow for the one cat we then had, but she did not show up. Later we found she had been shut up in the partly completed house. For the occasion I wore my white wedding dress and Mac a soft white shirt and the coat of his wedding suit. The trousers were still packed away somewhere and not found, so others had to be substituted. But it was a gala occasion.

One day in February, I snowshoed over to Thompsons' to spend the day. It was about a mile cross-country on the snow. I enjoyed talking to a woman again and seeing the baby, Mac came for us in the late afternoon, and after an early supper, we returned home just after sunset. We had a beautiful trip. Before [we reached] home, the stars were out while there was still lovely color in the western sky above the Teton peaks. Then a big full moon rose over the snow-covered hill to the east of us. This was the signal for the coyotes to start howling and a lone wolf joined in. Mac loved to hear them but they sounded much too close for me, and I was glad when we reached home.

By March the days were beginning to warm up. The snow on top would soften during the day, then freeze so solid during the night that one could walk anywhere in the early morning or drive a team on it. But as the crust softened again, one would sink through to a depth of several feet and be stranded if without snowshoes.

The early mornings were indescribably beautiful. Evergreen trees would be covered with frost crystals, which sparkled and glistened like diamonds in the sunlight and still sparkled as they fell from the trees. The snow, which stayed perfectly clean and white, would be crystal covered and sparkled with all possible colors. Unbelievably lovely—but so hard on the eyes!

During the snow crusting season, the mail man would have to travel at night or early morning as the roads were impassable except on the hard crust. Mail delivery was even more erratic than usual. Mac's occasional trips to the highway for possible mail would be made in the morning, but he would always take his skis with him for fear the crust might soften before he reached home. It was on one of those trips that the glare from the snow caused him to go snow-blind. He was still a mile from home. By closing his eyes for a few minutes, he could then squint ahead, get his direction and then with eyes closed cover as much distance as he dared, sometimes only a few rods. By repeating the performance, he finally arrived home but was unable to see much for three days thereafter. He had forgotten his snow glasses.

By now our new house was well along and we anticipated moving in soon. It had taken a long time for the ground to dry out so the flooring could be put in. Before the roof was on, much snow had fallen; this all had

to be shoveled out, whereupon the ground froze. We put a little sheet iron stove inside the house to dry and warm the ground, so finally most of the floors could be laid. The ceiling, except the living room one, [was] all in. That ceiling [for the new living room] was now the floor of the cabin [where we were living] so could not be put up until we moved. The sink was in the kitchen but no well as yet. Pantry shelves were in place and we had already begun storing things on them.

On March 11, we decided we could move and took our beds over. We let the fire in the kitchen range go out so we could move that when cool. To add to the confusion, Pilch, one of the boys who had come from Fargo last April, arrived unexpectedly, having snowshoed in. He had to have a cold dinner and then had the job of helping us move. The stove was loaded onto some boards at the cabin door, and Jet pulled it over to the house, where it was set up and a fire started. By then it was suppertime and in spite of the confusion, we had a hot meal.

Our beds were in the living room as that part had a floor in it, but we made up a bed for Pilch in the kitchen. He was really the lucky one as it was far warmer there. The next days the boys finished putting the floor in the living room and we could really begin getting settled. Furniture was uncrated, and we began to unpack more barrels and boxes for now we had room to place things. All winter the barrels had been out in the snow, covered with it, but [the] contents were safe. It was wonderful to have plenty of kitchen equipment, china, and silverware and so good to really be

Horses sometimes became bogged down during what Linda calls "the crusting season" and roads became impassable except in early morning or night. These travelers are bogged down on Teton Pass.
(JHHS&M, Evelyn Cherry)

getting settled. The following morning we heard someone outside the door and discovered [the] Thompsons had arrived. They had put the baby's crib on a sled and walked over on the crust. Things were surely in a heap: excelsior and partially unpacked boxes everywhere and the kitchen the only place in which to stay. With five adults and a sizeable baby's crib it was really crowded. But no one minded, though it was confusing to prepare meals, and we enjoyed the visit.

While Thompsons were there, the baby was weighed much to Emily's delight, as little Pearl had not been weighed since leaving the hospital six months before. The only scales we had were steelyards, and though [they were] never intended for weighing babies, this baby was successfully weighed on them. The *American College Dictionary* defines [a] steelyard as, "a portable balance with two equal arms, the longer having a movable counterpoise and the shorter one having a hook or the like for holding the object to be weighed." Pearl was placed in a blanket, the corners securely tied, and this knot hooked over the steelyard hook. Her weight had increased from eight to nineteen pounds.

Pilch left that afternoon but the Thompsons stayed overnight. Most of that day was spent just visiting as [the] Thompsons had to leave early in the morning while the snow was still crusted. After they left Mac took up the cabin floorboards and put the ceiling on the [new] living room. Then the rug was put down, dining room table and chairs [put] in place, also the bookcase, sideboard, and drop-side couch.

The next day, March 19, we had dinner on a real dining room table with luncheon doilies, napkins, china, silverware, and [an] artificial red rose for a centerpiece. In the evening we had a chafing dish supper. How good it was to feel we were really living and the table looking much as it did back in Washington for the Sunday night suppers there.

Our bedsprings finally arrived, but we had no bedsteads as the side rails had been lost on the way. My bedsprings and mattress were put on the folding cot, Mac's on the floor, until he [had] time to make frames for temporary use. But at least we had a bedroom, a place for our clothes and trunks. My treadle sewing machine was in there, too.

Although the burlap for the living room walls and ceiling had been ordered before Christmas, only part of it had arrived. It was May before we finally received all of it and then we finally purchased it from the Denver Dry Goods Company.

Later, in March, we were in the butchering business. We had bought a half hog from Billie, which had remained frozen all winter but now was thawing so had to be worked up. Since it weighed 117 pounds, this was quite a task. Using a government bulletin, we faithfully followed directions, putting hams and bacons in brine and using some of the less desirable cuts, with elk meat, for sausage. Head cheese was made and we even pickled the feet. We fried all the fat so obtained a wonderful supply of lard. Some fresh pork was thoroughly enjoyed after a winter of elk meat. It was a huge amount of work but the results much enjoyed later.

No wonder we sometimes were confused on the days of the week in that country. But the one long remembered was Mac's long trip to Moran on a Sunday when we supposed it was Monday. He went on business but it wasn't accomplished that day.

A few days later our neighbors from the main highway arrived for a visit. Mr. Lozier returned that afternoon, but his wife and small son stayed for three days. It was good to take care of overnight guests in comparative comfort.

Back in February people were beginning to get short on hay and were feeding the hay from their barn roofs. It was customary, partly for quick results, simply to lay poles across the top of the walls and stack hay on top, thus making a little extra storage for feed and incidentally a good temporary roof. By the first of April we were getting short, too, so Mac went to Walt Germann's on Buffalo Creek to see if he could finish wintering our three horses, providing Mac could get them over there. Not only was Walt willing but said he had been saving hay in case we needed it. That was the kind of neighbor, six miles away, who was refusing to sell hay in case these new homesteaders might need it. This is the way Mac described his trip:

"By starting early in the morning before the crust softened, I was able to lead the horses over the snow to Pacific Creek about one-quarter mile. My skis were tied on Nellie's saddle, Jet's lead rope [was tied] to the saddle horn and Ginger's to Jet's tail. Following down the creek, in the water, going was fairly good with the exception of two places. First, I came to a barrier of brush and logs, which had to be detoured, and that meant breaking a trail through four feet of settled snow. With the back end of my skis, I chopped the partially softened crust, and by leading one horse at a time, they were able to lunge their way back into the creek.

"The other obstacle was not apparent until too late. Water was crystal clear and depth hard to estimate. Suddenly Nellie stepped off into swimming water. As she dropped in, we sank up to my shoulders, but she swam right through to the shallower water below.

"There the warm sun had melted the snow back from the water's edge, exposing bare cobblestones. I peeled off my clothes, emptied the water from my boots and wrung the water from my clothes as best I could, then continued down the creek to the highway. I reached Germanns' sometime after noon and skied back home over the hill."

Harold Cole McKinstry:

We had hoped to be in the house by March 3, our first wedding anniversary. But nothing could stop the celebration.

Work on the doors, windows, chinking and daubing moved along pretty fast after that. Weather could not delay very much. By March 11, we were ready to move in, although, as usual, considerable finishing remained to be done.

The storm that had started in November seemed never to quit. The snow grew steadily deeper. The storm moaned overhead, wind driving the snow in relentless fury. The clouds were so heavy that often in the middle of the day the darkness seemed to indicate approaching night. Sometimes I wondered if it would ever quit.

"It always has," said Billie T., but at times we wondered if it always would.

Carefully I doled out the hay for the livestock. To each horse I gave a ration of oats twice a day. But the intense cold and constant storm required lots of fuel to keep their bodies warm, and the hay supply was dwindling faster than spring was coming. I skied over the hill and made a deal with Walt Germann to finish wintering the horses, if I could get them there.

The snow was too deep for them to wallow. The only way out appeared to be down the creek. It was open, although in some places [it] flowed between high banks of ice crowding in from both sides. Snow was melting in the daytime and freezing at night, forming a crust strong enough to hold up a horse. But soon after the sun came up in the morning, that crust softened, and any stock caught on it then was marooned right there until night, or until the temperature dropped enough to again freeze a crust.

I left home early in the morning of April 12, headed for the creek one-quarter mile away. Once there I started downstream in the water, riding one horse, leading the others. All went well for a while, until the creek canyoned up between walls of ice. Water was crystal clear and more than knee-deep, but between these high walls, deep in shadow, I did not see the abrupt drop-off. The surface of the water was smooth. The horse walked right off into swimming water. Down we went with ice water up to my armpits. But the horses did not hesitate. They swam smoothly, walking out into shallow water at the lower end of the gorge.

There the cobblestone banks were bare and the sun shone down on them [with] welcome warmth. I took off my clothes, wrung them out, emptied the water out of my boots and was again on my way.

By the time I reached Buffalo Flat, the sun had set. Walt was looking for me and had the mangers full of good hay for the horses. [After] eating a hasty supper, I got on my skis and headed over the hill. It was early in the night when I reached the creek. It had risen during the day and looked black and cold in the moonless night. But on the other side was Linda's light in the window. She knew by the barking of the dog that I was coming and stood in the doorway, listening for the hiss of my skis on the crystal snow.

On the first day of April another heavy snow came, and on the flat I measured six feet on the level. But the bitter cold did not follow. Instead, the sun came out clear and warm. Spring was struggling for birth. Day by day the tops of new bushes became exposed. At intervals, the snow settled with a muffled grunt. The top pole of the buck fence appeared. South slopes seemed to bare up as if by magic. Linda and I snowshoed over beyond the spring where the snow had melted and took off our snowshoes to get the feel of bare ground under our feet. There were buttercups right at the edge of the snow banks and grass already turning green. Spring was in the air.

A few days later we had company. Mrs. Bill Lozier from ten miles down country came riding in, horseback. Behind her saddle she carried a gunny sack full of watercress. She knew, from long years in the valley, the craving for green stuff after a hard winter. Of all the treats ever showered upon anyone, for Linda, that was supreme. Not only was Mrs. Lozier the first woman Linda had seen in several months, but coming with such a gift made the event one never to be forgotten.

Linda Preston McKinstry:

On April 8 we received a letter from the Ogden Land Office saying the land was now officially open for filing and that we would have first chance on it until May 27, after which it would be open to the public. Needless to say, we filled out the necessary papers and immediately made our application. By the middle of April, there were definite signs of spring. Although the snow on the flat was still knee-deep for me, it was melting fast on sunny, exposed hillsides, and almost immediately tiny yellow buttercups appeared. Pussy willows came out, too. [W]e began to hear the robins and to see occasional butterflies.

As the slopes became bare enough, feed showed up so horses could graze a little. Mac went over to Germanns' to bring back Nellie, although the snow was still too deep to break out a road. On the Buffalo side of the hill, there was very little snow left, so Mac decided to bring her over the hill, not realizing the depth of snow on our side or how slippery it had become. She was carrying his heavy saddle, though not Mac, and she slipped

April–July 1916

and slid most of the way down. Once the saddle horn caught on a tree and that was all that saved her losing her footing entirely. [They reached] Pacific Creek, and the snow on the bank gave way as they started to cross, and Nellie landed on her back in deep water. If Mac had not been able to hold up her head, she would have drowned. Coming to a shallow place, he got her up and they arrived home safely thereafter.

Laddie caused some excitement one day when he was found to be missing. We could not believe he would run away in all the deep snow, and before long [he] was discovered in one of Mac's coyote traps. Fortunately he was not badly hurt but was a very sheepish dog when he came home for he knew he should not have been there. He avoided traps thereafter, so perhaps it was a good lesson.

A few days after Mac brought Nellie home, there was enough of the trail to the main road so he could bring Jet and Ginger, as he wanted to use them. [Having turned] them loose after he reached home, he started out to find them the next morning, but they were nowhere to be found. After hunting all the morning, he started out again in the afternoon.

About four o'clock when I went out to feed the chickens and to chase the cow down by the pond where green grass was showing along the edge, Laddie, who had been up at the house, came down to me. As I started back through the woods to the house, I heard someone clearing his throat and thought Mac had returned. I called but there was no answer. Just then a man appeared in the pathway. Facing me was a big, red-faced, roughly dressed man, soaked to the knees from tramping through snow trails. He resembled a back-east tramp, and I was plenty frightened, being absolutely alone. The dog paid no attention to him, which surprised me, as he usually barked furiously at anyone arriving. He first words did not reassure me.

"Is your man anywhere around?" he asked in Irish brogue.

Trying to appear calm, I answered, "No, not right now but I expect him any minute."

His next comment was, "I wish he was here."

I knew he didn't wish it half as much as I did.

Soon I learned that he and his pal, who was somewhere out in the snowy trail, had been given wrong directions to get to Wind River, where they had been told work was available in a logging camp. They were supposed to have gone to Buffalo Creek, that road leading over the divide. Our road was hardly a trail through the snow, but they had been told to turn left at the first bridge they came to and so had turned at Pacific Creek. They had tramped those three miles through the snow before reaching our place. [When he asked] directions, I told [him] the shortest way was across Pacific Creek, if they could find a crossing, and over the hill, otherwise back the way they had come and then to Buffalo Creek. After getting some eggs and bacon, for which [he] left money, he called to his friend whom I never did see, and they went on their way. Looking back I am sorry that I was not more hospitable, but I was much too frightened at the time.

Mac finally arrived about two hours later, still without having found the horses, and was much disturbed about the incident. He had seen the tracks but thought Billie Thompson had been over. When he said he'd not want to cross Pacific Creek, even horseback, through so much water and ice, I wondered if I had sent the men to their destruction. We never heard anything more of them so guess they returned via the road and ultimately arrived safely somewhere.

We hoped the horses would come home themselves for oats. Sure enough, after supper they arrived. They must have crossed the creek, gotten into a deep hole and had to swim, for Jet was wet to her ears and Ginger almost all over. They were put in the barn then and the next day Mac went to Germanns' for some hay. The snow was soft and he thought he could get through. When he returned with the hay, he also brought a little light buggy, which he had been thinking of buying from Mr. Germann. He knew we should have a light rig for the trip to Jackson and we would have to be going next month. Dr. Huff had told us to come the latter part of May.

With the road broken out, we drove over to the Buffalo on Sunday, having dinner with the Germanns before Sunday school. The following Sunday we were invited to McClures' and that was quite a special day for the Sunday school meeting. Not only was the Baptist preacher from Jackson there, but a set of hymn books had been sent to us from Washington, and we had taken them over. The Congregational Church, CE [Christian Education], of which we were members before leaving Washington, had gotten new hymn books for their own use and sent the old ones to us. It was surprising that most of the folks knew the old songs, and we all stayed until after five o'clock singing them.

On the eleventh of May, Roy Lozier came up to use Mac's forge and brought word of the fire at Moran the preceding night. The post office had burned, [as well as] Mr. Sheffield's house and dude dining room, but the cabins had been saved. Most of the contents of the buildings were also saved, thanks to the help of the many men working at the [Jackson Lake] dam.

With May well started, we had to make plans for the Jackson trip, and we decided to start on the twenty-third. The Jack Fees, who lived fifteen miles down country, had invited us to stay there overnight, and we decided to do so rather than drive the forty miles in one day. Even in the comfortable little buggy that would be a pretty long trip for me.

Since the hospital was not yet complete, Linda and Mac stayed in the Episcopal Parish House awaiting the arrival of the baby. The baby was born in the second-story room above the three windows. This photo was taken soon after the parish house was completed in 1912.
(JHHS&M)

We hoped we'd not be away more than two or three weeks but had to arrange for everything at home. The cow and Betty were taken to Germanns', the chickens and cat to Thompsons'. We intended to turn Nellie and the colt loose, but Billie said he would like them in their pasture so Nellie would be available to ride. We would drive Jet and Ginger to Jackson and take Laddie with us. As the little log hospital there was not yet completed, we were to live in the Episcopal Parish House. Reverend Balcom was there part of the time but he was a young bachelor and took his meals out. He wanted only one or two rooms and the rest of the big house was ours to use. It was a two-story log building, a most attractive place, the nicest one in town.

We left home about noon, had dinner with Thompsons, then started for Fees'. The morning had been pleasant but during the afternoon it misted, rained or snowed. We arrived at Fees' in the late afternoon, had an enjoyable visit, and left about nine the next morning for Jackson. And how it stormed! Rain or snow all day. Mac insisted I use our umbrella and he got soaked and cold. At Kelly, where we stopped for dinner, we got warm and partially dried out. For the remaining sixteen-mile trip it poured, then turned to snow with a driving wind. The roads were dreadful and so slippery the horses could go no faster than a walk. It was a long, long trip, but we finally arrived at the hotel where we stayed for a few days.

Some people who had been living in the Parish House were delayed in leaving because of the storm, but we moved over as soon as they left and were assigned the guest room as our bedroom. The walls were plastered and the rooms furnished with mission furniture. It was very luxurious after our little house at home. Our room was one of three upstairs bedrooms, and there was also a reception room on that floor. One bedroom was reserved for the young Episcopal rector when he was in town. Downstairs was the large, main club room, which was used for Sunday services as their church was still unfinished. Also, there was a big kitchen, hallway, and a library room containing some 600 books. Everything was open to us and the modern kitchen was a joy to use.

A week later the baby decided it was time to arrive but complications prevented. After [I had endured] two days of suffering, Dr. Huff decided I could stand no more, so gave me ether. What a blessed relief! The baby was taken with instruments and when I came to, late in the evening, a baby girl was all dressed and awaiting me. No little squirmy red one either, but one with beautiful, natural color. A wee, tiny pimple on the tip of her nose was the only imperfection, if it could be so called, but that did not last long.

Mrs. Huff, who was formerly a nurse at Johns Hopkins, had been with me and assisting Dr. Huff during the critical days. She cared for me afterward until a practical nurse could take over.

Mrs. Huff was expecting a new arrival herself in September, and I know I worried more about her overdoing than she did. Both she and Dr. Huff came often on friendly as well as professional visits.

Eleven days later I was allowed to sit up in a chair. Mrs. Huff had entertained the Pure Food Club that afternoon, and in the evening she and Dr. Huff arrived bring[ing] meringues and ice cream.

One Sunday afternoon when they were there on a friendly visit, Dr. Huff's brother was with them and the conversation turned to books. We were interested to learn that Owen Wister, author of *The Virginian,* formerly owned a ranch in Jackson Hole. He came to spend summers there with his wife until after her death. We were told that the hero of *The Trail of the Lonesome Pine* by Harold Bell Wright came to hunt in Jackson Hole, [and] that story was largely a true episode except for the gunplay.[†] Maude Adams, the outstanding actress of those days, used to come into the JP dude ranch and later had a place of her own. We had many delightful visits [with Huffs], and also with the friendly Jackson people who came often to visit me.

Of course work on our ranch was at a standstill, and though so much needed to be done there, Mac would not leave me. Our first summer had been lost as far as getting started on clearing land and putting in crops, as our permanent location had not been definitely settled until September. However, he had all he could do to get building and fence timber and cut the wild hay in the fall and with the necessary building of the barn and

[†] *Though author Wright did frequent Jackson Hole, it was John Fox Jr. who wrote this book.*

chicken coop. During the fall and winter, he had worked on the house. Now, during our second summer, he had been unable to put in a crop. Before leaving for Jackson, he had plowed a garden spot and we had planted vegetables. We had expected to be back in plenty of time to care for them, but instead had to remain in Jackson for over two months.

Fortunately he had plenty of work there. The Episcopal Church was in the process of building, and he and Dr. Huff laid the floor for that. The property around the church and hospital needed grading and that furnished work for the team as well as Mac. Also he made trips for lumber [that] had been donated for church use and trips to Victor for hospital equipment and supplies. The church board was most happy to have someone to do the work, as all the ranchers were much too busy on their own places to take the time.

As we needed more than two work horses on the ranch, Mac was also hunting for some to buy. He had about decided on a couple of three-year-old unbroken mares, when an unexpected incident occurred. It seemed, as we were told the story, that a certain saloon keeper had gotten so involved with the law that he either had to go to the Pen or get out of the country immediately. He decided to go to the Klondike and offered to pay the way of any man who would go with him. A rancher took him up on the deal and offered his three horses, harnesses, and spring wagon for sale. Mac made an offer, which was taken, so we acquired Mike, Johnny, and Nugget, all extra good snow horses, having been used on the mail stage over the pass. Mike was probably the finest snow horse in the country. This meant that snow did not worry him, he could keep his footing on the narrowest snow road, or if he got into deep snow, was not frightened and did not fight it but climbed out with the least possible effort. He was a wonderful horse, gentle and always dependable.

The days and weeks passed and Dr. Huff said I would probably be able to return to the ranch by the end of July. Before returning [Mac and I] both needed dental work and the nearest dentist was at Driggs, Idaho, some eight miles north of Victor. So using the light buggy we, with the baby, started on the trip and it was 10:30 in the evening before we arrived at the Victor hotel. The next morning we drove to Driggs. The dentist had told us no previous appointment was necessary, "Just come."

Unfortunately it was on a Wednesday when we arrived and everything closed Wednesday afternoons because of the community football games. However, we made a 7:30 appointment for the next morning, and after one or the other of us spending most of the day in the dentist's chair, returned to Victor by evening. The next day back to Jackson [we went] and I was glad to return to the Parish House. A four-day trip for those hours of

dental work. Two nights in the Victor hotel and one in Driggs, besides the meals involved, added considerably to the cost of the work.

As Mac had some three or four hundred pounds of nails [and] some 1500 pounds of oats and barley, he decided to make a trip to the homestead, using the four horses. Those along with many miscellaneous supplies made a very heavy load. About sixteen miles from home, irrigation waters [that] flooded Ferrins' land also flooded the roadway. This caused the load to get stuck so the trip proved longer and harder than anticipated. But a few days later he was back and started packing so all the family could return home.

We had expected to return the thirty-first of July, but Dr. Huff said an outstanding Idaho physician, and a personal friend, was coming in August 1. Dr. Huff was still concerned about my condition and wanted this doctor to make an examination before we left. The examination was made that morning, his report was optimistic, so we were able to start for home. His orders, though, were to continue hot packs and do nothing for three months except to take care of the baby. Some program for a homesteader! He also said we were fortunate in having such a fine baby under the conditions that had existed. We were already intensely aware of this, and how fortunate we had been in having such an outstanding doctor.

Leaving Jackson about noon, we reached Fees', stayed there overnight, and [went] on home the next day, having dinner with Thompsons before arriving. How good it seemed to be home again after being away for nearly

Dr. Charles Huff and his wife Edna, a nurse, had left promising careers at Johns Hopkins to come to Jackson because of the doctor's throat and lung conditions. (JHHS&M)

ten weeks! We were so happy to find our garden flourishing. The weeds had not taken over and there had been enough moisture for good growth. We had an unexpectedly good supply of vegetables.

Harold Cole McKinstry:

With spring I started plowing. We had to have hay if our dreams for a cattle ranch were ever to come true. But the sagebrush was heavy. Scattered patches of small timber and old stumps had to be cleared. It was slow going. We needed a garden, and that ground had to be cleared. By late May I had succeeded in getting a few acres of oats seeded and a nice garden planted. There were still no fences; neither were there many cattle on the range. We hoped to get back home in time to fence our growing crop.

But our first "blessed event" was scheduled for early June. We had made arrangements to go to Jackson for the occasion. The Episcopal Parish House was to be vacated for the summer, and Dr. Huff had arranged for us to move in there. So on May 23 we drove down and soon were comfortably settled in the big old log house. The hospital was being built.

The days slipped by in a hurry. I went to Victor to haul in a load of equipment for the new hospital, graded the hospital lawn then took a load of our much delayed equipment to the ranch.

On June 6, Jeanne was born. Had not Dr. Huff been a most wonderful physician and Mrs. Huff an equally wonderful nurse, Linda or the baby would not have pulled through. To those good people we have always felt a debt of gratitude, but it was their nature to give their very best, and more. They knew no other way.

It was the end of July before Linda was strong enough to go home. Even then her strength was pretty limited, and only because we were young and foolish did we attempt it. But we felt that with the short summer so nearly spent, we should get home and at work.

Stocking Up for Winter

Linda Preston McKinstry:

The next day Mac went to McClures' on Buffalo Creek to get our milk cow and calf and to Thompsons' to get our chickens. Haying then had to be started and again we had to depend on wild hay. As two men could work to so much better advantage, Mac and Jack Fee had decided to help each other with the haying. The next month and a half proved hectic. Two days later they were to start work as the wild hay was ready to cut. So on August 4, all the family, which included Mrs. Fee, a 3½-year-old girl, and a year-old boy, also one milk cow, chickens, pig, and dog arrived. Upon leaving home, one had to bring all animals that could not be turned loose. We had planned to put up a tent and Dad [Mac] and I [would] sleep there, but it had been too rainy and the ground too wet. We were thankful for a four-room house.

After the long dry summer the weather did not cooperate for haying. Then, too, Jack was ill for several days, a flare-up from Spanish typhoid, and Mac sprained an ankle. It was taped by a government doctor at Moran, and that caused no delay. However, Mac had to work alone much of the time and the rain held back the work. Mrs. Fee took over running the house, as I could not, but I helped as I was able. But it was all very tiring and confusing.

This continued until the last of August when we moved down to Fees'. They had only a two-room cabin but were able to use a tent for sleeping. With better weather and health, that haying took less time, though a snow-storm caused a one-day delay. Also, Mac's brother was there for three days so he gave extra help.

But everyone, especially I, was thankful when we could return to our own house on September 16 and settle down by ourselves again. While at

August–September 1916

† *Nugget's name transitions back and forth from Nugget to Nougat.*

Fees' I had given Mac a haircut and it proved quite successful. His hair had grown out so much he said it was dreadfully hot working and he could not stand it, so to cut it someway. When in Jackson, and just beginning to get out, I had once gone to the barbershop with him. He had assured me it would not take long for a haircut and a little walk would be enjoyed as it was a lovely evening. I believed him, but his prediction was wrong. The barber proved to be a woman and evidently inexperienced. By the time she should have been through, she was just getting a good start, but I was already so weary I did not dare to start alone to walk home. Before she finished I felt as though I had taken a full course in barbering. But [I] was so tired I don't know how the short walk back to the house was ever made.

Nougat,† the third horse that Mac had purchased in the summer, was supposed to be a good riding horse. However, having been used in rodeos, he was not safe, and Mac promised not to ride him until someone had "topped him off." One day when Mac had the horse over at Thompsons', a man stopped by and wanted some horseshoe nails. He proved to be a horse wrangler for a big dude party going through, and said he would ride Nougat. He put his own saddle on the horse, got on and Nougat went up as though on springs. Only the adequate hazing of a young fellow who was also a member of the party kept the horse from going over the cut bank. Afterward, the wrangler said that of the thirty-eight horses he had broken out that spring, only one went higher, if as high, as Nougat. By the time they had all returned to our place, the wrangler wanted to trade or buy Nougat for himself. But we needed a good saddle horse and thought that

Nougat would calm down. He did, to a certain extent, and though Mac frequently rode him, [he] could never be depended upon. I never attempted to get on him.

Harold Cole McKinstry:

Haying alone proved quite a job, so Jack Fee, who lived about twelve miles down country, and I decided to work together. We started on our hay first, much of it in little meadows scattered around over the forest land and purchased from the U.S.F.S. [U.S. Forest Service]. But we made poor time. Day after [day], it rained, delaying the work far beyond our expectation. But we finally finished and then tackled Jack's hay. When at last that job was done, there remained little of the summer. It was well that I had done some fencing during the time Linda was recuperating. Otherwise none would have been done that summer.

There was still work to be done on the house. I had not completed the well under the house or installed the pump. That was a must before winter set in, and already there had developed a feeling of fall in the air. The late August frosts were turning the aspen leaves.

Linda Preston McKinstry:

September was the time to order our winter supply of groceries, and we gave our order to the representative of a Denver outfit who had come in to contact the ranchers. The groceries were to be shipped by prepaid freight to Victor, and then sent by parcel post from there, that being the cheapest transportation and most dependable. We had our last year's list, which helped out on the ordering:

 500# white flour @ $3.50
 100# cornmeal
  30# rice
  75# whole wheat flour
  50# brown sugar
  10# coffee
  3# cocoa
  2# tea
  25# navy beans
  10# macaroni
  25# each of prunes, dried pears, figs, and dried apples. Peaches
   and apricots on hand.
  1 case tomatoes, 24 cans
 1/2 case each of corn, string beans, and salmon
  10# each of lima, red kidney, and chili beans.

September–October 1916

From the Moran Government commissary, we purchased:
300# sugar @ $8.50
14# noodles @ $.50
1 case petroleum soap @ $4.50.
1 case Ivory soap. This was divided with Fees and each had
50 cakes.

Several hundred pounds potatoes procured rather locally.

These supplies with beets, turnips, and rutabagas from the garden, onions and cabbage, with elk for meat, made us ready for the many months when freezing weather and bad roads prevented getting supplies. [T]he cow furnishing milk and cream and eggs from the chickens when they would lay made well-balanced meals quite possible. Fresh fruit and green vegetables were badly missed.

Never will we forget when Mrs. Bill Lozier arrived one day in early spring, when our road was barely passable. Tied on the back of her saddle was a whole gunnysack of watercress. There were warm springs on their place so watercress grew all year. How good it tasted and I doubt if a leaf was wasted. It was a treat forever remembered.

After returning from Fees', we settled down for the winter and there was always plenty to do. Mac had wild hay to haul and often had to cut trees to get a passable trail from some of the mountain meadows. Tip-overs were not uncommon, causing more delays and extra work.

Several loads of dry logs had to be hauled in for the winter wood supply. These had to be cut into stove lengths and split. As all this had to be done by hand. Crosscut saws were used for cutting the logs, and as it was much easier for two men to work together, Billie and Mac exchanged work.

In October, the thermometer went as low as eight below and in November, down to minus twenty-three. The snow was coming and continued to come until there was no more bare ground until late spring. Long before then, the fences were completely covered and the whole country was just an expanse of glistening white. Every winter, on one or two nights, the temperature would fall to around fifty below. Yet the few days when it would not snow, and the sun was out, were beautiful. It did not seem nearly as cold as the thermometer indicated, though it seldom got above freezing.

Before too much snow came, more daubing had to be done to replace what had dried out during the summer. There was always timber work and fencing to be done. Indoors, the pump was finally installed and working well. What a joy to have water so easily available!

Feeding and caring for the livestock required considerable time, Nellie had to be treated for ringbone and there were minor casualties among the animals. Nougat's sore back required continual attention. He had been rented out to a hunting party, had had a poorly fitted pack saddle, and the resulting sore spot was very slow healing. Laddie tangled twice with porcupines. The first time he got his nose full of quills, the next time a mouthful as well. Mac had to get Roy Lozier to hold him while they were pulled. After those experiences, I think Laddie learned to leave porcupines alone.

The family, too, had upsets and colds. Once, Jeanne had us frightfully worried with a head and chest cold as she could scarcely breathe. With no phone, or near neighbors, bad roads and the doctor forty miles distant, I felt helpless. The nearest phone was at Moran seven miles away, but I thought if we could even phone the doctor he might tell us something more we could do.

So Mac started out to find the horses while I cared for Jeanne. He was gone for hours. At home the minutes dragged by as I tried to make Jeanne more comfortable. I was much relieved when she was able to breathe a little more easily. When Mac finally returned without having been able to find a single horse, she was definitely better. We were most thankful and I shudder to think what could have happened otherwise. I had never had any previous experience with babies, and had seldom even held one, previous to Jeanne's arrival. Hence, caring for [her] under such isolated conditions was especially difficult. Dr. Emmett Holt's baby book was the criterion of that day, but most of his views have long since been repudiated. However,

that and the government bulletin were the only guides. Poor Jeanne, I think she had her problems as well as we. But how we enjoyed her, and every new achievement was a miracle to us.

Harold Cole McKinstry:

The first snow came in early October. It was a reminder that the elk herd would be moving down out of the park and that all unprotected hay stacks were in jeopardy. So I started hauling hay from the far-flung meadows, trying to beat the elk to it. As I pulled up a long side hill through the timber, the upper runner of the sleigh hit a hidden stump and over we went. The thick stand of lodgepoles was all that kept the rack from turning upside down.

I threw a chain over the top and, with the team, pulled the rack back onto the sleigh. Then came the job of pitching the hay up the hill and re-loading. Again, it was far into the night when I got home, and again Linda was waiting anxiously.

By exchanging help with the neighbors, we all managed somehow to prepare for winter. None of [us] had enough stove wood ahead. We expected to saw that at odd times, but the time consumed in getting fuel ran into many days before the winter passed. The snow came so fast that work was slowed down to less than fifty percent efficiency. Trails had to be broken into the timber. Snow had to be dug away from the trees in order to cut them. Wallowing waist deep in the snow was hard work. An ax or a chain carelessly dropped could not be found.

Linda Preston McKinstry:

On November 7 we all were able to go to Moran to the polls. Wyoming had Women's Suffrage in 1916 so I cast my first vote. It was for Charles Evan Hughes for president.

On November 16, when Mac went for mail, the Lozier family returned with him. Mr. Lozier returned home that afternoon but Mrs. Lozier and the children stayed overnight. Although I did not know it at the time, it was truly a red letter day, for it was not until April 14, the following year, that I ever saw another woman. Almost five months.

A ranger or rancher would stop by, Will might come occasionally and also Pilch for a couple of days. The boys were always put to work on hay hauling, cutting firewood or whatever might be the most pressing job of the moment. When Mac had to be away overnight, the young schoolteacher from Elk would come up to stay and do the chores, for livestock had to be fed and the cow milked.

In late December several of the ranchers decided to haul coal to Jackson from a mine on Buffalo Creek. Three of the ranchers used four horse teams and one a single team. Mac used four horses. On the day they started, an extra severe storm started and the roads were very bad. The loaded sleighs would slide off the road or get stuck in the snow and it would take six horses to get started again. When the group finally neared Jackson, in early evening, one sleigh again slid off, hit a fence, tipped over, and dumped all the coal, completely blocking the road. All the horses then had to be un-hitched and driven into town, the men walking. Next morning they had to return, reload the coal and bring all the loads into Jackson. Altogether it proved to be a long three-day trip and a very difficult one. No more coal hauling trips were attempted. Mac had left home at four o'clock Monday morning and arrived back at 10:30 Wednesday night. Even at that, he had to leave his teams and the load he had brought from Jackson at Loziers' on the main road, as the horses were too worn out to travel the remaining three miles. Mac had borrowed Roy's skis and so arrived home that night.

The next morning he went back for the horses and brought back part of the load. We were glad to have those supplies as they were needed and otherwise would probably have remained in Jackson all winter. With the roads so bad, mail deliveries did not include P.P. [parcel post].

Mac had returned two days before Christmas. The following day a community Christmas dinner and festivities were held at the Buffalo school, but both Mac and the horses were much too worn out to make the trip over. We later learned that practically the whole community was there, except for us, but we were glad to be safely home together.

On Christmas Day the most enjoyed gift was the phonograph from

Mother. It was such a treat to hear music again, and Jeanne, too, was thrilled.

In later days it became a sort of toss-up as to whether Jeanne or the phonograph could outdo the other. Holt's book said, after putting a baby to bed he should never be picked up but cry it out until he went to sleep. Poor Jeanne, she did that all too often, and we would put on the loudest record to drown out her cries. To this day I never hear the "Robert E. Lee" selection without thinking of Jeanne's babyhood. We later learned she had a perfectly legitimate reason for crying for she was hungry. She had practically nothing to eat except her milk formula, and evidently not enough of that, but we were faithfully trying to follow Holt's directions. She was really half starved.

Harold Cole McKinstry:

As Christmas approached, the spirit of the season pervaded our little cabin. Christmas trees were all about us, but we found just the right one and set it up in the house. Linda's mother back in New Jersey was forgetting nothing. She had sent us a phonograph and records of some of the finest artists of the day. We loved them, and in that beautiful mountain setting those Christmas carols seemed to convey their meaning with a clarity found nowhere else. The box was packed with toys for Jeanne, useful articles for us, everything. Christmas was all around us. It was in the air.

But there was work to do. We had purchased two heifers down the valley, and they were to be brought up with one of the big cow herds being moved by one of the new ranchers in the valley. One of these heifers was, we were warned, on the fight and could not be driven. So, with the team and sleigh, I went to get her. Sure enough, she was on the fight. We had a rope on her, trying to coax her into the sleigh. Suddenly she charged one of the men. He jumped into the back end of the sleigh, she after him. He went over the top in front and she was trapped inside. It was no trick to haul her home, but she never tamed down. She would have taken to the tall timber had it not been for the deep snow, too deep for her to plow. After she got fat on the summer ranges, we sold her to the Army but had to shoot her. At sight of a rider she took out like a deer and could not be corralled.

[This is the extent of Harold McKinstry's manuscript.][†]

† *The McKinstrys' daughter, Stella, said she thinks writing his own account of these early years was an opportunity for Mac to recount some of the more hair-raising adventures they had—told from his point of view—and to share with his children and grandchildren the more alarming details he had originally kept from his wife, Linda. Occasionally, in the remainder of the manuscript, Linda includes first-hand accounts told from Mac's viewpoint, but Linda wrote them down.*

CHAPTER SEVEN

A Winter with No Women

In January, the ranger came and wanted Mac to get out logs to repair the Buffalo Creek Bridge. They went together to mark the trees, and the next week Mac started cutting and hauling. Mike and Johnny were wonderful in timber work as well as in the snow. They knew just how to skid the logs out of the timber and keep ahead of them down the steep pitches. Mac would just hang up the reins and let them go, knowing they would stop at the pile at the foot of the hill.

January–March 1917

Indoors I kept busy. There was much cooking to be done as Mac had a huge appetite from working out in the cold. On Saturday night we usually had the good old New England supper of baked beans and brown bread. A big pot of beans was baked and several loaves of brown bread steamed. White bread had to be baked two or three times a week, which meant three large loaves and a big pan of cinnamon rolls. Cake, cookies, and donuts were also much in demand, and preparing three meals a day required much time. With the cooking, the baby to care for, and the general housework, there was always much to be done. There were no electric appliances such as washing machines or vacuum cleaners in those days. Yet the most unpleasant part of winter living was the outdoor plumbing. With below freezing or near zero temperatures most days, and far below zero every night and morning, outside trips were far from pleasant. But some way we took it all in stride and did not think too much about it since everyone in the community had the same problems.

On January 27, the Markhams were giving a big dance at Moran, and we decided to try to go as I had not been away from the ranch all winter. The day before the dance Mac got the horses through the snow to the main road and thought we would be able to drive through with the light sleigh.

I made a big cake to take as everyone contributed to the supper. Mac covered the sleigh with a tarpaulin so it made a regular tent. He decided to use four horses as far as the main road then, if that road was in shape, would turn two horses loose to come back home. Only one team would be needed from there on.

After supper we got Jeanne all dressed and ready. She looked adorable in her little white dress and silk stockings and in her pink sleeping bag. I wanted to show her off! Putting her in a heavy blanket bag, [we] placed her in her box in the sleigh. With hay in the bottom of the sleigh, horse blankets over it, the lighted lantern, and a cover over all, it was made very comfortable. I was as warm as could be in my fur coat and the fur robe. Poor Mac had to be out in the open, though that did not worry him.

As our ranch house was so protected, we had very little wind, but as soon as we got out in the open, we found the wind blowing constantly and the road drifted full. The horses could barely keep on it at all, and after going about one-quarter mile, still on our own ranch, neither the horses nor Mac could see any road whatsoever and soon we were off. Mac got out [and] waded in the snow, trying to feel for the road, but could not find it. It was hopeless to try to continue. It was almost impossible for both man and beast to get the sleigh turned around and headed for home. If we had known how bad it was, and that it was beginning to snow, we never would have started out. We were truly thankful to reach the house again. Before

morning a terrible blizzard was raging, and if we had not gotten home when we did, I doubt if we ever would have. We did not attempt to attend any more festivities all winter.

February came and went. Two birthdays and Valentine's [Day] were celebrated in the only way we could, with special suppers. Our birthday gifts were the practical type. Mac received some special rope he needed and tin snips. He previously had been using my can opener, which was hopelessly hard on both him and the opener. March 3 was our second wedding anniversary and that called for another special occasion supper party. Jeanne was getting old enough now to take an interest and we centered things around her, of course.

One of Mac's added winter activities was cutting ice and putting it up for summer use. He got a trail open to Pacific Creek and was getting ice from a deep hole there. The ice was 2½- to 3-feet thick but not as good quality as we would have liked. This had to be sawed by hand, using the big crosscut saw. He removed the handle from one end so the saw could get below the ice and into the water. Thus he was able to cut the ice. The big chunks then had to be hauled out, loaded on the sleigh, taken to the little shed he had built on the back of the cabin, and packed in sawdust. During the summer he had been able to haul in a supply from a former sawmill across the creek. It had to be at least a foot thick on the bottom

Men harvesting ice for summer use just above Jackson Lake Dam. Though this photograph was taken in the 1930s, the process was much the same as when Mac did it in 1917. (Harrison R. Crandall)

and around the sides. Chipped ice was packed between the blocks unless they fitted snugly and then over all [he placed] another foot of sawdust.

Mac was also taking a refresher correspondence course in land surveying, having had only the minimum required in the Agricultural course in college. In addition to that, he also took irrigation surveying, as that was something almost unheard of when he was in school in North Dakota. The county surveyor was the only one licensed in the valley, and he lived in Jackson. He was so busy down there that he had no time for work in other parts of the country. Many ranchers, as well as us, needed lines and ditches surveyed. Mac knew he would have all he could do in any spare time doing that type of work if he had a license. Since the surveyor received five dollars per day and expenses, that would be a big help financially.

Even in March we continued to have very low temperatures. Water in the bedroom in the baby's boric acid would often freeze solid. The snow continued to come and was so deep, Mac had to give up trying to do timber work. By the end of March, the settled snow averaged five feet in depth.

Still the baby had her naps out-of-doors. She was warm as could be, snuggled down in the fur robe. This was put on top of a big box, which was in a protected place near the kitchen door, and she was most unhappy if she had to sleep inside.

We thought we had enough hay to carry [us] through the winter, but on the second of April, Mac decided to take the four work horses to Germanns'. He said he could finish wintering them and that would give us more hay for spring work. Again he had to take them down the creek to reach the main highway. The going was hard as there were so many deep holes and so many snags, and several times he had to tramp a path through the snow on the bank to get the horses around. It took five hours to reach the highway, and there he found the road had "gone to pieces" so that the horses broke through the snow with every step. After some four hours more, they had gone little more than one-half mile, but as they had reached Tom Carter's place, he left the horses there and skied home. By that time it was evening and I was becoming plenty worried as to his delay.

The next morning he was up by four o'clock and on his way. As it had frozen pretty hard during the night, that helped the horses in traveling the remaining four miles and they arrived at Germanns' before noon.

April 14 was really the red letter day. Billie Thompson was to come over to help Mac saw firewood, and Emily and the baby came with him. Early in the morning they could walk over on the crust, and Emily was the first woman I had seen since November 16 when the Loziers [had stayed] overnight. The Thompsons stayed overnight, too, in spite of a hard snowstorm, which lasted nearly all day. Billie and Mac sawed wood. The next two days, Mac helped Billie.

Though men in the valley tried to put in a supply of firewood in the fall, in cold winters they could run short. From left are Charlie Fester, Herb Whiteman, Ben Sheffield and an unidentified man. (JHHS&M)

April 1917

When Mac returned from taking the horses to Germanns', he brought back a fine piece of beef loin they had given us. They had butchered a young beef and the three meals of porterhouse steak was really a treat especially after an elk meat diet most of the winter. Elk meat was very good but one can tire of even the best.

During that spring we were glad our hens were laying well for they added much to our menu. One night when Carl Roice, a homesteader from across the creek, arrived, I scrambled five eggs with some leftover noodles. The next morning we had ten boiled for breakfast. In addition to having all we wanted to eat, several dozen were put down in waterglass for later use. Waterglass, a solution of sodium silicate, was the usual preservative used at that time.

As the calves arrived in the spring, most of them had to be dehorned. For several days Mac and Billie worked together, dehorning when necessary, and sawing more stove wood for the summer supply. It was the only fuel used, and good quality made cooking easier. They cut green timber, falling it on the crusted snow where it could be most easily sawed into stove lengths. It split easily at that time of year and was then left to dry out until the snow was gone and [it] could be hauled home in the wagon.

In late April there were wars, and rumors of war, but we knew very little of what was going on. Our mail was much delayed and when our newspapers arrived, they were often outdated by three weeks. But we did know that round the clock guard duty was being maintained at Jackson Lake Dam. A letter from Mac's brother, Will, who was then attending Wyoming University, said he was about to enlist. We worried about the draft. Our county seat was Evanston, 230 miles south of us, but the draft board was located there. In case Mac was called to report to them, it would take at least a week, probably longer, [to make the trip] as there was no direct travel route. It would mean a day to reach Jackson, another to Victor providing the road was even passable, a train from Victor the next day to Idaho Falls, hoping to make connections in Salt Lake, and from there back to Evanston, Wyoming. As yet he had not been required to register, but we knew that the call would come soon.

On May 24 the homesteaders who had succeeded in getting land adjoining our place arrived: a man, his wife, and a young boy, the son of the homesteader by a former wife. Mrs. Braman was much younger than her husband and the enterprising member of the family. She could do a man's work and seemed to enjoy it. We wondered if their cabin would ever have been built if she had been less efficient. Mrs. Braman was a fine neighbor in many respects, and the boy, about eight years old, was a nice youngster and well behaved. His father, however, soon gained the reputation of not being dependable, and in pioneer days the reliability of neighbors was all important.

It was early June when Mac received word to register for the draft and we all went to Moran. Although we were still having snowstorms frequently, Mac was already busy with plowing. We also got our garden started and those things [that] had been started indoors were transplanted.

Summer 1917

Then Jeanne became sick and was soon broken out all over. Mac made a trip to Moran to phone Dr. Huff and was glad to hear him say that it probably was not serious, although he did not know what was wrong. We never did know but in a few days she was quite recovered.

Soon after that, we were much excited when we received word from my mother that she would come out for a summer visit, leaving New Jersey on July 4. We were to meet her in Idaho Falls. We decided to make the trip to Ashton, a road open only in the summer. It was about a sixty-mile trip, but we thought it would be easier than going to Victor as there was no high pass en route. From Ashton we could take the train to Idaho Falls. Arriving there the day before Mother had said to meet her, we went to the railroad station on the following morning to meet the 8:20 train as arranged. To our surprise we found her already there. She had arrived the preceding day, a day earlier than she had expected. That proved to be a busy day, with dentistry, lawyer, and [purchasing] more supplies. As Mother took much of the care of Jeanne, they became acquainted very quickly.

Licensed surveyors were in short supply as many were working on federal projects. Mac studied and became a licensed surveyor which allowed him to work on irrigation projects. This provided an additional source of income. These surveyors are working in Snake River Canyon. (Wyoming Highway Department)

The following day we returned to Ashton via train and stayed at the hotel overnight. Early the next morning the horses were harnessed to the spring wagon and we started on the long return trip to the ranch. The first day we drove to Squirrel Meadows and camped there overnight. It was a hot, dusty trip, and the mosquitoes were terrible. In that country, in early summer, the mosquitoes were almost unbearable. We fought the mosquitoes, and the horse flies made life miserable for the horses. On hot days these flies were sometimes so bad that horses became almost unmanageable.

Although Mother was seventy-two at the time, she took everything in stride and did not mind the discomforts of camping in the open. The next day we drove to Ed. Sheffield's Snake River Dude Camp and insisted that Mother stay in one of the cabins overnight. She rebelled at not camping with us, but we knew that she would be more comfortable inside. She had already had a real initiation to the West. We arrived home late in the afternoon. Our little log house in a flower-covered opening in the pines, with the marvelous view of the Tetons, looked really beautiful, not only to us but to Mother, too. Laddie gave us all a most enthusiastic welcome.

The summer passed quickly. Mother enjoyed the country, although the altitude did not agree [with her] too well. Nellie could draw the light buggy, so Mother, Jeanne, and I took many trips to the neighboring ranches. Mother liked the young homesteaders and they all liked her, so we had many delightful visits. I know that Mother was glad to learn that her daughter, who had gone homesteading in the wilds of Wyoming, was really very comfortably located and happy.

About the middle of August, Mac took his examination for surveyor. By special permission from the state engineer, he was authorized to take this before the Moran postmaster, thus saving the long trip to Cheyenne. Within a few days he was notified that his surveyor's license was being forwarded to him.

Mother stayed until late September. At that time she was fortunate to obtain an auto ride from Moran through Yellowstone Park to Ashton [Idaho], which took only a few hours instead of nearly three days with horses. When Mac returned from that very early morning trip taking Mother to Moran, he said, "Mother said to be sure to look under the spread on the sideboard." So we went to look and there were two envelopes, one addressed to each of us. In each was a fifty dollar bill. We could scarcely believe our eyes for that was a pretty huge sum in those days. I know a few tears squeezed out of my eyes to think she had left us such unexpected and generous gifts.

It was surely lonesome for a while and Jeanne, too, sorely missed "Gamma." For days she would go to the little bedroom mother had had and was so disappointed not to find her.

By late October snow was coming again, we were using sleighs, and the thermometer went to minus sixteen. There was always plenty to do, but before winter really set in, the ranchers visited back and forth when work was not too pressing. Men riding for cattle, or hunting, often stopped by, were there for a meal or two and often overnight.

October–November 1917

With hay to haul from distant meadows where Mac had cut, fencing to put up, repairs to make, and the house to be daubed again before winter, his days were more than full. Also, after receiving his surveyor's license, he was in great demand for ditch surveying. Billie and we were taking water from Two Ocean Lake so those ditches had to be surveyed, too.

At Thanksgiving time Mac was hauling hay from Two Ocean Lake as elk were getting into the stacks there. It was snowy and slippery, especially on the sidehill roads, and on Thanksgiving Day, when [he was] hauling an extra big load, [the load] tipped over. He had expected to be back by noon and we were to have dinner then. As it grew later and he had not arrived, I was becoming really worried when he finally arrived with part of a load. But he was safe and sound. Our dinner was hours late but it was really a thankful one as the tip-over might have caused serious injury.

We were surely enjoying Jeanne for she added so much to our household. Each new development seemed more wonderful than the preceding, and each new trick or activity gave us joy. She had no playmates but seemed always able to find amusement by herself, and her imagination worked

Among other things, Gramma Preston sent Jeanne a photograph of herself for Christmas in 1917. Here, a little later, Jeanne is shown holding her prize photo of her gramma. (McKinstry)

overtime. Mother had sent her a picture of herself and that was Jeanne's prize possession and playmate.

By Christmas time she was old enough to be interested and to antici-pate it, although she must have wondered what it was all about. Her only acquaintance with Santa Claus was through pictures. We put up a tree in the living room and she "helped" string popcorn for it. Not nearly all our Christmas gifts had arrived, mail delivery was much too uncertain, but we had plenty to make a joyous, happy day. A little red cart was Jeanne's special joy. Our relatives and so many Washington and Springfield friends remembered us so generously, we felt very humble knowing we did not deserve so much.

CHAPTER EIGHT

Frustration, Flu, Frigid Weather

January came and it was at this time that the whole Jackson Hole community began to be upset about the proposed Yellowstone Park extension.[†] We did not know how the ranchers would be affected, whether or not we would lose our range rights, or even our ranches. We did know that our part of Jackson Hole was definitely not a winter range for elk, with snow several feet deep on the level for months. However, several Washington people were advocating the extension for use as a winter feed ground.

In late January Mac received his draft card. He was listed 4-A[‡], so we felt he was not likely to be called, although one never knew what might happen. Then, too, almost all the unmarried young men in the country enlisted and they more than filled the quota for that community. Joe [Chapline], the young school teacher at Elk, was among them.

Almost before we knew it spring had arrived. About the first of June, Bob Tidwell, a young lad, came to work for us and was with us for about five weeks. Ten days after he arrived, he came down with the mumps and was one sick boy. We thought Jeanne would surely have them, for she loved to be with Bob and Bob liked to play with her, but she never did. It was a week and a half later before he was able to work again. The preceding day he made a trip to Moran, which proved to be very fortunate. Laddie seldom ran away but evidently had gone to Moran that day. Possibly he might have followed Bob, who went horseback, but he did not know the dog was there. An electric storm came up. Laddie, who was always terribly frightened of thunder, had crawled into a cellar. He refused to come out and someone was about to shoot him as he was thought to be a stray dog. Fortunately, Bob happened on the scene just in time, recognized Laddie, so all ended happily.

January-May 1918

[†] *Almost from the time Yellowstone Park was established in 1872, proposals to expand it into the Tetons were made, at first mainly to protect the migrating elk herds. After the National Park Service was formed in 1916, talk became more serious and included the idea of a separate Grand Teton National Park. See the foreword of this book, p. xii.*

[‡] *4-A was a hardship deferment. Mac was temporarily exempted probably because he had a spouse.*

Laddie, a stray dog with some Collie ancestory, joined the McKinstry family. He was a faithful companion of Jeanne's. He was succeeded by a dog who looked so similar they called him Lad. (McKinstry)

In June, some unusually warm weather after the deep winter snows made the creeks very high. Buffalo Creek caused special difficulties as the approach to the bridge was flooded. People on horseback crossing the creek would get wet feet even when standing on the saddle. Small horses would swim through. People in wagons would stand on the wagon seat. Mails were delayed more than ever and only first class mail was brought. It was on June 30 that we received our first supply of magazines and newspapers, and the dates on them went back as far as June 1. We really did not know what had been going on in the outside world.

It was in the latter part of June that Joe received his call to report to the Service. Before leaving he spent a little time with us and was hoping to collect a bill from our neighbor, which was due him, but was unsuccessful. The money was badly needed and I doubt if I ever saw my husband more angry than he was at Joe's lack of success. Joe had asked Mac to come with him as a witness. The neighbor insisted he owed nothing, although he had purchased considerable food stuff and many other items on credit from Joe's little store at Elk. He denied owing anything and Joe accused him of being a crook, whereupon the fight started. Braman had bragged about his pugilistic ability, but Joe met his first pass with [one] straight to the chin, knocking him flat. As he got up he threw his arms around Joe in a clinch but never was able to do anything more. He was thirty years older than Joe and no match for him. Mac asked if he hadn't had enough, why not pay what he owed. Braman then said he'd pay when he could but typically never did. He did tell around the country, after Joe had left for the army however, that if Mac had stayed out of it he would have killed Joe.

Mail was frequently delayed because of snow, high water, mud, and world events. This is the mail stage from Jackson to Moran traveling across Antelope Flats in 1915. (JHHS&M)

A day or two later Joe had to leave. No stages were running because of high water, so he had to hike to Moran, cross on the dam, and go down the road on the west side to Wilson, at that time a little used road. Then over the hill to Victor. We never did learn just how many of the seventy-five miles he had to walk, or if he was fortunate in getting a ride part way.

An incident, a few days after the fight, emphasized the attitude of our neighbors. En route to Moran they had driven across Mac's newly plowed and seeded oat field, as it was a few rods shorter than going the usual road way. When Mac objected, the man said, "Well, we already have a track there now." The track did *not* get deeper, however.

In early June we had planted a big vegetable garden near the house. With such a short growing season, we were limited on varieties, but the cold nights produced the sweetest peas imaginable. Other things planted were lettuce, radishes, onions, chard, and such root vegetables as carrots, turnips, rutabagas, beets, kohlrabi, and potatoes. Of course caring for the garden took much time, and Jeanne, at least, greatly enjoyed it, though her help was pretty questionable. But she loved everything out-of-doors and was happy amusing herself. She had an imaginary family named Eboe, as I remember, so they could always be with her if she wanted. We would often hear about their many experiences and problems. She loved all the animals and considered them her friends and never tired of going on walks and picnics.

On the Fourth of July there was a picnic at Moran and a benefit Red Cross dance that evening. After the dance of early June, which we had attended, we were not enthusiastic about Moran dances. At that time the

Summer 1918

high water had caused many delays in people arriving. The dance did not begin at all until twelve o'clock, and it was nearly two o'clock before the people who were supposed to be furnishing the music reached the hall. Before that someone had been trying to play a fiddle, which was hopeless, and little better when someone accompanied him on the little old foot-pump organ. After the eats the people did not have to wait long for daylight. Although we were about the first to leave, it was nearly five o'clock when we reached home. Jeanne had been awake all through it, good as could be, and thoroughly enjoyed it, but surely slept thereafter.

In mid-July I had to make a trip to Idaho Falls for dental work. Mr. Banks, a U.S. engineer at Moran, and a U.S. inspector were driving out [of the valley] in their car and offered to take all three of us. Mac felt he had to stay at the ranch and would keep Jeanne, but I appreciated the offer of getting to Idaho Falls so easily. As the road to Ashton [Idaho] was very rough, they decided to go through Yellowstone Park, out the west entrance, then on to Ashton.

Leaving Moran soon after 8:30, we drove the eighty miles to Canyon Camp, arriving in time for a late lunch. After that we drove on to Ashton, arriving about 9:30. After a very late supper, [we] started for Rexburg as there was an excellent hotel in that town. As they stopped to pull an auto out of the ditch, it was after midnight before we arrived. Since leaving Moran at 8:30 we had traveled 212 miles, a delightfully fast trip in those days. In the morning, [we] drove the thirty miles to Idaho Falls in less than an hour and a half. The trip would have taken three days via the stage—to Jackson [the first day], over the hill to Victor the next day, and [then] taking the train from Victor to Idaho Falls the third day.

Dentistry work was started the day I arrived, but since it was Saturday, I had to wait until Monday for completion. It was nine o'clock in the evening before he finished pulling a wisdom tooth, which was the last of the work done. The next morning I took the train to Victor. I had to stay overnight there, but the evening was well spent arranging for our freight, some of which had been stored since last December to be brought over to Jackson. Arrangements by letter had brought no results. The next day I took the stage to Jackson, and all the passengers had to cross Snake River in a rowboat as the bridge was still out. It was then Thursday and I had to spend the day in Jackson as there was no stage to Moran until the following day. However, I was too ill to have left Jackson, even if the stage had been running. It had been very hot on the Victor-Jackson trip the preceding day as the stage had no top. We did not arrive at Crandall roadhouse until three o'clock, so evidently [I] overate when we did arrive. It was no wonder I was ill the next day, but [I] felt better by evening and visited with some Jackson friends.

On Friday I took the stage for Moran, and Mac and Jeanne met me about ten miles down country from the homestead. How good it was to see them after being away seven days [just] to have some dentistry work done. Arriving home, I found the living room all completed with burlap on ceiling and walls and woodwork stained. It looked wonderful to us. How glad we were to have it finished when one evening, a few days later, a big car drove up to the door. The occupants proved to be Mr. Horace Albright, assistant director, National Park Service; Mr. Howard Hays, U.S. Railway Administration, Western Park Service Lines; a Mr. Goodwin, chief engineer, and another young man who was the official map taker, and Joe Markham. The chauffer drove the car. The party had come to Moran the day before on an inspection trip concerning the proposed Yellowstone Park extension.[†] They came to see Mac because of his correspondence with Mr. Mather, then Head of the National Park Service. They were going on to Jackson the next day but wanted to give us more information about Park extension plans. We found them to be very friendly [and] most complimentary about our house, and [we] much enjoyed meeting people from Washington. We were glad to learn that grazing rights would not be withdrawn by the proposed extension and they convinced us that [the extension] might be to our advantage. So our opposition was eliminated and we now rather favored the bill.

One day in late September when Mac was surveying at Moran, he received a telegram, via phone call, from Max Ball, a former Washington friend. The telegram stated that he and his party of four would arrive for an overnight visit within a day or two. We immediately put up a tent [and] borrowed beds and bedding so were all ready for them. However, it was several days later before they did arrive, but their visit was the highlight of that fall season. Max was a native Coloradoan, graduate of the School of Mines, and when we knew him in Washington was with the U.S. Department of Geology, having been instrumental in its organization. He was now with the Shell Oil Company, with his headquarters in Cheyenne, and was on a business trip. The group included Max, his wife, Molly, and two girls recently out of college. One was a geologist, the other, his secretary. They had planned to stay only one night, leaving the following day, but rain and some light snowstorms were an excuse to lengthen their visit to a week. They loved the country, horseback riding, and herding cattle.

We had a never-forgotten picnic the day after their arrival, going far up Pacific Creek. Mac and the two girls rode horseback, while Molly, Jeanne, and I went with Max in the auto, as far as we could drive. After hiking some distance farther, eating a late lunch, and enjoying the wild country, we started for home. It had been raining a little in the afternoon,

[†] *For a summary of the extension of Yellowstone Park and the formation of Grand Teton National Park, see the foreword beginning on page vii.*

September 1918

but by early evening it was raining harder and harder. On an especially steep pitch, made slippery by the rain, the auto stalled. Only with the help of Mike, with the rope tied to his saddle horn and everybody pushing, were we able to get up. That was repeated on another hill less steep and later [due to] deep ruts. Then as we neared home, [the auto] high centered and could not be moved. By then it was pitch dark and pouring rain. Mac put Jeanne and me on Mike, and he was given his head. Max held onto Mike's tail and with his other hand, led Molly. The girls rode Shorty. Afoot, Mac took the lead through the timber, leading Johnny as he was too wet to ride bareback. We trailed through the inky blackness, taking down the bars into the hay field, and then the last quarter mile to home. Arriving there, we soon had a hot fire and cocoa, which warmed us, our clothes were drying, and all agreed it had been a lot of fun.

After [the] Balls left, we settled back into routine. The Red Cross chairman for the community was Mrs. Miller in Jackson, and she sent up considerable work—khaki—comfort kit material. This was to be made up and Emily and I worked on it.[†] Mac had hay to haul, wood to get, the innumerable chores, and more survey work than he had time to do. Winter vegetables from the garden were dug up and stored, and I canned and dried the more perishable garden stuff.

Cattle were rounded up to be sold and we had a few head to sell. Having so few, [we named] each animal, and the paragraph below is a quote from a letter:

> "Betty, being a cow, we could get only nine cents per pound for her, but as she weighed 1100 pounds got ninety-nine dollars. Roany, you may remember how small he always was, weighed 900 pounds, but at eleven cents per pound it amounted to $105.05. Just imagine! He is only two years old and never had a good start. He was nice and fat but small. I don't wonder meat is high when buyers in here will pay prices like that and take all they can get."

Mac's [surveying] transit, ordered last August, finally arrived, October 18, thanks to Mr. Banks who brought it in from the railroad for us. We were glad to [be] able to return the one borrowed from Moran, and Mac was glad to be using his own.

Thanksgiving day was spent at the ranch and the Banks family were our guests. We greatly enjoyed their visit and the day.

A couple of days earlier Joe Markham borrowed two of our horses to make a trip to Kelly after gasoline for the government. He brought our kerosene, which had been a year en route.

Ever since early September, having been unable to get a telephone, we had been considering the advisability of getting out on the main highway

[†] Even into the 21st century the American Red Cross supplies comfort kits to American and Allied soldiers and sailors as well as civilians who have need of them in combat areas. They also provide the kits to survivors of disasters. The kits contain basic food, clothing, first-aid, and personal hygiene items. Linda and Emily were probably making the "kit bags" that held the comfort kit items.

for the winter. After being completely snowed in for months the preceding winter, with no way of getting help no matter how much it might be needed, we felt it was unwise to stay there through another winter. There was a possibility we might be able to live at the Allen ranch, about a mile east of Moran, and on the highway. This ranch had been bought in early spring by the Loomises, but in July tragedy struck.

⁓⁓⁓

[Mac recounted the fateful events.][†] The horse pasture on this place was not fenced on the river side because the constant high water made crossing for the horses uninviting. Early one morning Loomis had gone to the barn to get his saddle horse to run in the team. He used only the halter, no saddle. When he did not return for breakfast, his wife went to the door and called. There she saw his horse grazing in the yard with [the] halter rope dragging. Immediately suspicious she went to the barn but he was not there; then [she went] to the phone and called Joe Markham, water superintendent at Moran a mile away.

Within a short time, men began to arrive and the search was started. They found where three horses had gone into the river; two had crossed but the saddle horse returned, evidenced by the track of the trailing halter rope on the soft bank. They theorized that Loomis might have tried to head the team back when they started into the river, but when his running horse hit the water, [it] fell, throwing him

With rowboats and grappling hooks, dragging began, but the water was deep and swift. Occasionally great chunks of earth and rock fell into the swirling current from the cut bank on the far side. Even though Joe shut down some of the gates at the dam to lower the water level, the search proved futile.

However, the belief that Loomis was drowned was not unanimous. There were those who maintained that he had good reason for wanting to disappear, something we never could understand. There were occasional unfounded rumors that he had been seen in one city or another over the country. But when some folks got together later to discuss the episode, there was usually someone to declare that the ranch must be hoodooed. And to that there was no argument.

⁓⁓⁓

Mrs. Loomis was leaving, so if another buyer was not found, the house would be available. Mr. Allen said we could move in for the winter, asking only that Mac try to repair the barn enough to keep it from falling down. I was almost superstitious about the place, as many years before, a son of Mr. Allen's had drown[ed] in Snake River while attempting to ride a horse across. And we understood another son had been killed by being thrown from a horse. Then this recent drowning.

[†] *Mac did not write his account of this event but seems to have recounted it to Linda who wrote it down. Mac was present at the events. His input seems to end after four paragraphs.*

But we would be glad to be so near Moran and to have a telephone available as there was already one in the house. Therefore, after Thanksgiving we made preparations for the move. Hay had to be hauled up there for winter feed [and] logs for firewood, besides our household goods, including the big kitchen range. On December 12, the final loads were taken. The men set up the range and some of the furnishings [were] put in place. Jeanne and I were staying with Mrs. Lozier as the Allen ranch house was still too cold and Jeanne and I could not move in alone.

On December 13, Mac, with Joe Markham and George McClure, had to go to Jackson. December 14 was "proving up day" for our homestead, and there had to be two witnesses. The winter that far had been unusually open and roads were good so they could drive through in Joe's car in a day. But even at that it meant a three-day trip with horses and wagon. However, they arrived back about the middle of the afternoon on the thirteenth, so we moved up to the Allen place.

The ranch house was a big, log, two-story, ten-room house, sitting back about 200 feet from the highway. The main part had been added onto the original homestead cabin, a one-story, three-room structure. In this was the kitchen, a small bedroom, and a storeroom. We were living in

this part and one adjoining room, which we used for a living and dining room. But we had an impossible task keeping even that much warm. Then, too, Mac had gotten hold of some poor logs for firewood, which added to the difficulty. He had not had time to get a better supply, nor to get a bigger supply.

Besides the main house there was an assortment of other buildings belonging to the ranch. These were along the roadway leading to the barn. The first building to the east was the meat house, next to that a combination ice and storehouse. The bunkhouse was the third building, next to that the chicken coop, then a small blacksmith shop. Beyond that was the carpenter shop and then finally the big barns, really two joined together. Close to the main road was an old, unused store building with a false front, in which dances were sometimes held. All were log buildings and the ranch was almost a community in itself.

Soon after [we moved] into the ranch house, Mac had to make another trip up home for more equipment and supplies. Jeanne and I continued to try to get settled and keep warm, which was an impossibility. On the twentieth of December, Mac went to the Elk post office to bring some sacks of potatoes, which had been left there for us. He had been having a bad cold,

Linda and Mac spent the winter at the Allen place in order to be closer to a road and telephone. They found the house very difficult to keep warm. (JHHS&M)

Keeping warm was a continual struggle for Jackson Hole residents. Not only did they need to have a good supply of firewood, they had to keep it accessible. Billie Braman (shown here at Moran) and other residents had to shovel new snow off paths almost every day even if they were ill. Snow eventually accumulated in huge piles making paths almost like tunnels. When the wind blew, snow drifted into the tunnels, sometimes filling them to the top. This required even more shoveling. (JHHS&M)

but two days later he was really sick. That was the winter of the terrible Spanish Influenza epidemic. Some of the huskiest Jackson Hole boys who had enlisted for service had already died in camp. Jackson was in quarantine and no meetings were allowed. Many people were sick. Mrs. Brown, the Elk postmistress, was half sick but insisted it was not the flu. However, it evidently was for many people who had contacted her were down with it in a very brief time. And Mac, having had a cold for several days, was especially susceptible.

He was so ill by night that I phoned Dr. Huff in Jackson. He told Mac to go to bed immediately and he would send up medicine the next day on the mail stage. However, neither mail nor medicine reached Moran that day. We heard later that so many people were ill with the flu that a driver could not be found. Thanks to having a phone, we learned that someone in an automobile was bringing up medicine, but as he did not come to Moran, we thought the medicine might be at Elk. It was a bitter cold night, but Herb Whiteman insisted on making that fifteen-mile round trip, horseback, only to find the medicine was not there.

Herb was a neighbor living about half mile away, who had immediately come to help us [on] learning of Mac's illness. Besides his own work he did all of our outdoor chores, which included milking, feeding the livestock,

Dr. Charles Huff was nearly overwhelmed when treating patients during the influenza epidemic of 1918. He and his wife, a nurse, saved many lives. (JHHS&M)

cutting wood and bringing it to the door, and keeping us supplied with water, which came from a pump away from the house. And beside all that, [he] found time to cut a little tree to bring to Jeanne the day before Christmas. Jeanne and I trimmed it that evening.

Christmas and the days following that year were a never-to-be-forgotten nightmare. Except for our wonderful neighbors, I honestly doubt if we would have survived. On the afternoon before Christmas, Beth and Leah Clark, two attractive girls in their late teens, who were living with their mother at Herb Whiteman's ranch, arrived. They did not come to the house but went to the log pile where they sawed and split wood the rest of the afternoon, helping out with the desperately needed wood supply.

On Christmas Day Mac could scarcely raise his head from the pillow. Jeanne and I were already coughing, and I was so tired I could scarcely keep going. Dr. Huff had said we probably would get the flu, but the important thing to do was to stay in bed, much easier said than done. No one was much interested in presents and only a few packages had arrived, but Mother's boxes always seemed to contain just what was wanted, and there were toys for Jeanne. The one always-to-be-remembered gift, which Mac and I had ordered together, was the record *Dinorah*, sung by Galli-Curci[†]. We usually did not care for classical music, but that beautiful record helped

[†] *Amelita Galli-Curci was a very popular opera soprano in the early 20th Century.*

carry us through the day and was played over and over many times.

Two days later Jeanne was down in bed and I was up and down until after noon when I had to give up. Mac had gotten up but was so weak he could hardly move around, even to prepare a little food. Herb had continued with all the out-of-door work. We were so thankful to have the phone so we could keep in touch with Dr. Huff. Although he'd had the flu himself, he insisted on getting up and helping other people and when unable to get out of bed would answer phone calls.

On the last day of the year, he made a trip all the way to Moran. He came up in his car but had trouble with it and had to be taken back to Jackson in a big Yellowstone Park touring bus, which happened to be at Moran. That winter had been most unusual with very little snow, so a big car could get through easily. He stopped to see all the sick people en route so arrived at our house. When he learned that I was nearly three months pregnant, he really [laid] down the law. The one admonition I have always remembered was, "You absolutely cannot cough." And I didn't, although I'll never know how I kept from it. After feeling better I was ordered to stay in bed another week before I was allowed to be up and dressed and do a little work.

Time to Start Over

The new year arrived. Mac did a little more each day and soon insisted on doing the outside chores though not really able. Jeanne had recovered quickly. But we all had survived the flu and were most thankful. I, too, had been allowed to get up and dress by the end of the first week.

We were still remembered by our neighbors. All our wood supply had been used, so Herb, with some men working on the dragline at Moran, got a logging sled [and] four horses from Sheffield, and they brought in a huge load of logs. Although we had never before seen the dragline men, they would not accept a cent of pay. Herb would have been insulted if offered any for his many, many hours of work.

Never were we able to keep comfortably warm in the house though [we were] using only three rooms. We had the range in the big kitchen, and a small heating stove in each of the other two rooms. We had had relatively little snow all winter, but the weather had been intensely cold. The kitchen was very large, and our supplies of waterglass eggs were kept in there though on the opposite side from the range. That part of the kitchen remained so cold that they never did thaw out after freezing. We had been able to purchase some local coal to use in the heating stoves, hoping to keep a fire in them overnight, but it was of such poor quality it gave little heat.

When I was allowed to be up and dressed on the sixth of January and out-of-doors for the first time on the thirteenth, we felt that all was really going well again. Sometimes it is fortunate if we do not know what is ahead.

On January 15, just two days later, Mac had gotten up before 5:30 as usual. He had started the fire in the kitchen range, replenished the fire in the living room, and gone out to milk.

I got up soon after 6:30, stopped in the kitchen to put more wood in the stove, then went on to the living room to dress as it was warmer there.

January–April 1919

Soon I noticed a crackling sound over my head—that was the one room we were using of the double story part of the house—and wondered if it could be fire. Looking out the window I saw a bright yellow light reflected on the snow. Then I knew it was.

Rushing out, I ran toward the barn screaming at the top of my lungs. Mac was just finishing milking, heard the screams, and came hurrying around the barn with a pail of milk. Immediately he saw the blazing high roof of the house. Setting down the pail of milk, he grabbed the only ladder on the place, and that was long enough to reach the low roof only, and ran toward the house. I followed and brought him the Pyrene fire extinguisher by the time he was going up the ladder. Going back inside the house, I pulled Jeanne's crib into the kitchen near the door so she could be quickly carried out. It was so bitterly cold we did not want to take her out until necessary. Then [I went] to the telephone in the front hall to phone to Moran for help. There were still some unpacked boxes in the front hall so I pulled those out through the front door.

Returning to our part of the house, I found that Mac had come in, saying that all he could do was to check the fire a bit. Since the living room was directly under the blaze, he thought we should get those things out first. We had no idea the fire would envelop the whole house so quickly, so [we] took out [the] dining room table and chairs before we realized how fast the fire was spreading.

He carried Jeanne out on her mattress and placed it in the snow some distance from the house. She was good as could be and stayed quietly in bed. I suspect she might have enjoyed watching the big "bonfire."

After my phone call, Herb was there in a matter of minutes and within ten or twelve minutes two men from the dragline and Joe Markham arrived. But even then there was little time left to do anything.

Knowing how important it was to save our kitchen range, most of the men started dragging and shoving it to the kitchen door. Water slopped from the reservoir onto the floor and immediately froze. Between the icy floor, hot stove, darkness—for it was still barely daylight—the smoke, and flames bursting through into the room, it was a difficult and dangerous job. But they reached the door and there, when part way through, the range stuck. The men were outside by then, except for one big man from the dragline, who had gathered up Mac's mattress bedding and fur robe and headed for the door. Reaching there and finding it blocked by the stove, he had to drop all the things and climb over as best he could to save himself for flames were reaching there then. Outside someone had gotten an ax, chopped the doorframe, and with the help of all the men, the range was pulled to safety.

After that nothing more could be done except to watch the house burn to the ground. Due to the tinder dry logs and intense heat, there was nothing left in about an hour's time but a pile of ashes. If we had had just a few minutes more, even one or two, with the help of the men, many more things could have been saved. But we didn't have those minutes. As it was we could barely think about our furnishings, equipment, and all our grocery supplies and clothes in the storeroom, knowing they were burning to ashes.

I remember wondering what the real temperature was that morning and wandered over to the bunkhouse to look at the thermometer hanging by the door. It was twenty below zero.

❧

[Mac recounted the events of the fire to Linda.] On the morning of January 15, I had gotten up before daylight, started a fire in both stoves as usual, and gone out to do the chores. I was just finishing milking when I heard Linda screaming, screams that can never be forgotten. Running out I saw her standing part way down to the barn and the peak of the high roof in flames.

As I ran, I grabbed the only ladder on the place, leaning against the shop.

"Where's Jeanne?" I wanted to know.

"She's all right. The fire's in the other part."

As I set the ladder against the eaves of the lower roof, Linda brought the fire extinguisher.

"Call Moran."

She ran in and I reached the base of the high, steep roof, but the pressure was too limited. The roof was too steep to climb. I backed off along the ridge of the lower part to get a running start, but before quite reaching the top and a hand hold, [I] slid back. I could barely reach the fire with the spray, but even so thought I was gaining. Just then the surrounding, dry, curled shingles exploded into flames, and the extinguisher failed entirely.

Jumping down I, too, began carrying things out. Even then we did not realize how fast the fire was traveling. I grabbed Jeanne, rolled in her mattress and blankets from the crib where Linda had dragged it near the door, and set her down out in the snow, swathed in all the bedding we could get around her.

We got out the dining table and some of the chairs. By that time the men from Moran were there and helping. They started to take out the kitchen range, hot though it was. Water slopped from the reservoir and instantly froze to a glare of ice on the floor. In the doorway it jammed.

This photograph shows the Ward Hotel and old Post Office being burned in Wilson as practice for the fire department many years after the McKinstrys' fire, but it illustrates how a log building becomes totally engulfed in flames. (JHHS&M, Olie Riniker)

Behind them came a big fellow from the dragline, an ex-con, carrying a mattress, blankets, and the fur robe. Just then the fire broke through the ceiling, and he had to drop his load and jump over the stove to save himself. From somewhere Herb had grabbed an ax and was chopping out the door casing. That done, the stove was pulled to safety.

By that time the whole house was in flames and there was nothing to do but watch it burn. The logs fell together in embers like the fuel in a seething fireplace. The heat was terrific. In an hour there was nothing left but a pile of hot ashes.

Jeanne, bundled in all the blankets we could get around her, watched, entranced by the spectacle. In a hazy sort of way we reckoned our loss, but looking around we could not help but be thankful that we had all got out, and no one in the crowd had been hurt or seriously burned.

It was time to start over.

Sometime [later] we got Jeanne up, but [I] don't know how we could have dressed her. Most all of her things were in the house so burned up—even the clothes she had worn the day before. She may have had to keep on the nightclothes she was wearing. Reaction was setting in by then and the events of the next few hours were always pretty much a blank. As soon as the men were sure the burning embers could not reach any of the other buildings so that it was safe to leave, Mac hitched up the team and took Jeanne and me to Mrs. Clark's on Herb Whiteman's place. We remained there the rest of the day. She was much concerned about me and insisted I lie down all the time, which was about all I could do anyway. Between the overexertion so soon after the flu, the shock of the fire, and my pregnancy, I later learned there was far more cause for worry than I realized at the time.

That evening we were taken to Mrs. Markham's and Jeanne and I stayed there the next two days. Mac and the men got the range into the bunkhouse, cleaned up the place, which had not been used for years, and got it in livable shape. Mrs. Markham was a trained nurse, and although I did not need any help of that kind, it was good to know it would be available if necessary.

Three days after the fire we moved into the bunkhouse [at the Allen place]. Again we were down to a one-room cabin, much smaller than our original one, and with little to go on. But at least we could keep warm as we had not been able to do before, and we were thankful to have any place in which to live. People loaned us cooking equipment, serving dishes and utensils, and even groceries, for practically nothing was saved from the kitchen except the range. Later we found an iron frying pan and an iron muffin pan in the ashes of the fire and they were still usable.

Fortunately, most of our winter supply of white flour and sugar had been stored in the bunkhouse and we were most thankful for that. But everything in the storeroom in the house was a complete loss. This included some seventy-five pounds of dried fruit, nearly 200 pounds wheat substitute (that was war time and people were supposed to be using substitutes for white flour), all our canned goods, and the innumerable miscellaneous supplies. Also in the storeroom were all our medical supplies, so necessary to have on hand in that country, which we had replenished for winter use. As there were no closets in the rooms we had been using in the big house, our clothes [had been] hung in the storeroom. How I hated to think of my lovely brown velvet corduroy riding skirt going up in ashes. But as we had survived the flu, and the fire, with only minor burns, we knew conditions could have been much worse.

Mac put up frames for two bunk beds, and Jeanne's mattress was placed across two chairs as her crib had been burned. But some sort of routine was soon established, and it was the least of Jeanne's worries that when she went out-of-doors in the snow, she had gunny sacks tied around her feet in lieu of overshoes.

As days and weeks went on, we acquired needed articles. Mother sent china, silverware, cooking utensils, and innumerable other supplies. Our faraway friends, relatives, even little-known acquaintances, upon hearing of the fire sent blankets, towels, clothing for Jeanne, and all kinds of useful household items. We were able to replenish our grocery supply and most necessary clothing needs via parcel post, though it took time. Ultimately living became quite normal, and borrowed equipment and supplies could be returned.

Mac was busy with outside work doing far more than he should after his serious bout with the flu. Coal was needed to fire the dredger at Moran so all the ranchers were hauling coal from the mine on Buffalo Creek when weather and roads permitted. Also he was busy getting out logs for the U.S. Forest Service to be used as stringers on the Buffalo Creek bridge. These were nearly sixty feet long and each made a load for four horses. Roy Lozier was also helping with his team, and [they] hauled the logs on the ice the full length of Emma Matilda Lake in order to reach the road.

In March a dentist came to Moran and, as always, I needed more work done. We were fortunate in being so near Moran as appointments could easily be kept. Ranchers from farther away usually had to stay overnight as Sheffield's lodge, as the roads were very bad, the spring breakup having started.

I had to have several appointments for sixteen small fillings were needed. Three were gold. He told Mac he never charged less than five dollars for a gold filling but because he hurt me so much, and had to "push my gums up nearly to my eyes," he was charging only three dollars! The other thirteen were silver fillings at two dollars each. The total bill, which also included cleaning and polishing, was thirty-five dollars. In some ways those were "the good old days."

In April some of the ranch ladies, who had been wanting to start a domestic science class, got together and one was formed. Since I was the ex-Home Ec teacher, I was to give the lessons, but I was glad to do it. Sometimes there would be about as many children as adults but that was expected. At one of the meetings, there were ten ladies and sixteen youngsters, eight of whom were [younger] than two years old. [It was] almost a baby show but the youngsters seemed to get along nicely. As it happened, the subject for that day was "The feeding of children." At least it should have been appropriate. Dr. Holt's baby book was the authority in those days. Since then most of his rules of feeding have been repudiated.

May–August 1919

In early May we had to make a trip to Jackson as Dr. Huff said we must come for an examination. We decided to make that trip before moving back to our own ranch. The report was satisfactory but the doctor said I must come to Jackson by July 1, although the new arrival was not expected before the seventeenth. In the meantime I must be extra cautious.

Moving back to the ranch was somewhat delayed as there was so much surveying the ranchers wanted done. They needed irrigation ditches for their crops.

About the middle of May, Mac started hauling furniture and equipment to our own place and soon after we moved back in. It seemed good to have more room and be back in our own attractive home again. Coming from Moran, and with Jeanne, I drove the loaded spring wagon. Mac followed with the big wagon, well loaded, to be sure we got along all right. Just as we started up a very steep, dugway hill[†], the back right wheel of my spring wagon gave way and down it went. It was lucky Mac was near. He got the broken-down wagon pulled to one side so not to block the road, and we all continued on in the big wagon. Then he had to go back, and in place of the broken wheel lashed a pole under the axle to support the load and act as a skid. Thus [he] was able to bring the load home.

† A "dugway" is road sunk below the surface of the land. Sometimes it is a road dug along a precipitous place otherwise impassable, like into a steep hill or alongside a riverfront.

Ranchers on Buffalo Creek as well as ourselves had long been trying to obtain telephone service from Jackson. Finally Mr. Lovejoy, owner of the telephone company, said he would put another wire in the main line. However, all who were to use it would have to purchase and put up their own wire from the highway to their home. For us that was a distance of three miles. We first put our phone in Loziers' house as they were on the main road, and we did not want to give Mr. Lovejoy a chance to change his mind before we could get our wire up. We knew that would take considerable time, but to have a phone three miles away would be better than eight. We had to order three miles of wire and when it arrived in Victor had to make the seventy-mile trip to haul it in.

Spring work had to be done, plowing and planting. As we planned on getting more cattle, we would need more feed so [we] arranged to have the use of the land at the Allen place where we had wintered. It was established meadow but needed irrigation to produce.

We had many visits from Buffalo Creek friends, whole families arriving unexpectedly. There was no way to contact us ahead of time, but plenty of groceries were always on hand and garden stuff in season. On June 6, Jeanne's third birthday, some six members of the Germann family arrived. They came just at noon but had brought so much lunch I had little to do. They had started out for a picnic but someway missed the group and came on to visit us. She had a big supply of potato salad, bread, cookies, and

St. John's Hospital was in their new building by the time the second McKinstry baby, Neal, was born. Here the hospital is under construction. (JHHS&M).

such, besides a quart of thick cream. For a late afternoon lunch before they left, I made muffins, salmon salad, cocoa, and with the remainder of the potato salad and with Jeanne's birthday cake we had plenty. I had planned a little party supper for Jeanne, but she, as well as I, was too tired to care about any more celebration.

Less than two weeks later it suddenly seemed advisable to go to Jackson at once [and] not wait for July 1. If we could get the man who was to take us down in his auto, we would leave that very day. We found he could, and after a hectic time getting ready, we left about 3:30 that afternoon. We arrived in Jackson just after seven o'clock and it was a joy to make the forty-mile trip in three and one half hours! A room at Mrs. Deloney's, a Jackson family, had already been arranged and would be ready for Jeanne and me whenever we wanted it. Mac returned home on the stage the next day as there was so much to do at the ranch.

Jeanne and I took our noon dinners at Mrs. Crabtree's hotel, fifty cents a meal, but usually had breakfast and supper in our own room. It was nice to have fresh fruit available even though high in price: oranges at eighty-five cents a dozen or more, bananas at seventy-five cents a dozen. Those were the first bananas Jeanne had ever seen and she wanted to know what they were.

As it turned out I need not have hurried down quite so quickly, but our young son arrived July 9, considerably earlier than expected.

When we learned he was about to arrive, the doctor had the telephone operator notify Mac who was surveying at Moran. I had phoned at noon and told him that I was not feeling well but did not expect to have to call him that afternoon. It was nearly five o'clock before he received the call as the line was busy and the operator could not get through. Joe Markham had filled up his car with gas at noon when Mac remarked that I was not feeling well.

A later photo of the hospital and church shows the changes and expansion. This photo is undated. (JHHS&M)

"Just to be ready," Joe said.

Arrangements had been made with a man in Kelly to go after Mac when needed, but Joe said he would drive until they met. As it turned out Joe drove almost to Kelly as Mr. Spicer had had car trouble after starting out.

Early that afternoon Jeanne and I had started out to visit Mrs. Huff and Gretchen, their little girl [who was] about three months younger than Jeanne. We had gotten only to the telephone office when I had to phone Dr. Huff, who came for us and took us both to the hospital.

Jeanne did not ever want to be away from me. I had hoped she would become friends with children in Jackson and play with them, but she was timid and did not know how to make friends. Since she had played by herself practically all of her young life, and with her lively imagination was quite happy doing so, [she] was quite content to continue. She was not interested in other children but insisted on being near me for all else was a strange world to her.

The hospital was small, not more than three or four rooms for patients as I remember, and one friendly nurse in charge of all. So Jeanne could be with me just as well as not—[as] long as I was up and around.

As the baby had not arrived by seven o'clock, Dr. Huff took Jeanne home with him. From later reports I learned about her reaction. She was very unhappy but did not cry. Every time she heard an auto, [she] would exclaim, "Maybe that's Daddy!"

He did not arrive at Huff's until around nine o'clock, and Jeanne [was] asleep then. Little Gretchen was ousted from her bed and Jeanne was put in her bed in Huff's bedroom. Mrs. Huff said that Jeanne did not cry aloud but just sobbed and sobbed until she finally fell asleep. The next morning she started sobbing again, but when Dr. Huff told her she had a baby brother at the hospital, she was momentarily happy. But the joy did not last long. She ate breakfast with tears running down her cheeks, but not making a sound, and eating whatever was set before her. The Huff's said they never saw such self-control in a youngster.

By the time she had seen Mac and gotten to the hospital, she was very happy and thought the small baby pretty fine. Much excited then, she told how she had slept in Gretchen's bed, had orange juice and such good things for breakfast, and evidently enjoyed the memory if not the experience.

We had quite a time deciding on a name for the baby. I rather wanted Preston, but that sounded jerky with McKinstry. Then we thought that with a one-syllable first name he might be called by that rather than "Mac," so decided on Neal Preston McKinstry. Needless to say he was called Mac anyway.

After two days, as all was going well with both Neal and me, Mac returned to the ranch taking Jeanne with him. We knew she would be most unhappy staying with anyone in town and maybe she would stay with some of the people near Moran while Mac was surveying.

As for Neal he was one cute infant! He had such a funny, adorable expression that the hospital nurse would even wake him up to show him off to visitors. Mac said I would get somewhat peeved at that, but [I] guess I was remembering the long waking hours we had with Jeanne. I surely wish they'd had, at that time, the hospital picture-taking facilities of today.

In those days having a baby meant ten days in the hospital even if all went well. It was a wonderful period of rest and relaxation. Even though the little hospital was being enlarged so was plenty noisy at times, it was still a pleasant place to be. As I remember there were only three or four rooms for patients, and the friendly, young registered nurse was in charge of it all, so [it was] was far different from present-day hospitals. Meals were sent in from one hotel or another, which was the most unsatisfactory part, but that was not too important.

As the doctor wanted me to remain in town for more than the ten days, he said I could stay in the hospital if I wished. Room was available, the nurse always there, and it would be far easier than going to a hotel with the baby. Also [the hospital was] much nicer, and [I] am sure it was very little if any more expensive. I was glad to stay.

At the end of two weeks the doctor said I might make the return trip home if I could return by auto. We did not own an auto but Mac and Jeanne came down via stage the day before and made arrangements to hire one. We left around noon the following day and arrived at the ranch about four o'clock on July 23. It surely seemed good to be back together again in our own home after some six weeks in Jackson.

That was the summer of the terrible drought. It was usually dry and dusty in Jackson, and although everyone was talking about the lack of rain, I had not realized how serious conditions were elsewhere. Usually at that time of year, the yard around our ranch house would be beautiful. Wild flowers, most golden buckwheat, would be a mass of bloom. But this year there were no blossoms, even foliage and grasses having dried up and turned yellow.

In the spring on our own place, Mac had planted many additional acres of oats, anticipating a big supply of oat hay for winter feed. He had also arranged for the pasture and all the hay from the Allen ranch. All this would enable us to buy enough cattle to start a real herd. But then came the drought, something almost unheard of in that country. Seeds did not germinate and what grasses grew soon dried up. Our land was on the reserve, [where] there was still abundant feed for the wildlife and the few cattle allowed thereon, but on fully stocked rangeland the feed soon ran out. Ranchers were forced to sell their cattle at hopelessly low prices as there was nothing to feed them. Many horses, though needed for work, had to be sold also, as all that section of the northwest was in the drought area. It was reported that in Montana, beautiful big draft horses were sold for a cent per pound, bringing only fourteen or fifteen dollars.

Here a stagecoach crosses the Pacific Creek bridge. Mac and Jeanne took a stage from Moran to Jackson to pick up Linda and the new baby, then they all returned to Moran by rented car. This photograph was part of a movie scene directed by Sam Woodring. (Harrison R. Crandall)

Every day people hoped and prayed for rain but none came, unless it was a wee shower, never bringing enough moisture to do any good. Our hopes for a start in cattle were completely gone. We would be lucky if we had enough feed for the few head we already had.

We probably would have been utterly discouraged had it not been for Mac's survey work. People in surrounding states were also suffering from the drought and were searching for any additional irrigation water. A land and livestock company, located in Idaho Falls, came into the valley hoping to acquire some Wyoming water rights. They wanted to construct an eight-foot dam at Two Ocean Lake and a smaller one at Emma Matilda. The Wyoming state engineer had been contacted and he favored the project. He knew that water from these lakes had limited use in Wyoming and that water was desperately needed elsewhere.

Since there was a possibility of the proposed Yellowstone Park extension including all that country, the National Park Service was much opposed to the idea. However, [as] the extension bill had not been passed by Congress, [and since] the Wyoming state engineer favored the [water] project, the company decided to go ahead with preliminary work on the chance the official permit would ultimately be approved.

Two or three days after I arrived home with the baby, Mr. Milner, who was head of the Idaho Falls project, came in. Much survey work would be needed and Mac was hired to do it. This meant permanent work for an indefinite time.

The company first wanted a survey made for a feeder ditch from high up on the Pacific Creek to Two Ocean Lake, designed to catch the early runoff. The outlet from the lake would carry water from Two Ocean Lake down to Pacific Creek, thence to the Snake River and on into Idaho. That survey was started at once. Mr. Milner and a couple of ranchers helped Mac for a few days to complete the survey before Mr. Milner returned to Idaho.

We were also directly involved in this whole project since Billie and we had already acquired the first water rights on Two Ocean Lake. These represented the top two feet of water. We had already started work on the dam and ditches, although not much had been accomplished due to the pressure of other work. Three other homesteaders nearer Moran, Markham, Lozier, and Snell, all had similar rights on Emma Matilda Lake. Their work on the dam and ditches also had been started but little accomplished.

In order to get a state permit to increase the storage by raising the dams, the company first had to obtain from all five of us the "Consent to Enlarge." For this consent they offered $1000 to each and a guarantee that our water rights would always be protected. This agreement, too, was approved by the state engineer.

The very last of July, Mr. Albright, who was then superintendent of Yellowstone National Park, was again at Moran. He sent word asking Mac to meet him, but the message was not received until Mr. Albright had left for Jackson. However, through Joe Markham, we learned the Park Service was still very much opposed to the project.

Although Mr. Milner had decided to go more slowly on any actual construction than first planned, after the continued opposition, he wanted much more surveying done. This included mapping contours of the lake so Mac was busy surveying every day.

Also a little actual work was started as a better road was needed to Two Ocean Lake and Emma Matilda. This gave some needed work to a few ranchers and their teams could be used when hauling gravel.

At the house, we were getting on nicely with routine activities. We had been fortunate in getting the help of a young girl when needed, Helen Taylor by name. She was a willing worker and cheerfully did whatever was asked, all for the magnificent sum of a dollar a day, the going wage of that time.

People from Idaho were frequently in to see about their proposition and, although they stayed at Moran, they were frequently at our place for meals. People from all around the country would also stop by.

Neal was a happy baby and much admired. His hair was curly and at least one curl was usually standing upright on top of his head. Jeanne was quite delighted with him and usually happy to hold his bottle. One day, shortly after we returned, I overheard her pretend to make a phone call. She made believe ringing the bell for the connection, then the brief conversation. "Dr. Huff? Thank you for that nice baby brother, Dr. Huff."

Of course the drought had ruined our garden and we greatly missed the fresh vegetables. Peas for only one meal, an occasional lonely, tough radish or other vegetable, and a little lettuce. Unfortunately, the cow found the lettuce, too. Some of our Buffalo Creek neighbors who had water enough to irrigate their gardens were most generous in sharing their vegetables with us. We surely appreciated them.

On August 25, Mr. Albright and other government people interested in the Park extension program were again at Moran. They were having lunch there and then going to Jackson that evening. It seems that Mac had been invited for the luncheon and trip, but thanks to our inefficient mail service, the letter did not arrive until the following day. Unfortunately he and Mr. Albright missed one another again.

About four days later, Mr. Emerson, the state engineer, and several of the officials of the Idaho company met at Moran to discuss the irrigation project and to see what had been done. After inspecting the work, they all

Little Neal was soon back with his sister and parents on the homestead. "He was a happy baby and much admired," Linda writes. (McKinstry).

came to the house for supper. Besides Mr. Emerson, some of the others in the group were Mr. Milner, Mr. Johannessen, attorney for the company, and Mr. Brunt, another official. I was very glad to meet them all and enjoyed the evening immensely. Mr. Emerson was continuing to favor their project but said some Wyoming people opposed having the Wyoming water go outside the state. He felt that if it would not be used in Wyoming and was greatly needed elsewhere, others should have it. But he said he did not have the final authority in the matter as the Board of Control, or some committee, had to be consulted. Usually that group was in agreement with the engineer's recommendations; all were very hopeful that the company would ultimately receive the permit.

Although the company had begun construction of the dam, they were very careful not to exceed the two-foot limit for which the ranchers had permits. However, they hoped the foundations were heavy enough to support a higher dam.

The Park officials were still opposing any increase in the height of the dam, but it was not until the first week in October that any real authority was found for stopping the work. At that time a presidential order of 1918 was brought to light, which said all work in the proposed Park extension area was prohibited. That made it impossible to build more than a two-foot dam, so all work was stopped, although the Idaho company did not give up hope of being able to continue later.

September was a busy month. There was much demand for survey work all around the country, but it was only on Sundays that Mac felt he could take time from the company project. One Sunday he went to a ranch on Buffalo Creek, which had been recently purchased by a wealthy man from "outside." I think that what most impressed Mac was the fact that the man could not understand why the ditch could not be surveyed so the water would run uphill. From his report I was most intrigued by the fact that dinner was served by a maid and served in several courses. That wasn't the way the homesteaders did. Mac was also offered fifteen dollars a day for a continued survey job but of course could not accept even if he wanted to.

Another little event of that day made us unhappy. That was when the cat brought in a flying squirrel he had caught. I think it was the first I had ever seen.

By the last of the month, Neal had outgrown his clothesbasket and his bed was made in a big box. The crib Mac had made for Jeanne was burned in the fire, but Neal was happy in his box.

As well as being imaginative, Jeanne was a practical youngster. Mother had sent her a little box of animal crackers, which delighted her, but they were soon gone and she asked me to send the box back to Mother for a refill. I asked her if she did not have any left and she replied, "Yes, one, and I broke off the foots to make more."

She loved a little flat iron Mother had also sent. At night, regardless of the weather, she would wrap it up without bothering to warm it and take it to bed with her. Other times she would let her dolls use it, but then [she] always warmed it before wrapping.

In those days a good haircut was hard to come by, as wives and fellow ranchers were not too efficient. So when an ex-barber came into the country and gave one to Mac, and also to Mr. Germann who happened by, it was a real event. The man, a Mr. Riniker, was working at the dam, and his wife was so appreciative she came over and gave my house a real good cleaning, just out of kindness of heart. Helen did a pretty good job but could not do it as efficiently.

More complications developed regarding the building of the dam in September and early October. A man by the name of Carlisle, who evidently was trying to gain control of Wyoming water and block the Idaho project, arrived at Moran. We never knew just what it was all about, but he was surveying and spreading erroneous reports about the company work being done. But then came the presidential order, so all work was stopped anyway, at least for the time being.

That gave Mac time for needed ranch work. Billie Stilson, another homesteader, had cut hay near Emma Matilda, had hauled most of it the seven miles to his place, [and] then told Mac he could have any that was left. So we were fortunate in getting one big load. Hay was precious and we appreciated getting that much more.

With October came cold weather, and early in the month icicles were hanging from the porch roof. We were still short of bedding and had to resort to using the daytime go-cart blankets and even coats, until something more could be obtained. In October the ranchers had a surprise party for McClures on Buffalo Creek. They had sold their ranch and were soon to leave for the outside. As Helen could stay with Neal, Mac and I rode over the hill horseback, Mac carrying Jeanne on his horse. It was then we met the Cowles, an older couple, who had bought the Mc-Clure ranch. Mr. Cowles had sold his business in Detroit; they had been touring the country and come into Jackson Hole, liking it so much they decided to locate. We enjoyed meeting them and invited them over for dinner the following Sunday.

We were glad that our Milky cow had a calf the middle of the month as that meant a good milk supply during the winter. [Milk was] a very welcome and important part of our food supply.

Mac's next project was getting ready to string our telephone wire. Although the needed wire and equipment had not yet arrived, we hoped it would soon. Postholes had to be dug across Loziers' flat, but trees could be used much of the way for the next two miles. Where a swamp had to be crossed, he set the needed poles as that would be very difficult to do after freeze-up. One never knew about freight, and the bedsprings and mattress ordered after the fire in the spring had not yet arrived. We were hopeful that the wire would come.

Soon after the McClure party, Helen's father insisted that she return home as he was teaching school and thought he needed her. However, before the month ended he said she could return [for] thirty dollars a month and stage fare both ways. We were glad to have her again, if for only a month.

Just about that time we heard that the whole Park extension bill had been withdrawn. Some work on the small dam at Emma Matilda Lake had been continued by the ranchers as they wanted it ready for spring irrigation. On November 3, Mac, Holland, and Snell finished the cement work there. Already there was over ten inches of snow so little possibility of doing further work thereafter. As it was, a fire had to be built to thaw the ground for excavation.

We had sold five of our few head of cattle and were well satisfied with the returns, especially considering market conditions. The "old cow" brought only five cents a pound but the others ranged from $7.75 to $10.50 per cwt. In [the] present day market, the price would range up to twenty-five dollars. However, our five animals brought approximately $440, out of which were shipping expenses of $61.50. But that gave a net of $378.50.

That fall the rangers and game wardens began to crack down on hunting on the reserve. Although always against the law, it was generally accepted that the relatively few ranchers living thereon would not be disturbed if they did get their winter meat there. Then, rather unexpectedly, a young rancher who lived just off the reserve, but came there to hunt, was fined seventy-five dollars for killing his elk. In another instance, the zeal of the wardens brought unexpected results. It seems that Elmer Arthur, a part Indian homesteader living near the Loziers, was crossing Loziers' place one morning and had his rifle with him. Noticing a horse had gotten out, he left his gun on the fence and went after the horse. Returning he found Ohl, the local ranger and also a deputy warden, and Nelson, another game warden, waiting for him.

Ohl said, "I'll take your gun for carrying it on the reserve."

Elmer replied, "I guess you won't," and after some argument the men rode on.

Later in the day when Elmer was at home sawing wood, the men came back.

Ohl said, "You're under arrest. Go to Jackson tomorrow for trial."

Elmer inquired, "What for?"

"Carrying a gun and hunting on the reserve."

Elmer replied "I wasn't hunting. If you have me arrested, I'll have you arrested for killing that elk on the reserve three years ago."

It seems that Elmer and Carl Roice were on the reserve and hearing a shot soon found Ohl dressing out an elk.

Nelson entered the conversation and said, "If you swear out a warrant against Ohl I'll arrest him."

So Elmer did.

Elmer had to go to Jackson the next day, and his wife had to go down later as witness, but they were back in a few days. He was found not guilty and it was reported Ohl's trial would come off as soon as Carl returned from the cow camp. However, Elmer never did press the charges because of the time and expense that would be involved. So that blew over, but it seemed as if the wardens were then more careful about tangling with homesteaders who might know too much. Of course it was generally believed that Elmer had started out that morning to go hunting, but since he had not taken his gun off of Loziers' land, evidence was surely lacking. So much for local color.

Other work that had to be done was getting the winter supply of wood hauled in or available. That took considerable time and work. With months

Evanston 05516   4—1004—R.

The United States of America,

To all to whom these presents shall come, Greeting:

WHEREAS, a Certificate of the Register of the Land Office at **Evanston, Wyoming,**
has been deposited in the General Land Office, whereby it appears that, pursuant to the Act of Congress of May 20, 1862,
"To secure Homesteads to Actual Settlers on the Public Domain," and the acts supplemental thereto, the claim of

Harold C. McKinstry

has been established and duly consummated, in conformity to law, for the   **southeast quarter of the north-west quarter, the east half of the southwest quarter, and the Lot four of Section seven in Township forty-five north of Range one hundred thirteen west of the Sixth Principal Meridian, Wyoming, containing one hundred sixty-six and fifty-four-hundredths acres,**

according to the Official Plat of the Survey of the said Land, returned to the GENERAL LAND OFFICE by the Surveyor-General:

NOW KNOW YE, That there is, therefore, granted by the UNITED STATES unto the said claimant   the tract of Land above described;
TO HAVE AND TO HOLD the said tract of Land, with the appurtenances thereof, unto the said claimant   and to the heirs and assigns of the said claimant   forever; subject to any vested and accrued water rights for mining, agricultural, manufacturing, or other purposes, and rights to ditches and reservoirs used in connection with such water rights, as may be recognized and acknowledged by the local customs, laws, and decisions of courts; and there is reserved from the lands hereby granted, a right of way thereon for ditches or canals constructed by the authority of the United States; reserving, also, to the United States all coal in the lands so granted, and to it, or persons authorized by it, the right to prospect for, mine, and remove coal from the same upon compliance with the conditions of and subject to the limitations of the **Act of June 22, 1910 (36 Stat., 583).**

IN TESTIMONY WHEREOF, I,   **Woodrow Wilson,**

President of the United States of America, have caused these letters to be made

Patent, and the seal of the General Land Office to be hereunto affixed.

GIVEN under my hand, In the District of Columbia, the   **TWENTY-SEVENTH**

(SEAL)   day of   **SEPTEMBER**   in the year of our Lord one thousand

nine hundred and   **NINETEEN**   and of the independence of the

United States the one hundred and   **FORTY-FOURTH.**

By the President *Woodrow Wilson,*

By   *W. P. LeRoy* Secretary,

S. A. C. Lamar,

Recorder of the General Land Office.

RECORD OF PATENTS: Patent Number **708784**
6—2283

On September 27, 1919, Harold McKinstry was granted the patent for his homestead in Jackson Hole. (BLM, General Land Office Records)

of winter ahead, temperatures way below zero night after night, and with all heating and cooking done with wood, a huge supply was needed. As all cutting then had to be done by hand, it was a major project. Usually two ranchers would work together sawing the logs into stove lengths, after which they could be split as needed or as time permitted.

In early November Mac also daubed the house again as the summer heat had loosened it. This made the house much warmer and cut down on the fuel needed.

After the Park extension bill had been withdrawn, the Idaho company wanted more survey details and asked Mac to come to Idaho Falls to work with their engineer in computing earth yardage and water shortage. Their attorney then was to take these specifications to Cheyenne for consultation with the state engineer and, hopefully, for the continued approval of the project.

Mac decided to drive [a team] to Victor to take the train, using only the front bobs of the sleigh. He knew it would be quicker than going by the mail stage, which was not at all dependable. Also he hoped to find the veterinarian to check on Ginger's teeth, but there was none in either Jackson or Victor. As it took two days to reach Victor, he could not get a train until the third day. In Idaho Falls he worked early and late, sometimes until midnight, with their engineer as all were anxious to complete the work. We were glad when he arrived home after a ten-day absence.

While [Mac was] away, Joe Chapline came to do the necessary chores. He had returned from Service, married, and was teaching at the Buffalo school. His wife came and stayed part of the time but was anxious to continue getting settled in Germanns' bunkhouse where they were to spend the winter. We were having some severely cold November weather with the thermometer going from thirteen to twenty-one below on three nights, and his help was surely appreciated. We had only three head of cattle left at the ranch and hardly enough hay left for that many and the horses. But they had to be fed and cared for. Germann helped us out by wintering four head of our cattle.

In early November articles, long awaited, finally came through on the mail stage. Mac's surveying rod, which had been ordered several months previous, also a wringer, which Mother had ordered for us more recently. The wooden box holding the latter was broken apart, but the wringer was intact and really needed after having been without one since the fire.

When Mac returned he brought some of our freight, which had been long delayed in Victor, also the telephone wire, which had arrived quite promptly. He also brought food items that were much enjoyed. He also brought half a young sheep [that] he bought in Victor, which made a welcome change from our elk and chicken diet. We had previously had one change when someone had brought us a piece of meat from a young bear he had killed. It was delicious and we liked it but had the feeling one would tire of it quickly. Meat from an old bear is said to be too strong to eat. Mac also brought oranges, celery, and a box of apples. His gift to me was a locket, as one I had enjoyed wearing was burned in the fire. This lovely new one was oval shaped with an engraved edge and center and four tiny diamonds. He got it in exchange for a few elk teeth he had taken out, and as only one pair of teeth was first class, we were well satisfied with the exchange.

In later November we had 500 pounds of potatoes brought in for winter use. A couple of ranchers drove to Victor to get a winter supply for themselves and neighbors. It was so cold en route that all the potatoes had to be unloaded every night and a fire kept burning all night long to keep them from freezing. We were glad they arrived safely. After Mac returned he helped Joe for the first day. Joe was to get out the winter wood for the schoolhouse, and since he had been coming to our house every night after school, he had not had time to do it. We were glad to help that much.

Mac then started on the telephone work. More posts had to be set, and the dirt from the holes dug earlier had frozen, which made extra work. By the first of December, he had almost finished cutting tree branches and putting on insulators, and all the needed poles were in place.

The weather continued very cold, twenty-seven below on Thanksgiving morning. Generally it was ten to thirty below or even more, but [it was] surprising how it warmed up on sunny days. Later in the day it was relatively comfortable out-of-doors until the sun was low in the west. Except for taking a day or two off to complete a ditch survey at Kelly, he continued work on the line. When he was ready to string the wire, Roy Lozier offered his services and said he would refuse any pay. I think he appreciated having had the phone in [his] house for some months.

Most mornings Mac was up before five so as to be ready to start out by daylight. Milking, feeding, and getting the horses ready all took considerable time and the horses were needed for hauling, stringing, and stretching the wire. Later in the morning Roy would meet him and they would work together. At noon they came to the house for dinner so both men and horses had time to eat and rest.

Getting the wire fastened to the poles and trees was a difficult task since it was three miles to the highway. Three and a half miles of wire had been purchased and most all of it was needed. The snow had weighted down the trees so much they were leaning badly, and they had to be chopped out to make way for the wire. [Mac and Roy] had hoped to finish on the seventh of December, but when Mac arrived home about 6:30 that

Mac was responsible for stringing his own telephone wire for the three miles to the road. He often used existing trees as poles. When completed it was a seventeen-party line. This photograph shows utility poles in Jackson in snowdrifts. Mac's poles were much smaller, hand cut, and rougher. (JHHS&M)

night, he said they had had bad luck in the afternoon and the wire had broken twice. It had been a very cold day, barely above zero when I went out at 4:30 to feed the chickens, so [it] had been doubly hard to handle the wire. However, Mac expected to finish up the next day working alone and then he'd be ready to put in the phone.

Mr. Lovejoy, owner of the phone company, had promised to have our new phone come on the stage two days later. Mac went to the highway to get it but no telephone. Mr. Lovejoy had phoned to Loziers' earlier in the day and said the mail stage had too big a load to bring it up. We couldn't understand that. Since the Victor train had stalled, no mail was coming in over the hill; the mail stage was never [full] with the small amount of mail from Jackson only. Mac telephoned Mr. Lovejoy, who finally admitted he had not gotten up in time to get the phone on the stage but would surely send it on the next one. We were surely disappointed. One never knew in the winter when the next stage might arrive. It finally did on the seventeenth of December and the phone was soon installed.

Even though there were seventeen subscribers on the line, and when anyone rang a phone number, most of those seventeen receivers came off the hook, at least we had contact with the outside world. Of course the whole country knew everyone's business, but they would sooner or later anyway.

By mid-December the snow was getting very deep. Paths could not be kept cleared and as the snow came so often, it was hard to keep dry when out-of-doors. I had finally hit upon the idea of ordering black tights and by pulling them up over my dresses I could get along very well. Those I had had been burned so [I] ordered more.

Hanging out clothes was a special problem when the snow became three and four feet deep. Sometimes I waded through it and other times [I wore] snowshoes. Another difficulty was the fact that the deep snow made the clotheslines just a few feet above it, and I would have to lean over to put the clothes on the line. Needless to say the clothes had to be so doubled to hang at all, [and] they were a long time drying.

Although so deep, the snow was still loose enough so the horses could walk through it, and we could drive to the main road. Jeanne and I drove down for mail one day and although the horses had to walk every step of the six-mile trip we enjoyed the jaunt.

Our Roany cow, which we had been wintering at home, had her first calf the sixteenth of December. It was minus five degrees that evening and Roany was not at all interested in the calf. Mac wrapped it in hay hoping she would care for it soon. When he went to the barn to check a little later, he found all was well, though it was a very cold world in which the little creature had arrived. A cold barn, too, but I was glad it wasn't necessary to bring him in the kitchen to keep warm.

With Christmas approaching we tried to interest Jeanne in Santa Claus, thinking she might be missing some childhood pleasures. She was not at all interested. Her emphatic responses were, "Grandma sends me my toys."

We were concerned about our own Christmas needs. Our bedding supply was still short as we had received refunds on blankets ordered earlier. And the blanket Mac had ordered for my Christmas brought more refund. I had the same experience on the bathrobe I had ordered for him and by then it was much too late for substitute orders.

But we had a wonderful Christmas anyway though the delayed mail had brought us only a few packages. Those were opened early Christmas morning. After enjoying the contents, we got ready to go to Cowles'. We had been invited there for a two o'clock dinner and to stay overnight.

Neal was put in his box bed and loaded in the sleigh with any needed warm winter bottles and flat irons. Mac, Jeanne and I sat in front on the wagon seat. It began to snow soon after we started and kept on all the way. We were plenty wet and snowy when we arrived but it was a part of the fun. We covered Neal's box so he was warm and comfy and he had slept all the way. When we reached the mail box we found a big box from Mother awaiting us, so knew we would have another Christmas when we opened it the next day.

Our visit with the Cowles was much enjoyed. It was so nice to visit in a home where they had lovely china, silver and glassware, and such nice furnishings. Dinner was delicious, and in the evening after Jeanne and Neal were in for the night, we played "500." I believe that was the first time we had played since Washington days, and it recalled so many former happy evenings. "500" was the popular card game then.

The next day was cold but sunny and lovely, and we left for home about noon. We stopped at Germanns' to pick up our long awaited heating stove. It had finally arrived in Victor, a storekeeper had it brought to Jackson, and then sent it up to Germanns' by some men hauling coal from the Buffalo [Creek] mine. The coal haulers passed by Germanns' ranch. Nearby we found that Gregory, a rancher living next to the Germanns, had cleared a road to the top of the hill as he had been hauling out wood. Mac decided we would take that road, trusting that we could get down on the other side. That would save many miles via the main road and was the way we went on horseback. I wondered how he could possibly find the way through a mile and a half of timber and deep snow, with the sleigh and two horses, but he did. Safely reaching the bottom we crossed partly frozen Pacific Creek and in a few minutes arrived home. There we were enthusiastically welcomed by the dog and cat, and the livestock were awaiting their quota of hay.

Mother's box was as wonderful as anticipated. As always she seemed to know just what to send. Little puffs, or quilts, were especially appreciated as well as our individual gifts. Jeanne was right when she figured that Santa Claus could not be nearly as efficient as Grandma. One gift she especially appreciated were her Bubble Books[†] [and] her own little phonograph records, and she was most careful of them. They had recently come on the market and we enjoyed them as well as Jeanne.

Neal had a cough [that] had persisted for quite some time so we decided to phone Dr. Huff. He said to try rubbing his chest with olive oil and kerosene, two to one. We had no olive oil but Mazola seemed equally effective and were glad the mix brought good results in spite of, or because of, the smell. There was no use trying to send liquid medicine via mail stage. Twice we had tried ordering Milk of Magnesia; each time it had frozen solid and could not be used.

[†] *Bubble Books were a series of books and records published together. Produced from 1917 to 1922, the books focus on a little boy who receives a magical pipe that blows Mother Goose characters, who sing songs with the boy on the three records that accompany each book. Children could play the records and sing along as they read the stories*

The very last of the month we received word from the Idaho company that their conference with the Wyoming state engineer had been quite successful. Since Mondell had withdrawn his Park extension bill, they were quite sure they would receive their water permit so planned to continue work on the dams as soon as weather permitted.

Then came 1920, our fifth year homesteading.

The following paragraph is not related to homesteading but [regards news] taken from a letter received from Mother in December 1919 and is a tribute to a fine man.

Dr. Stocking, who was pastor of a very large Congregational church in Washington D.C., had performed our quiet marriage ceremony on March 3, 1915. He had left Washington and had been transferred to some location in New Jersey. Mother was then living with my sister in Upper Montclair, N.J., and when she wrote that Dr. Stocking had called on her we were amazed. With his thousands of parishioners, among whom we had been very ordinary ones, it was really wonderful of him to remember her, or us, and contact her nearly five years later. A most kindly act and much appreciated by all of us.

CHAPTER TEN

Water, Water Everywhere

January 1920 arrived. We felt pretty well ready for the New Year with the telephone installed, logs out for the woodshed [that] Mac planned to build on the back of the cabin, a good supply of stove wood, and many more minor jobs completed.

Our wonderful horse, Mike, was taken on his last long journey. He was old, had always done more than his share of the work, and the long cold winters had taken their toll. [As he was] stiff and hard to get about, another winter would be misery for him. If a horse could look back on his life and accomplishments with satisfaction, Mike sure could. Usually horse hides were sold, but we decided to have Mike's tanned for his long white hair was almost fur. We would have liked to have made it into a fur robe but the twenty-dollar cost was more than we could afford. Just the tanning was around eight dollars.

We were enjoying our Christmas gifts and the handwoven wool blanket Uncle Lester had sent to Neal was especially appreciated. He had sent one to Jeanne when she was a baby. Those blankets were made from sheep wool produced on the farm in Minnesota, made into yarn, and handwoven. He had kept them stored away for many years.

Our ice cream freezer from Mother was really enjoyed. Previously we'd had mousse, freezing the flavored, sweetened whipped cream simply by setting it outside. With our plentiful supply of milk and cream, ice cream was enjoyed for a change. Fresh apple pie, made with dried apple of course, and served ala mode was one Mac's favorite desserts.

Thus far our winter had been a comparatively mild one and we had relatively little snow. Horses were still able to travel our road to the highway so we could drive down for mail. They had to walk the entire three miles

Left: Mac became very proficient with his skis, traveling crosscountry with one pole for miles at a time. (McKinstry)

Right: Jeanne, too, became adept at traveling by skis using the small skis that Mac made for her by hand. (McKinstry)

each way, but it was lovely out-of-doors on sunny days since we were accustomed to below-freezing temperatures. If horses could not make the trip, Mac would have to go the six miles on skis. If there was parcel post to bring, he would take the little sled with ski runners.

January 3 was such a lovely day, even though it had been twenty-four below in the early morning, we all drove down for mail in the forenoon. The cold trip made Jeanne's cold worse. She'd had many colds during the winter, which may have been the result of the flu the previous winter. We knew her tonsils were enlarged so [we] decided to contact Dr. Huff and were thankful to have the phone. Ever since Mac's flu attack, he'd had to use a throat spray and the doctor said to try that for Jeanne. As he had said before, he hoped Jeanne would outgrow the tonsil difficulty and it would never have to be necessary to operate. However it ultimately had to be done a few years later, as the spray gave only temporary relief.

While our road was still passable, Mac drove over to Buffalo Creek to the mine, hoping to buy some coal. It was very poor quality coal but would help out on the wood supply and hold the heat a little longer during the night. He was unable to get any. Their carbide for lights had given out and until more could be obtained from Jackson, no mining could be done. We were much disappointed for we never knew when roads might be completely closed.

One weekend we enjoyed a visit from the Cowles, the new Buffalo Creek neighbors whom we enjoyed so much. We celebrated the evening playing "500" until after midnight, an unusual event for us. Our Sunday dinner ended with ice cream and rich chocolate sauce, all we could eat, and we really had appetites in those days. Ice cream was an extra treat enjoyed by company as well as ourselves.

Mac had coyote traps set in the open spring water about a quarter mile from the house. Roy Lozier and a neighbor of his were trapping some ten or twelve miles up Pacific Creek where martins could be caught and these pelts brought more [income] than the coyotes. Although they asked Mac to join them, he could not as they were away several days and nights at a time. Money from pelts was one of the few sources of income during the winter so was very welcome. He succeeded in trapping over twenty coyotes and most of the pelts were beautiful. They usually sold for fifteen to eighteen dollars or thereabouts.

Our hens helped us out financially, too. They started laying generously in January when eggs were bringing sixty cents per dozen. Mrs. Lozier, living on the main highway, could sell all we took down. When the price dropped below fifty cents, we started putting the eggs in waterglass for summer use. When a little new calf arrived in January, we were assured of a good milk supply and rich cream. That was especially appreciated in the wintertime.

On January 19 Neal's first tooth came through, which was a real event for us all. He was then just a little over six months, a husky, happy, cute baby [who] made lots of company for Jeanne as well as for us. He had one unfortunate experience that month. Jeanne and he were playing in the kitchen, Mac and I were in the living room, and suddenly Neal started screaming at the top of his lungs. Hurrying to the kitchen, we had difficulty locating the trouble but finally discovered severe burns on one little hand. The go-cart was nowhere near the stove then but quite evidently had been. Huge blisters developed on three fingers and he was pretty miserable for a few days.

One day in late January we enjoyed a daylong visit with Loziers. Roy was to butcher a pig, an awkward job for one man, and he asked Mac to help. Of course meat was always shared and pork was a welcome change from the regular elk meat diet.

It was during that winter that various magazines, especially the *Saturday Evening Post,* started publishing many articles about the Jackson Hole country and the proposed Park extension. Occasionally an article would appear in a magazine opposing the Park extension but most were solidly on the side of the Park Service, favoring extension. The *Saturday Evening Post* was one of these and many of their articles were far from accurate. Those by an Elizabeth Frazer made us especially unhappy. She seemed to know nothing about the country except its unsurpassed beauty, inferred that all the elk were being butchered by the ranchers, rustling was a regular pastime, and holdups were usual things. Local and county newspapers wrote articles reversing her reports but of course they had limited circulation. Ultimately E.W. Nelson, chief of the Biological Survey, issued a statement denying the truth of these allegations concerning the Jackson Hole ranchers and their slaughtering of elk. As a matter of fact some ranchers shared their feed with the hungry animals, sometimes willingly and other times because the elk helped themselves to the hay stacks. One group of ranchers was cooperating with the government, which was already starting to buy winter feed for them. This was the beginning of the extensive program [that] has been developed.

While our road was still passable, Jeanne and I would sometimes drive [a horse] to the highway for the mail. On a sunny, relatively warm day, it would be a beautiful trip. The whole country would be snow covered, the snow always clean and glistening white. Going down was mostly toward the west so the jagged, snow covered Tetons were ahead, marvelously beautiful. If we did not see any little wild creatures along the way, at least we saw their tiny tracks in the snow. Mac could tell whether they were made by mice, weasels, squirrels, or birds. Although we'd had comparatively little snow during the winter, the men trapping up Pacific Creek reported six feet on the level there. We knew we still might have that much before the winter was over and we did.

One trip for mail brought another of Mother's much enjoyed boxes. Among other things was a book for Jeanne, which was called *The Selfish Fox*. Usually she wanted a story read several times before she liked it nearly as well as those she already knew. But not this one. In a very short time she would "read" it herself. Looking at the pictures, she would repeat the story almost word for word. Then she spent hours acting it out. I wish I could remember the story but I can't. Another of her favorite pastimes was playing with an imaginary family she invented. I believe their name was Eboe, though I'm not sure, and she now has no recollection of them. At the time they were very real people to her and she enjoyed them immensely. She had a marvelous time with her vivid imagination, which was fortunate.

Neal was growing fast and wanted to stand on his feet whenever anyone would help him. Because he was so bowlegged, we tried to discourage his efforts to stand. When sleeping he lay flat on his back, his head turned sideways, his legs up against body. He looked dreadfully uncomfortable but evidently wasn't. We were afraid he would grow up bowlegged so I spent considerable time rubbing his legs hoping to help straighten them. I doubt if this did any good but soon nature took over and all was well. Although most of the time he was a model, happy baby, and good as could be, he had a temper of his own. What he wanted he wanted right now, which I guess was perfectly normal considering the inheritance from his mother.

In late January we had our first instant coffee, probably the can was received in one of Mother's boxes. Then, as we saw it advertised in our grocery catalogs, we sent for about all of the available brands. It usually came in little three or four ounce cans, as I remember. Not the quality we have today, but a thrilling innovation. We found we liked Great Barrington's best, although the George Washington was very good, too. Hire's had a satisfactory flavor but was less easily dissolved. We did not care for the Faust brand.

Valentine's was celebrated in the only way we could, a supper party with extra eats. Of course [we had] a Valentine cake with white frosting, three red candles, and red hearts painted on the frosting with food coloring. Valentine's Day was written across the top. Jeanne received some valentines from relatives and outside friends but I wondered what special significance any of these special days must have for her. Christmas and birthdays meant presents; other days must have been extremely vague. But she always loved any extra party decorations.

In early February I had to can elk meat as a brief warm spell had thawed out some of our frozen elk meat. No pressure cookers then and it had to be boiled on three days. The meat had to be cut in stew size pieces and packed in the jars. My wash boiler would hold fourteen quart jars, which had to be covered with water and the water kept boiling for one or two hours on each day. It took a great deal of fuel to simply bring that to a boil then hold it there. Plenty of work was involved in the whole process but it was the only way we could be assured of meat during the summer, other than our chickens.

We had an opportunity at that time to buy ten pounds or so of pork, probably for about twenty-five cents per pound. For several days we feasted on pork chops and roasted the last of it. We surely enjoyed the change from elk.

At the danger of repeating, I must tell about our tapioca pig, as we called him, which we had raised a few years earlier. The commissary at Moran was closing and selling out the leftover food stuff at the lowest prices imaginable. Their tapioca had come in 125-pound sacks and it was cheaper to almost give it away than to ship [it] out. Since tapioca is almost pure starch, Mac thought it might make good pig feed and as it was much cheaper than any grain available, we purchased a couple of sacks, and how that little pig thrived on tapioca and skim milk! He grew unbelievably fat, which would be most undesirable on today's market but was just the type wanted in those days. The lard from the fat was most welcome.

In February we sent some of what we believed to be burned black, melted silver, salvaged from the fire, to Daniel Low Company. Whether it really was melted sterling we were not sure, but some must have been for soon we received a credit for three dollars, quite a bit in those days. As we needed more silver[ware], we added a little more to the amount and received a half dozen heavily plated teaspoons. [We] also purchased an extra one with Neal's name engraved thereon as Olea Wood, a Washington friend, had sent money for a gift for him.

On Mac's birthday, the twenty-third, we celebrated in the usual way, extra decorations and eats. His birthday supper was just as requested: omelet, apple salad, hot rolls, ice cream with chocolate sauce, birthday cake, and cocoa with whipped cream. It was good.

We had borrowed Joe Chapline's big sleigh for some hauling that had to be done, so Mac started out early one morning for Buffalo Creek intending to return it. I had expected him back before noon but it was evening before he arrived. Then he returned, still with Joe's sleigh, but hauling a load of wonderful ice. Pacific Creek had thawed and refrozen so many times no usable ice was available. We'd had to resign ourselves to expect a summer without any so were delighted to get a supply from Buffalo Creek. Mac had helped Walt Germann with his feeding in the morning and Walt had helped him get the ice in the afternoon. Our phone was surely appreciated that day for I would have been more than worried over his lateness if I had not received word over the phone. We had so much snow during the preceding week, our road was in very poor condition and he'd had to leave half the load at Loziers', returning for it the next day. With the added shed room [that] he had completed at the back of the cabin, we had a good icehouse and ice packed in plenty of sawdust would keep for months.

In those days, of course, we had to make our own butter and made it whenever we had sufficient cream. Over the years we must have made hundreds of pounds. We did not wish to sell any until after we purchased a separator as we used large quantities and if kept cold, packed in ice during the summer, [it] would keep fresh for weeks.

At first we had had to put the milk in large pans, set them in a cool place for twenty-four hours or so to let cream rise, then skim it off as best we could. Later we purchased a separator (in 1920) so the cream could be separated as soon as the milk was brought in. This was a far more economical and satisfactory way as the cream would always be of the desired thickness and fresher. To make butter it had to be soured by adding some sour milk or sour cream and allowing time for souring, or ripening, to take place before churning.

In time we purchased a six-gallon barrel churn to replace the original one of a tin pail with the up and down wooden paddle, which Mac had made. The barrel churn was rotated by turning the crank. If the cream was of the right consistency, thirty-five percent butter fat as I remember, properly ripened, and of the right temperature, the butter would come in less than half an hour. Otherwise it would take much longer.

Walt Germann, feeding a foal in the Buffalo Valley. Walt and his wife, Pearl, were good neighbors to the McKinstrys. (JHHS&M)

We could tell when the butter came by the sound of the cream in the churn. Instead of just a splashing sound, it would chug down as the barrel was rotated. The butter formed in tiny bits, sort of kernels, and after a few more turns, the buttermilk would be drained off by removing the cork from the outlet at the bottom of the churn. And was it good buttermilk! Some flecks of butter always came out with it.

Cold water was added to the churn and the bits of butter were pressed together with the wooden butter paddle then lifted into a large, wet wooden bowl. Here it was washed several times in more cold water [and] pressed with the paddle until all traces of buttermilk were removed. Salt was added and after [it was] thoroughly mixed in, the butter was pressed into a one-pound wet mold, pushed out, and wrapped in parchment paper. Altogether it took quite a bit of time but [was] just one of the things we took for granted and we were always well supplied with butter. We made considerable cottage cheese, too. This gave us added protein if we were low on meat and was always a welcome addition to meals as it could be used in a variety of ways.

To return to March 1920. Our fifth wedding anniversary was celebrated on the first instead of the third, which was the correct date. Mac had agreed to do some surveying in Jackson if he could get someone to stay with me and thought he might be away on the third. We celebrated in the only way we could, extra eats and some kind of decorations, but always the duplicate wedding cake. Our wedding cake, made by a Washington bakery, had been a large, round, white frosted cake with a beautiful cream colored rose in the center. That had been a real one, but Jackson Hole roses had to be made of paper; not even plastic ones [were] available then. They looked nice to us anyway and the children were always thrilled.

Mac could not leave on the third after all as Helen Taylor, the girl who had been with me before, could not come until that day, so he left on the fourth. Mr. Braman was to do the milking and feeding. If Helen had not arrived, Sonny, the Braman boy, ten years old or so, was to come over and stay nights. He was disappointed to have Helen arrive. She came on the evening stage. They phoned about suppertime from a ranch down country that the stage was there and Helen on it, so Mac had to ski down to the main highway to be sure she found her way safely.

That night about 2 A.M. Mac heard the phone ringing. When anyone rang central, the bell rang at all seventeen ranches en route. Sometimes this was fortunate as help might be needed in ringing through. Ordinarily Mac would never listen on the phone just because it rang, but a ring at that time of night indicated an emergency so help might be needed. The call proved to be Joe Markham who was making arrangements to start for Jackson as soon as possible. Their oldest boy, about six years old, had been ill for several days and had taken a turn for the worse. He, his wife, and boy were to drive to Eynons' ranch, some twelve miles down country and would arrive about daylight. There they would change horses and the Eynon boy would drive them the next ten or twelve miles to Kelly. Owing to the bad roads, horses could not make any kind of time and were not able to travel long distances. From Kelly a Mr. Kafferlin would take them to Jackson if the road was sufficiently open for a car. Otherwise another fresh team would be waiting and take them on. There was nothing local ranchers could do but all were concerned and awaited more details regarding the boy. Since Mrs. Markham was a trained nurse, we knew she must consider the situation critical.

Mac left early the next morning to take the mail sleigh to Jackson. We had much snow the preceding couple of days and it was piling up fast. It was still storming at our end of the valley so he had a long uncomfortable trip although there was little storm further south. All the roads at our end of the valley were beginning to be almost impassable but the mail sleigh was usually able to get through although much delayed.

Upon reaching town, Mac was able to get a report on the Markham boy and phoned back. Mrs. Markham had feared appendicitis and the appendix might have ruptured. Dr. Huff was more optimistic. He did not believe an emergency operation necessary [and] said they were to await further developments as the boy was feeling slightly better. The Markhams were thankful to have arrived in Jackson as quickly as they did, although the trip had taken seven or eight hours. It really was good time, considering road and weather conditions. Mrs. Markham's sister who lived near Moran took care of the younger children while their mother was away.

Although we had celebrated our fifth wedding anniversary a little ahead of time, there was at least one gift for me on the third. Mac had not had any recent success trapping coyotes, but when he checked his traps that morning an extra large coyote was caught in one. Although furs were apt to be less desirable that late in the winter, this one was exceptionally beautiful. Mac said the pelt was to be half of a fur set for me.

While Mac was away, Helen and I got along nicely. She was pleasant to have around and always willing to do what was asked. The children liked her and she liked them. With Mr. Braman to do the outside work all went well even though the weather was plenty stormy. I wondered how Mac could do any surveying but most of the storms were not reaching Jackson.

When Mac was in Jackson Jeanne invented a new playmate. It was an imaginary piggy, which she put to bed every night, fed, and played with. One evening when Mac was phoning, she said she had something to tell him whereupon she shouted into the phone, "Daddy, I had a little sick pig in bed with me this afternoon." I don't know what all the listen-inners along the line must have thought, but I can imagine!

Another of her favorite pastimes was opening imaginary packages from Mother. She would wrap some of her toys and Neal's, pack them in a box, after which they would be opened with proper expressions of surprise and delight. A cooking utensil might be wrapped up for me. One evening when she had been especially mischievous, I asked, "Jeanne, what makes you act that way?" Evidently remembering that she had once heard someone remark, "She has mischief in her eyes," she announced, "I guess the mischief in my eyes got down into my hannies."

❧

While Mac was away I checked on his traps, which were only a short distance from the house. First I found a duck caught in a martin trap. Roasted later, he made a treat for us and a welcome change from elk. Another day something caught in a coyote trap, which was over the edge of a bank, gave me quite a start. I was almost upon it when I stopped short. Above the edge of the snow was a big head and two yellow eyes blinking at me. For a moment I couldn't imagine what it was then realized it was an owl. I wondered how I could ever set him free for [an] owl can scratch and bite viciously. However, the foot caught in the trap was badly injured and [as] he was exhausted from struggling I had little difficulty. Then I watched as he hobbled across the meadow to the woods for he would be easy prey for any enemy and eagles were plentiful. Among the trees I thought he

In several instances, Linda included letters to her mother as a part of her manuscript. Here she includes the original letter:

"Jeanne was getting into all kinds of mischief. Scolding and spanking seems to worry her but little. Just before she was ready for bed, she climbed up in my lap and wanted me to 'love' her.

"I asked what made her do so many naughty things, etc., and she finally said, 'Oh, because—because—. I don't mean to.' She thought a minute then said, 'I guess the mischief in my eyes goes down into my hannies.'"

April–June 1920

Snow was often so deep that horses bogged down in it. (Harrison R. Crandall)

might be safe. I was glad no coyote was caught while Mac was away, but one was caught soon after he arrived home.

Although Mac had been able to do considerable surveying for a few days after reaching Jackson, the storm finally arrived there. Fortunately he was able to complete the most necessary work but returned home earlier than expected. He walked in about 9:30 in the evening, having come up on the mail sleigh, and skiing in from Loziers'. It was surely good to see him and he was glad to be back to see all was well with the family and check on ranch affairs.

A few days later he went to Moran to print survey maps at the U.S. Reclamation office. We then learned more of the details of the trip on to Moran the night he came up on the mail sleigh. Mrs. Markham and little Joe were also returning on the sleigh that night. It had been a long cold trip all the way up, [and they did not arrive] at Loziers' until nearly eight in the evening. But the three miles on to Moran were far worse. The snow was so deep the horses just had to flounder through. It was after eleven before they reached Moran and Mrs. Markham suffered a frozen ear. The boy had been kept warm and suffered no ill effects. It was fortunate the road had not been so bad when they made the emergency trip to Jackson.

Of course our mail was very irregular in arriving and I had written Mother not to worry if she did not hear from us. We did receive some mail about the nineteenth. It was then an Eversharp pencil arrived, which had been ordered in plenty of time to have been received before Mac's birthday on February 23. On the same mail were some much needed shoelaces. I had asked Mother to send some for "medium high black shoes." Whenever

packages were received, regardless of what they were, Jeanne would immediately sit down and write "Thank yous." [As she was] three years of age,
they were hardly legible but probably good training for her.

On March 21 the calendar said spring had arrived but it didn't apply
to Jackson Hole. It was ten below the day before and on the twenty-first
wind and snow continued. Out on the flat a regular blizzard was raging.
These conditions were hard on livestock, and horses several ranchers had
wintered some twenty-five miles beyond Moran were in trouble. During
the winter they depended on tall swamp grass in the area but with heavy
snows and late spring, their feed was giving out and the snow was too deep
for any early spring range. The young men in charge tried to take oats to
them. They planned to make a road across Jackson Lake, and then go the
remaining eight or more miles by toboggan. Starting out with two teams,
they did not get far on the lake before one of the teams broke through the
ice and went down. Fortunately the men succeeded in getting chains around
the horses' necks and the other team pulled them out. Since that plan
didn't work, they had to go by toboggan all the way, a terrific trip of twenty-
five miles or more through loose snow. However, they succeeded in getting
some feed to the animals and planned to take hay later, but it was reported
later that only forty-two of the sixty-six horses survived. Roy Lozier and
Elmer Arthur both suffered losses.

It surprised me when I realized how we used to dress babies. I could
hardly believe it when I read in one of Mother's letters, "Neal has worn
only white dresses so far but will need something else when he gets to
creeping." He was already rolling around the floor and pulling himself up
if possible. Fortunately we were well prepared. Mac's sister had two boys a
few years older than Neal and she sent a wonderful supply of outgrown
rompers. They were surely a blessing. It was then that Jeanne's old playpen
was brought out and for a while Neal thought it was a big joke.

March went out like a lion for the wind was blowing hard all day and
the cold continued. The snow was still three feet deep on the level. Helen
was to leave the next day to go down home for a week or so. As our road
had not been open since before the middle of the month, she had to ski to
the main road but that [was] nothing unusual. Mac went down with her,
taking more eggs for Mrs. Lozier to sell.

Our snows continued well into April and we wondered if spring would
ever come. So much snow at that time of year was not appreciated. Yet on
the twentieth of March, Mac had found pussy willows in spite of the snow
and the cold.

By the second week in April, the warm sunshine was at last having its
effect and the breakup began. Even though frequent snows continued

throughout the month, they could only temporarily delay the thawing process. The main highways went to pieces. Horses would fall through the snow and go down so deep they could not travel. Sometimes the mail carrier brought mail, first class only, on a toboggan, using skis or webs. During the day [the snow] would thaw a little on top, then with the thermometer dropping at night to fifteen degrees below zero or even more, a hard crust would form. This was wonderful to walk on for a few hours, but one would be in serious trouble if caught away from home when the crust softened. We would often go for a morning walk. Putting Neal in a clothesbasket and tying it on Jeanne's sled, we all enjoyed some wonderful outings. With so much snow to melt, one would have thought the mud would have been a terrific problem but it wasn't. Practically all the water soaked into the loose gravelly soil and little early spring flowers appeared right at the edge of the receding snow. It was almost unbelievable.

Mac made me an Easter gift of a chiffonier frame.[†] He doubted if he could make anything decent of unseasoned lumber, but it looked wonderful to me even before being stained. It was a big relief not to have the chiffonier drawers piled on the floor around the bedroom, but there had been no other place to keep them since the fire.

We had hens setting and the baby chicks were arriving. Often they had to be brought in the house to dry off and keep warm so we would have newly hatched chickens in the little box, either at the back of the stove or up in the warming oven. Of course the children loved to have them. They really were not in the way and much preferable to a newborn calf having to be brought in and warmed by the kitchen range.

Late in the month the roads around Jackson were getting well broken out and for some miles north but [were] still impassable at our end of the valley. We had expected Helen back in about a week when she left in March, for she had left clothes, but she had not yet returned. With road conditions as they now were, she could hardly get back.

In Jackson gasoline was fifty cents per gallon, sixty cents at Moran. All gasoline was brought over the hill in steel barrels and that was expensive. In Jackson a few people had automobiles and Mr. Kafferlin in Kelly had one. There were almost none farther north except for Joe Markham's government car at Moran. There was little use for them anyway, as some of the creeks had no bridges and the water [was] usually too deep for autos to cross. After high water and during the summer, temporary bridges were put across some of the creeks enabling the use of autos, if needed.

It was around the middle of the month that a letter from Mr. Johannessen, the attorney for the Idaho irrigation company, arrived. He wrote that within two weeks they expected to get all the affairs settled with the

[†] A "chiffonier" is often a tall chest of drawers, but sometimes the term is used to describe other furniture with drawers.

OVER
TETON PASS
TO VICTOR, IDAHO

state and government offices so that work on the dams could be started as soon as weather conditions permitted. That meant Mac would be busy all summer with that work and that many other men and teams would be needed.

April brought a new innovation to our attention. It was a pamphlet about a flat iron [that] contained a liquid, which would burn and heat the iron. I remembered a lady in Jackson had something of the kind and liked [it] but [I] never did own one. It wasn't too bad heating irons on the stove since we usually had to have a fire going anyway.

It was in the same month, Mac's sister and brother-in-law made a big change. They had been living on the original family farm in Audubon, Minnesota, and decided they wished to move to New York state. They held a big auction, the farm was sold, and they bought a place in the east. I think they hoped for less severe winters and greater opportunity for their two growing boys.

We were having bad luck with our baby chicks. Something seemed to happen to them in the night and Mac would find dead ones in the morning. We had no idea what happened. Finally there were only seven left. But we continued setting hens and hoped conditions would improve.

There was another midnight phone call and Mac got up to listen and see who was in trouble. As I may have said, it probably was fortunate that people along the line did listen because often one could not ring through to Jackson. Then the people along the way could help by ringing from

Automobiles made more frequent appearances in Jackson Hole by the 1920s, though gasoline had to be brought over Teton Pass in steel barrels and rocky roads, snow, mud, and deep water presented obstacles. (JHHS&M)

their phone so the call would ultimately reach through. It seemed that little Joe Markham was sick again, [but his condition was not] so serious this time and evidently Dr. Huff could give needed instructions over the phone.

The latter part of April we sent to Baltimore, Maryland, to the Calvert School for their Kindergarten Course. We wanted to have it for Jeanne's birthday in June but did not plan to start on the lessons until fall when regular school opened. This course consisted of wonderful daily lesson plans and we felt it would be the next best thing to real kindergarten. We were sure she would love it and she did.

May 1 arrived but no baskets of flowers. Skis still [were] needed so we were glad when it froze sufficiently hard at night to form crust that could be walked on for a while in the morning.

The highway was beginning to clear and mail came through on the first. We even received one of Mother's boxes, always an anticipated treat. Jeanne was overjoyed.

We thought it would be interesting to check our egg report from January 1 to date and were surprised how well our relatively few hens had done. They had produced considerably more than 1600 eggs. We sold over forty dollars' worth as the storekeeper at Elk and Mrs. Lozier on the main highway were glad to have them as they received many requests. We used at least fifty dozen ourselves besides several dozen for setting. Our little chicks were doing better so we set another hen or two when they were inclined.

Down country it was opening rapidly and people at Kelly were very anxious to have Mac come down to survey a ditch. Since Helen had not returned, he had to find someone else to stay with me. A young couple, who had come into the country the preceding year and [were] living at Moran, agreed to come. They were very pleasant people and Mrs. Grimmesey [was] especially attractive as well as very efficient. They were like friendly company to do your work.

Mac left on the eighth of May and had to ski to the main highway for the mail stage. On his return four days later, he still had to ski most of the way home.

We already had some bare ground around the house, and then as the days warmed and the sun seemed to become hotter, it was amazing how quickly the snow began to melt, although not in the timber. Our garden was still snow covered but that had not deterred the rhubarb, which was growing right through it. In just a few days, the horses could walk through the remaining snow to reach the highway. Mac had already broken out the road to Thompsons'. Although the [Thompsons] had left for the winter, the hay he had stacked there was needed. In spite of all the melting snow, we had practically no mud as our soil was so loose and sandy.

After Mac returned, the Grimmeseys stayed a few days longer; then Mac took them to the Hatchet Ranch over on Buffalo Creek. They were going there to work. As the horses were not in working condition, they had to walk almost all the way. It takes a long time to go some twenty miles at that speed so it was ten o'clock before he reached home that night. It had been a long tiring trip, but milking and feeding still had to be done. He reported much mud and standing water on the Buffalo Creek road.

Mac was also busy checking on the dams at Two Ocean and Emma Matilda Lakes. At Two Ocean he found water had found an outlet at the end of our dam so he and another rancher went up and filled cement bags with sand for temporary repair. There was still far too much snow there for teams to get through.

As our road to the highway was at least passable, we decided on Sunday to go to the Buffalo schoolhouse for Sunday school. It was quite a treat for me as I had not been out among people all winter. Neal slept in the clothesbasket under the seat of the big wagon all the way over and back, even though it was a bumpy trip. Mrs. Cowles had charge of the Sunday school and we all made the most of what equipment might be available. Sometimes a little wheezy organ was brought to accompany the singing, other times perhaps a fiddle, or maybe nothing at all. But the music was always quite a thrill to Jeanne. Sometime later Mother sent her a harmonica and she started blowing on it as she walked around the house. After a few minutes she stopped and remarked, "Sounds something as if we had Sunday school, doesn't it?"

It was a long slow trip over to Sunday school and back but we enjoyed it. Thousands of little yellow and white flowers were blooming right around the edges of the melting snow. [It] just seemed impossible.

The Idaho people remained quite confident of their project going through and that they could raise the dam, but until they received a definite permit only the two foot [versions] would be allowed. These would give the ranchers more water than they could use and as the Idaho people could have the surplus, they were anxious to have the dam kept in perfect condition. More work and grading was needed on these present ones and they were willing to pay for any work that was done.

Helen finally returned a couple of days after Grimmeseys left. She would have returned sooner, perhaps, if she could have brought her twelve-year-old brother with her as her father wanted her to do, but we objected. She was uncertain how long she could stay but was hopeful. However, it was less than two weeks later when her father phoned that her younger brother was sick. Helen was unhappy as well as we and said she guessed she would have to quit trying to work out. But she remained nearly a month anyway.

Linda was glad when the snow was gone, but spring run-off usually created new difficulties. This was J.D. Beckley's Ferry which crossed the Snake River near Wilson, near the present-day bridge. (Harrison R. Crandall)

There were always quite a few girls available for helping at housework as that was the only opportunity for them to earn money. They were especially anxious for work when school was not in session. Since the girls were used to working at home, they were fairly efficient in their way but it was a problem to find one that fit in best. We hoped to get a Lena Feutz next but she had already accepted work. In early June Marion came; Connel was her last name I believe. She stayed even a shorter time than Helen. It seems she had applied for work at the Bar BC ranch and her job became available earlier than expected. We were not too sorry to see her go although she was a pretty good worker. The dude ranchers were reported to be paying fifty dollars per month, but thirty dollars, or less, for a girl without experience was the usual rate paid by the ranchers. We paid Helen thirty-five dollars.

Since Mac was having many records to keep for the Idaho project as well as our own, a desk was needed. One, formerly used by the Reclamation people at Moran, was for sale so he decided to purchase it. This was a big solid oak affair, so big that in order to get it into the house, he had to take off the kitchen door and remove a piece from the front of the desk. Then he and Helen succeeded in shoving it through. It took up a lot of precious living room space but proved a most useful piece of furniture. He paid ten dollars for it, and since Joe Markham included a lot of leftover paper and blotters, quite essential in those days, we felt the price was very reasonable.

Our baby chicks were doing better and we had twenty-one thriving so [we] continued to set more hens. Jeanne could even play out around the house without even the need of rubbers now and she really enjoyed the out-of-doors. Although she loved the real baby chicks, she still kept her imaginary one as well as her other animals. She would come in the house and ask for a bottle of milk and a spoon as she said her chicken was hungry. I only had to pretend to give them to her as she would start out quite content. Knowing nothing of child psychology I was sometimes concerned about all her imaginary pets and friends but need not have been.

Her uncle once sent her a phonograph record called "Train-time [at] Pumpkin Center" in which a train roars into a station. It was never a particularly popular record as the train was utterly beyond her comprehension. She had ridden on one when [she was] two years old but of course had no memory of that period. We were never able to explain the train to her as we certainly had nothing comparable in Jackson Hole nor could [we] find a picture. As for Neal he kept us busy. Although not yet walking, he could go anywhere is the briefest space of time crawling flat on his tummy, and incidentally wiping all the dirt en route.

We enjoyed our trip to Sunday school so much we decided to go again a week or two later. The Baptist preacher from Jackson was to be there that day. This trip proved less enjoyable. We again had to use the big wagon, we on the front seat and Neal in the clothesbasket underneath. [It was] sunny when we started out but it closed up and began to sprinkle before we reached the schoolhouse. There were quite a few people present but some way it seemed to lack the usual friendliness and informality. Perhaps we expected too much of the preacher and should have realized an outstanding minister would not be sent to the little Jackson Hole church. The rain continued and we had a long trip home. No overhead protection of course but we wrapped whatever was available around us and let it rain. It was so cold riding high up on the seat that I forgot Neal might be warm and dry in the clothesbasket underneath, so he was wrapped too warmly. He was really wet when we reached home but it was perspiration, not rain. As for the front seat riders, we were plenty cold and all our outside clothing was dripping. We were thankful no one suffered any ill effects, but we decided to omit Sunday school until we could get a more comfortable means of transportation.

Mac had finally succeeded in getting another wheel for the old spring wagon to replace the one that had broken when we were moving back home in the spring. It still needed the reset. This involved heating the iron tire until red hot, replacing it on the wooden rim of the new wheel, then pouring cold water over it, thus shrinking it tight on the wheel. That conveyance was much smaller and lighter than the big wagon [and] was equipped with springs so [was] more comfortable riding.

June arrived and although [the roads] were now all open, there was still much difficulty in traveling. High water had started so creeks were flooding and overflowing. Much of the parcel post was still stacked across the Snake River from Jackson and all mail was considerably delayed.

With most of the snow gone around the ranch, Mac was starting spring work. However, he needed more horses. Ginger, our white mare brought from North Dakota had barely made it through the winter and could not be worked. Mac thought her teeth were giving trouble as she seemed unable to eat or chew her food. He had to use Nugget, really a saddle horse, to work with Jet. They surely made a funny looking team and were not too efficient. He looked for more horses and decided to buy two from Jack Eynon.

When he went for them, one horse had gotten loose and was missing but he brought home the one named Belle. She proved a good mate for Jet although not as heavy muscled and with her, [Mac] finished plowing and seeding barley on more land. After discing, he started plowing another meadow.

A few days after getting Belle, [we received] a phone call from Eynons [who] said they had the other horse and would bring [him] up to Loziers'. So Mac went down to get [him]. This horse could be either worked or ridden. As the horse was bay in color, [Mac] called him Bay. Later he learned the horse's name was originally Fred. Bay made a good mate for Nugget and they made a good team for lighter work.

On June 6 Jeanne was four years old and she proudly announced, "I'm past four now." Marion was with us then and, although a willing worker, was not as neat as Helen. To celebrate, Jeanne wanted a picnic lunch over near the garden so we prepared one. Just as we were about ready to start, Carl Roice, a young rancher from down country, arrived. That meant I had to stop and prepare an indoor lunch, but then Marion, Jeanne, and I went over and had the picnic. The men ate indoors but joined us for dessert, a birthday cake I'm sure. After lunch Jeanne opened her box from Mother. It had arrived well ahead of time although with the uncertainty and scarcity of mail, I don't know how it happened. "The Three Little Kittens" Bubble Book record gave her special joy.

With the large supply of milk we were getting, we were enjoying our separator and were surprised at how much faster the cream collected. Marion had already churned over five pounds of butter, then she churned eight pounds, and more cream was collecting. We used quantities ourselves with rich cream on the table for every meal. Soon we were so far ahead on butter, we took several pounds to [the] Elk store and also to Mrs. Lozier to sell.

It was early June when we planted our garden and [we] were always surprised at how quickly things grew. This was very fortunate as our summers were so short and the frost had been known to arrive every month. Before the end of June, we were eating radishes and lettuce. This is even more surprising because on June 25 it was so cold one night that ice formed on the water.

Spring brought many elk as they were returning to the upper range and hundreds would follow through on the elk trails. They were most interesting to watch. More moose were seen, too, although they had been in the vicinity all winter. One morning a big bull moose ambled out of the woods near the house and on by the kitchen door. Jeanne was out with Mac and suddenly she said, "What's that, Daddy, a moose?" He looked up and sure enough it was. Just then Tip discovered it, barked, and started to chase it. The moose just trotted off but did not seem much worried.

A couple of weeks earlier Mac, Jeanne, and I were over on the south side of the beaver pond. We heard Tip barking and almost immediately a big bull moose came tearing out of the woods heading right toward us. Mac tried his best to hurry us to a nearby tree but [I] guess I was too busy watching to hurry. Fortunately the moose went by instead of over us. Mac was quite exasperated with me and asked why I didn't hurry. I replied that I knew he was carrying a gun. Still disgusted, he said, "Yes, I have your little .22 rifle." After that I think I hurried when requested.

One morning when riding I saw an elk and her baby just crossing the creek bed. They made a lovely picture. Those many unexpected wildlife pictures were always so much enjoyed.

It was about that time that Mac brought home a baby elk that had started to follow him. They are so tame and gentle. Tip had found it and barked so Mac went to see what he had. Mac petted it and then it followed. Tip immediately took it upon herself to guard it and for a while growled if Laddie, cats, or chickens came too near. We gave it a little milk from the baby's old milk bottle and nipple and although it took a little, it preferred poking its nose against Laddie, evidently hoping for something better. Soon Mac took it back where [he] found [it]. The next morning when he checked, he found it was gone, so the mother had probably claimed it as we thought she would.

In the spring Mac had happened to find a Canadian goose nest and also a crane's. As some of our hens still wanted to set, he took a couple of eggs from each nest to see if the hens would hatch them. They had to continue setting longer than for chicken eggs, but ultimately two baby geese and two cranes hatched out. The baby geese were so soft and downy with a wonderful protective coloring, with a sort of yellowish green and grey.

The baby cranes were a soft light brown and [had]huge feet. Their legs seemed to be too weak for them to stand on very much. They did not live long and the stronger one died first. We thought the hen did not know how to care for them and let them walk too much, and perhaps they did not have the proper food.

The little geese surely thrived. Both the hen and babies were shut up for a time, which was fortunate as some of the baby chickens suffered a sad fate. The mother hens were shut in small pens, as a hen is apt to ramble around too much for the tiny chickens, but the little chicks could go in and out. Suddenly Mac discovered that the cats were eating them and five had already disappeared. We had to dispose of the cats as he said they could not be trusted again. We were sorry as we liked the cats and they were really needed around the ranch.

The geese were perfectly happy with their hen mother but they soon outgrew her in size. Nevertheless they still wanted to sleep under her wings at night and she wanted to have them. They made a funny picture: the hen trying to cover birds as big as and soon bigger than herself. The geese became delightful pets. They did not want to be touched but wanted to be near and know what was going on. They would eat out of our hand and when they became more independent of the hen would follow us around like dogs when we went walking. They soon learned that the sound of opening the bread box meant another handout and would walk right into the kitchen if they had a chance.

With warmer weather and the roads open, there seemed to be many extra people arriving at the ranch, several staying overnight. Andy Chambers brought loads of grain for horse feed, which was an all day trip from down country. Some was for our own use, the rest for use of the Idaho people who planned to bring more teams to work on the dam. They were still optimistic about the project going through and fully expected to get their permit although both Park and Forest Service were now bucking them. Of course Andy had to stay overnight so had supper and breakfast with us. One night we had a very unexpected guest. A young man arrived who was entirely alone herding bulls on an unused homestead several miles up the creek. He had gotten so lonely he evidently couldn't stand it and wanted to visit and stay overnight. Of course we made him welcome although we were all strangers to one another.

Ranchers riding for cattle, checking range, or on some errand would stop by almost any time of day and maybe overnight. We never knew who would arrive next. Although often it was long after mealtime, it frequently meant getting another lunch for them as they had not eaten.

When Marion received word to come to the dude ranch in a couple of days, it was fortunate that Andy happened to arrive with grain that night.

That made it possible for her to ride down country with him, saving Mac a trip to the highway to take her to the stage and the trip for her on the mail stage. He was really busy plowing and planting, checking dams, and working on our own ditch. When he was ready to seed oats, I was to drive the team for him, expecting Marion would be there to take care of Neal. As it turned out both Jeanne and Neal had to be taken in the wagon [during] seeding. Of course that was the day extra people showed up for both dinner and supper. There was still alfalfa to be harrowed in after the oats were planted. But things got done some way and it was all in the day's work.

We were glad when Pearl arrived on June 23. Jeanne and I drove down to meet her. She proved to be very satisfactory and we were glad she stayed several months.

It was about the middle of June that I had a wonderful surprise. Just as I was finishing up the afternoon work, I saw four rigs and an auto arriving. I couldn't imagine who was coming but it proved to be a surprise party arranged by members of the Domestic Science Club, which we'd had last year. They brought lunch [and] a delicious array of pies and cakes. [They] also brought me a lovely cut glass bowl because I had organized and taken charge of the club. All wanted to continue the club meetings and this year include sewing. Mrs. Cowles said she would take charge of that. No definite date was set for the first meeting but Mrs. Cowles and I were to let people know the time at the community picnic July 3.

One morning, almost the last day of June, the phone rang and to our surprise, it was Dr. Huff phoning from Moran. He had been called there the night before for the premature arrival of the Chapman baby. With that case taken care of, he and the group with him wanted to go fishing. With him were Mrs. Huff and little Gretchen and two nurses as a little outing had been planned. They wanted to go to Two Ocean Lake for fishing and a picnic and thought it would be fun. We did, too, [so] stopped in the midst of a washing and put up a lunch. Then we waited. They expected to arrive by 10 or 10:30 but they did not show up. We phoned Moran and learned they had left quite some time before but could not be located. Loziers had seen no one pass although they would have to go by there. Mac thought Loziers might have missed seeing them and maybe they were having trouble on the dugway en route [to our house], so [he] rode down. No one was there. By noon they still had not arrived and all we could learn was that they had left Moran. We didn't know what had happened but about one o'clock we went out under the trees and ate our picnic lunch. About 2:30 they drove in. It seems the tire had gone bad about a mile from Moran and he'd had to fix that, or some other, tire six times! In those days flats had to be repaired where they occurred and each took considerable time. Punctured tires occurred far too often. By that time it was far too late for the anticipated picnic, so we had time for only a little visit before they had to return to Jackson.

❧

July arrived and the day before the big picnic, Mac just escaped what might have been a serious accident when working on our ditch. Mr. Cowles had happened to stop by that day as he was riding for cattle and after dinner went over to see if he could help. Mac was plowing a ditch on a very steep side hill and was using Jet and Belle. Mr. Cowles was holding the plow. For some reason Jet got frightened and tried to jump uphill, lost her balance, and went down the hillside backward, dragging Belle and the plow with her. Fortunately Mr. Cowles was able to hold the plow so that it did not go over on top of the horses. Otherwise they might have been seriously cut, but as it was, no great harm was done.

The big July 4 picnic was held on Pacific Creek on the third, about two miles from our place. There were over 100 people there and quantities of marvelous eats. Tables were set up on which to put the food and people helped themselves. There was always plenty left over for later snacks. This year a beauty contest for babies under a year was held. Three bachelors were the judges and Mrs. Lozier's baby won first prize. Although everyone ate their fill at noon, there was still much of the good food left: fried chicken, roasted meat, salads, wonderful homemade bread, richly frosted cake, freezers of ice cream, and plenty of coffee and lemonade.

Mrs. Cowles and I decided to start the Domestic Science Club meeting on the eighth if it was agreeable among the members. They agreed on the date and it was to be held at Mrs. Stilson's, which was about eight miles down country. When the day came, Mrs. Braman, usually called "Billie," and I planned to ride down horseback. She would ride Nig, a big old work horse they had, and I would ride Bay, but when the time came Bay couldn't be found. I had visions of both [of us] having to ride poor Nig and could well imagine how we would both feel after riding eight miles on his back. By luck Elmer Arthur happened to arrive, for dinner probably. Of course he came horseback and happened to be riding a gentle horse and offered to let me have him that afternoon. Being a real saddle horse, he was irked to have to travel as slowly as old Nig but ultimately we all arrived safely. There was a large attendance and the meeting was mainly a review of the subjects discussed the preceding year. I was surely surprised that they had remembered so much. The next meeting was to be in two weeks, a sewing meeting with Mrs. Cowles in charge.

Neal's birthday was the ninth. He was a fine, big active baby. Jeanne and I found the first wild strawberries that day and Jackson Hole wild strawberries are surely delicious. Later berries were quite plentiful and were luscious with so much thick cream. Jeanne remembered she had seen some blossoms at Two Ocean Lake when we were there one day quite some time before. She inquired, "Do you think those blossoms are hatched out yet?" She was confident there should have been time.

We were glad when a dentist and an oculist arrived in Moran the [first] part of the month. I always needed a dentist and Mac did, too, this time. Pearl wanted an appointment with the oculist. It meant a good deal to have people only six miles away instead of 125, a three-day trip each way by mail stage and train. Once when I lost an inlay in the middle of winter, the Idaho Falls dentist sent in some cement and told me how to replace it. On the tenth we all went to Moran and the dentist filled cavities for both Mac and for me, and Pearl visited the oculist. It proved to be a rather strenuous day but we ate lunch in a lovely spot on the hill across the dam, which gave us a beautiful view of the lake with the peaks reflected in the water.

The next day both youngsters started being sick. Jeanne asked if we thought Neal had the "peasles." A recent letter from Mother had said her young cousin back [home] had the measles. Soon both children felt miserable. I phoned Dr. Huff and he said they probably had the measles although neither youngster had broken out. He thought they probably got them the day of the picnic and for a few days they were really sick. As this was the time the annual hordes of mosquitoes were getting underway, they made matters worse. Our only consolation was they were worse on the highway and over on Buffalo Creek.

I don't know what happened to me the first night they were sick. I had gotten up to check on them, and getting back into bed [I] gave my knee a bump in such a way it hurt frightfully. Getting onto the bed and starting to rub it, [I] was so sick I could not sit up and remember flopping on my back. Next I knew, I was trying to think who, what, and where I was, conscious only of a throbbing ache in my head. That lessened and I gradually remembered what happened. In the morning all was well, not even a sore knee.

We were beginning to wonder what had happened to the Idaho company. No letters were being received and payments were overdue on the

Neal's first birthday on August 9 was celebrated with wild strawberries. Here Jeanne offers support. (McKinstry)

† *Royal Dutch Shell was formed in 1907 by merging two companies to compete with Standard Oil. It is head-quartered in the Nether-lands and incorporated in the United Kingdom. By the end of the 1920s, it was the world's leading oil company. In 2016, it is one of the world's most valuable com-panies and the world's second largest oil company.*

‡ *Willem A.J.M. van Water-schoot van der Gracht was a prominent geologist and mining engineer who also held a degree in law. Born in Amsterdam, he was en-gaged in worldwide mineral explorations. He spent the 1920s researching the mid-dle of the U.S. for Royal Dutch Shell and became one of the leading geologists in North America. He also re-searched prehistoric geol-ogy and was one of the authors of the first research studies on the Theory of Continental Drift. His wife was Josephine Rudolphine Maria Gisella Ferdinandeine Frelin (Baron-ess) von Hammer Purgstall.*

ranchers' ditch rights, and Mac also owed money on the oats they had or-dered. Mac had already borrowed money from the bank to pay Andy Chambers as it had been promised and he needed it badly. Joe Markham wired the company and they wired back immediately that a letter had been sent. We were glad when the letter arrived some days later. Also some of the Idaho people were expected in soon.

In June, Max Ball, our friend in Cheyenne, had written about some business friends who wanted to vacation in Jackson Hole a couple of weeks. They hoped we could take care of them or find other accommodations. The man was a Hollander, president of several Dutch Shell† companies, and Max had charge of one of the subsidiary companies. There would probably be six in the party; Max would come with them but could stay only a day or so. They were to come about the middle of July.

I thought it would be fun and interesting to have them since Pearl was proving a real help. Mac was a little doubtful because if work at the dams really started on a full scale he would have no time. But there had al-ready been so much delay, more seemed probable. So we decided to have them come.

Since the Idaho project had not started, Mac could use two of the large company tents. We could borrow cots and bedding as needed and arrange for extra riding horses and saddles. Getting meals did not worry me at all; [we had] more milk, cream, and eggs than we could possibly use and the garden for fresh vegetables. Mac also put a couple of loads of wild hay in the barn so the saddle horses could be kept in rather than running on the open range.

The group arrived about the twenty-fourth of July and proved to be wonderful people: Mr. Van der Gracht, the Hollander whose whole name, or part of it, was A.J.M. van Waterschoot van der Gracht,‡ his wife, and young son. Mrs. Van der Gracht was an Austrian countess in her own right and was really charming and lovely. Although quite out of her line, I'm sure, she insisted on taking care of their own tent [and] often helped with the dishes and any little household task she noticed. They seemed to appre-ciate being on a home ranch instead of an organized dude camp. The chauffeur was Swiss and as Mrs. Van der Gracht spoke of a Belgium maid she had, they must have had quite an international household. Mr. Van der Gracht was widely traveled, having been to many places throughout the world, including Africa, South America, the Near East, [and other locations] so could tell of many interesting happenings. At that time people were not the world travelers of today since airplanes were still in their infancy.

The geologist that came was not the one expected but a Mr. Plummer. It was a real surprise to learn that his sister and I attended the same teacher's college [at] the same time back in Massachusetts, even living in the same dormitory. Dormitories were smaller then, we had only two anyway, so all students were at least acquainted. I did not know the girl well as she was taking the regular two-year teaching course and I had the three-year household arts [course] so all our classes were separate.

The weather cooperated while our guests were there and they seemed to thoroughly enjoy everything. Mrs. Van der Gracht remained pretty close at home as they had been driving for five or six weeks previously and preferred to just relax. All did some horseback riding but Mac and Mr. Van der Gracht spent many hours riding over the country. Since he was a geologist, he was interested in the rocks and formation of the country and Mac enjoyed his fascinating explanations. He was also interested in the trees and flora as well as the wildlife, really just everything. One evening they arrived home after ten o'clock instead of 7:30 as expected. We were becoming concerned but evidently they were simply enjoying the beauty of the night and hoping to see some wildlife by moonlight. But before they left Mrs. Van der Gracht insisted they drive to Jenny Lake so the children and I could go. We took a picnic lunch and surely had a delightful trip.

They had been there barely a week when Mr. Van der Gracht was most unexpectedly called back to his headquarters so [they] were forced to leave. They were so delighted with the country, definite plans had already been made to have a little cabin, like our first one but with a large screened porch, built southwest of our garden. They wanted a young boy and little girl to come for the summer and the adults whenever possible. Mr. Van der Gracht fully expected to return in the fall for hunting so left his bedroll and tent. Unhappily, none of these plans worked out as they were called back to Holland. We never learned just what happened but evidently unfortunate events occurred, and I think a young son was killed in a rabbit hunting accident.

August arrived and our next club meeting was to be held August 4 at our place. We had decided to prepare a luncheon and have it ready within an hour. The women also wanted to learn correct table setting and serving. We never knew how many to plan on as the weather, whether or not cars could get across the creek, [whether] saddle horses [were] available, [and] unexpected delays at home all affected the number attending. Except for Billie Braman, all had to travel from three to fifteen miles. Usually fifteen or twenty could be counted upon, although there might be six to thirty. As it turned out there were nineteen adults and six children. The menu planned was macaroni and cheese, graham muffins, lettuce with French dressing, pineapple pudding, toasted crackers, cocoa and whipped cream. All went well and we had a lot of fun although a thunderstorm nearly interfered.

A few days after the club meeting Mac had an accident, which was a near tragedy. Starting out on horseback early one morning, he said he would go for [the] mail but would be late returning as he wanted to work on the telephone line. Much of the wire from the highway to our house was attached to the trees. During hard winds some of these trees swayed badly and tended to break the wire. The wire had broken at one tree, and to prevent further expected swaying, many tree tops needed to be cut as well as some of the upper branches.

Much earlier than [he was] expected home, I heard the horse coming and went out to meet him. I wondered if something might have gone wrong and when he reached the house I knew. I was stunned and terribly frightened. He had his big bandanna handkerchief tied around his head, [and] it was soaked with blood and dripping. The blood was running down his face and over his clothes. [After he got] down from his horse, we removed the kerchief and found the blood still coming out in spurts from his forehead. I feared he was going to bleed to death then and there for what little could be seen of his face and neck was plenty pale in spite of his tan. We did not know what to do except use compresses and cold water and [we] started in at once, and I got details of the accident.

It seems he had climbed the tree that had the broken wire and was up about thirty feet. Holding onto the tree with one hand, he started chopping with the other. Unfortunately there was a wasp's nest in the tree beside him and the wasps did not appreciate his presence. When they began to swarm around, he tried to hurry and got a little careless. The result, the hatchet went into his head a little above the left eye, cut an artery, and went through to the bone. Blood spurted. Getting out of the tree as quickly as possible, [he] crossed the road to the creek, leaving a trail of blood all the way. Lying on the ground, he kept his head in the cold creek water, coloring it red as it flowed by. However, the bleeding would not stop so he decided to start for home. Mounting his horse, he began the two-mile trip. Every movement of the horse must have increased the spurts of blood and I don't know how many quarts he must have lost. Finally the compresses of cold water had some effect and the blood stopped coming in spurts. I figured he didn't have enough left to spurt but was thankful to have the bleeding lessened and finally stopped. Then we could put on a compress and small bandage. "I feel all right," he said and he was ready to start out. It was only at my emphatic insistence that he agreed to lie down until dinner was ready. After dinner he was quite determined to go out to work but finally compromised by staying in the cool cabin and making a much needed high chair for Neal. It was fortunate the cut had been two inches more to the left or it would have hit the temple and there would have been no bone to stop the blow.

By August various officials of the Idaho project were coming in and out quite frequently. They did not stay with us overnight but were often there for various meals. One afternoon Mr. Johannessen, the attorney, came and had his son with him. Roy Lozier and his son were there and Joe Markham as the ranchers had papers to sign regarding the ditch permit. Mr. Johannessen was supposed to have brought the papers ready for signing but [as he] left them in Idaho Falls, new ones had to be typed. That took considerable time so all were there for supper.

The name of the Idaho group was now officially Osgood Land and Livestock Company. Since they had their definite state permit to use the extra water above our needs, it had to be measured. On August 9 a state engineer by the name of Schlopkhol arrived to put in the water gauges at Two Ocean and Emma Matilda Lakes and Mac went with him. After those were in, Mac had to read the gauges daily and telephone the report to Idaho. The men were supposed to be back for a noon dinner but it was near four o'clock before they arrived. We had to be ready to serve a meal any time of day, but Pearl, the youngsters, and I tried to keep a respectable schedule.

Mac was continuing farm work, too. We did not get any alfalfa hay but were not expecting to the first year. The barley, planted with it, was doing well. He again had the permit to cut wild hay north of Thompsons' and could trade some of that with Mr. Germann for tame hay. Our garden was furnishing lettuce, peas, and hardy vegetables and the Germanns were always generous with anything we might not have.

The middle of August I was expecting Elizabeth Smith, a former Framingham College friend whom I had not seen since 1910. She was living in California with her family, keeping house for them. Her father, a retired Yale professor, had offered her a better proposition than teaching and as her mother was not well [and] her two older sisters were working, she accepted that responsibility. On the sixteenth we went to the highway to meet her as she had phoned from Jackson she would arrive that day on the mail stage. It was a real treat to see her again and we had a wonderful time. She lived in a big tent, which she much enjoyed, loved the country and horseback riding. Morning rides to Two Ocean Lake with Mac, to read gauges, meant a good start on the day's riding. Elizabeth helped most efficiently with any household duties and I never knew anyone [who] could defeather, clean, and cut up a chicken as quickly as she. And she didn't mind it in the least. We canned three quarts of chicken while she was there besides all those that were prepared for eating. It would have taken me hours of time but not Elizabeth.

One morning when Mac and Elizabeth went to Two Ocean Lake to read gauges they found six dead cows evidently poisoned by larkspur.

Coyotes and bear were after the meat. Mac took a shot at a bear that was among the trees but missed.

Although Mac was busy getting barley hay, he took one day off and we all went to Moran taking lunch. It was hot in the sun but lovely on a hillside across from the dam. The cool breeze and the view across the lake were wonderful and we surely enjoyed the day.

We had many temperature changes and at night it was always cool or cold. On the eighteenth, we had a heavy frost. It was so cold that night that an inch of ice formed around the edges of the pans of water out for the chickens. That surely finished any peas we may have had left but other things [were] not especially hurt.

Just a few days after Elizabeth came, the Domestic Science Club meeting was with Mrs. Brown at Elk. This was held at the Skinner bungalow. Mr. Skinner was a newcomer who had built quite a house there, then bought a big ranch some miles up Buffalo Creek. Elizabeth and I rode over the hill horseback to the Germanns' as they had an auto then and were driving down. It was a lovely ride over the hill and much shorter than the ride to Elk by the roadway. She was much interested in everything at the meeting and the ladies enjoyed having her there.

Sunday the twenty-ninth was the last day of her visit as she felt she had to leave on the thirtieth. Mr. Brown, the storekeeper at Elk, was going to Ashton [Idaho] early that morning to pick up a load of groceries for the store. Elizabeth could take the train at Ashton more quickly than at Victor. Mac made the trip with her as he had to see a dentist. He was suffering with a bad tooth that ached to the top of [his] head and he was getting desperate.

On Sunday Elizabeth and I went for a farewell ride. We had planned a light lunch for everybody at noon and arranged to have dinner about three, after we returned. We took our lunch with us and ate at our original homestead site up Pacific Creek. Then we rode on up the creek, enjoying the scenery and the country. Quite unexpectedly, we met Roy Lozier and Elmer Arthur as they were hunting [for] cattle but saw no one else and usually met no one when riding. We arrived back before 2:30 and started the chicken frying. Pearl had gotten the other things ready. That panful was about cooked when Roy and Elmer arrived, for dinner of course, so more chicken was put on to fry. When that was about ready, Joe Markham and Mr. Grimmesey came from Moran so more chicken was started. Fortunately we had plenty on hand thanks to Elizabeth's efficiency. By four o'clock we all sat down to eat and we really ate. Elizabeth could not understand how we could ever plan our meals and I assured her we couldn't.

The men had scarcely left when the Schlopkhol family arrived. They were going to Thompsons' and on up to Two Ocean Lake and as I had to read gauges while Mac was away, Mac, Jeanne, and I went with them. It was a nice trip but [it] had been a strenuous day and I was tired. It was 9:30 when we arrived home and I still had bread to mix. We would have to get an early start in the morning in order to meet Mr. Brown at the highway, and I would have to drive them down.

It was not a very happy group that started out around five in the morning. Mac with his aching tooth [and] Elizabeth and I regretful at her leaving, and it was cold. They must have had [a] long tiring eighty-mile trip to Ashton. Roads were rough, the old Ford had hard rubber tires, and it remained pretty cold but it was much the easiest way to reach the railroad. Evidently it had rained in the night and there was already the winter chill in the air. Elizabeth's coat was well spattered with mud before she realized it and put on her raincoat for protection. The all-important part for Mac was the relief after arriving and the dentist pulled his tooth.

Mac returned from Ashton the next day. The people at Grovont were having a meeting that evening regarding the Kelly Ditch. Mac had surveyed the ditch but they were having difficulty receiving their necessary permits for water and might want Mac to go to Cheyenne to see the state engineer about them. Some of the Grovont people met Mr. Brown and Mac at Buffalo Bridge to take him to the meeting then brought him up home the following morning. He brought a treat of fresh vegetables: sweet corn, cucumbers (forty cents per doz.), and a crate of tomatoes, which he had gotten in Ashton. They were much enjoyed as none of these things could be raised in our garden.

Early in the week Tip had become the mother of nine tiny puppies. Two died and three [were] disposed of, but since some had already been spoken for, four were saved. We wanted to keep only one for ourselves. They were plenty cute, grew fast, and the children enjoyed them.

In spite of Jeanne's overworked imagination, she could be very practical. One noon when we'd had chicken for dinner, Jeanne happened to have the wishbone and when [it was] nice and clean, we asked if she had wished on it.

"Oh yes," was her quick reply. "I wish Grandma would send me another box."

The children surely loved the contents of her boxes.

They had just recently received some lovely and unexpected gifts. The Van der Grachts, still in St. Louis, sent Jeanne a beautiful Effanbee doll. It was seventeen inches long, opened and closed her eyes, [had] real hair, and all clothes could be taken off. Jeanne put her to bed every night and gave her a make-believe bath every morning. Neal received the cutest little grizzly bear imaginable. It was about twelve inches long and looked like a real baby cub. He surely loved it.

September–Christmas 1920

† *This was written on the back of a letter to Linda's sister in New Jersey:*

"Jeanne is much interested in the 'skin' and 'hide' proposition. Tonight we had baked eggs for supper and there was a little egg white and cream covering the yolk. She proceeded to scrape it off and said she was 'scraping off the skin.' Then she ate it and remarked, 'My, that hide tastes good.'

I partly covered a box (to put in a chair to make it higher for her when eating) with green burlap a while ago. Now the box is mostly broken and the burlap loose, but it is still used. The other day Mac asked her where her handkerchief was and she said, 'Oh, I guess it's in the hide on my box.' And ever since she speaks of the burlap as the 'hide.'"

About this time or earlier, Jeanne started calling all coverings hides. The wooden box with her things was covered with brown burlap and this was a "hide." Searching for a lost handkerchief one day, she suddenly remembered "Oh, it's under the hide in my box." Any loose covering was the hide coming off. One wonders where the youngsters get these ideas.†

Mac had hardly returned home before he left for Cheyenne, but that day there was another Domestic Science [Club] meeting. Since we could leave the children with [Mac], both Pearl and I attended. I was surprised at the good attendance since Jackson Frontier Days began on that day. The women all seemed to enjoy the meetings very much and I enjoyed being out among them. The next meeting was to be just a social affair but I knew I'd have to miss it. I knew Mac would either be away or too busy working at the lake to take me, and Pearl would have to leave before then for school. The club meetings were about the only community activity available except for attending Sunday school and none of us liked to miss them.

Just a day later Mac left for Cheyenne, as Mr. Brown was going to Ashton again. [Mac] wanted to combine the Kelly Ditch business with the Idaho Falls lake project, which was more important to us. By staying overnight in Ashton, he could take the very early morning train for Idaho Falls and spend the day there before leaving for Cheyenne in the evening. The company wanted him to work on obtaining the permit to build the dam higher. They wanted permits for a seventy-five-foot dam at Two Ocean Lake and a forty-five-foot dam at Emma Matilda, but much lower dams would provide the water necessary to prevent a lawsuit the following summer from the sugar company.

[After] arriving in Cheyenne, [Mac] checked in at a hotel [and] contacted the Balls, our friends there, and they insisted he stay with them. Max Ball introduced him to Mr. True, who was the ex-state engineer and, although not on speaking terms with Mr. Emerson, the present engineer, gave Mac some information that was of value. Most of the day was spent with Mr. Emerson, and on the second day, [Mac] felt he had made some real progress. Mr. Emerson said he would send permits for ten-foot dams. As soon as he arrived home from Cheyenne, [Mac] was to start work for the Idaho company and to contact as many men as were available to work. The Idaho people also sent in men and teams. Although they could not start on the actual raising of the dam until the company had received their permit, there was considerable preliminary work needed.

Below the outlet of the lake, the beavers had dammed up the water, forming little ponds, resulting in a large area of willow growth, some of which was standing in three or four feet of water. These had to be dynamited to make a direct channel into the original Two Ocean Creek stream. Men and teams could do this work. Fresnos were sent in, which were much like scoop shovels but larger and drawn by four-horse teams.

There was [a] dance at Moran the night Mac returned, and since it was a farewell for Loziers, we thought we should attend. Mac also thought he might contact more men there to work at the lake. We did not arrive until nearly 10:30 and the dance was just starting. [It was] nearly 3 A.M. when we reached home, and we knew these dances were not for us. The Loziers left a day or two later and Elmer Arthur and his wife started living on their place. Loziers' house was much better than their place and much more accessible being on the main highway.

Cold weather was really coming. Milk froze in the pantry [in] the middle of September and, of course, there was always ice outside in the early morning. We were glad that soon melted when the sun reached it.

Pearl had to return to Jackson for school so the children and I were alone all day. Mac was working with the men all day at Two Ocean Lake and took his lunch. Mrs. Roice was cooking at Thompsons' house as they had left and the Idaho workmen needed a place to board. Carl Roice was driving four of our horses on fresno work.

The fun meeting day of the Domestic Science Club arrived but I had to miss it. Without Pearl, the housework and children kept me more than busy and Mac could not take time off. Sometimes Jeanne's kindergarten lesson had to be postponed until evening, which was regrettable. Neal was never still unless asleep. He was into everything but knew what "no no" meant and would temporarily remember. He was a happy baby although he had a temper of his own. Usually that did not last long and he could give the sweetest, as well as the wettest, kisses imaginable.

We would not receive mail for several days at a time as the men were much too busy to go to the main highway. The weather was unsettled and it frequently snowed, especially in the night, so the men were working against time with both cold and snow.

One night, Tip and Laddie got after a porcupine and Tip especially had the worst of the deal. She had so many quills in her head, we wondered if we should not put her out of her misery and later were almost sorry we hadn't. We kept trying to get all the quills out and finally got all we could find but many must have been left. Later, she was blinded in one eye as one came through that. Yet two days later they tackled another porcupine for Tip never did learn to leave them alone. They had fewer quills then but enough. Mac would have to hold the dog while I pulled quills with the pliers, which evidently hurt plenty. The almost invisible barbs on the quills kept them working deeper and deeper but to be pulled out, they were pulled against the barbs. After those two experiences it was several days before Tip was interested in chasing anything.

Toward the end of the month we had more snow interspersed with a day or two of Indian summer. Though the nights were so cold, with the temperature down to fourteen, the days would warm up nicely. In spite of the cold, some things in our garden still remained green. One day we had fresh beet tops, and several heads of lettuce remained in excellent condition.

Johannessen, Brunt, and Shane from Idaho Falls were in the last of the month and quite happy to see how much progress had been made. In their work, the men had uncovered an old Indian campsite. A ring of large cobblestones was found around what must have been where they had their campfire. Among the cobblestones were quantities of obsidian chips, imperfect arrowheads, and beads. They also found a stone, sharp at one end, which evidently had been used as a fleshing knife for cleaning hides. One of the men whom I had previously known sent it down to me.

That late in the summer, few people were passing by the ranch house, but one day Mr. Germann stopped by in time for dinner. He was riding for cattle to head them off from returning home because of the snow. Germanns had just had a new son arrive and Mrs. Germann was in the Jackson hospital. Mrs. Chapline was helping out [with] their housework and Joe was working at Two Ocean Lake.

It was in the early fall that Mac purchased a new saddle horse. He was a beautiful black gelding, gentle and friendly. I had difficulty in holding him in as he loved to race and never wanted a horse to pass him. When Mac said his name was "Slop," I couldn't imagine how anyone would give a name like that to a horse until Mac offered an explanation. Slop was a pacer, a gait some horses have naturally but other horses may be taught, [which is] supposed to be especially easy for the rider. The cowboys called it a sloppy gait.

As early as September we were discussing the possibility of going outside for the winter months if Mac could be sure of making expenses, but there was a general shortage of work and money that year. Mr. Banks, an engineer friend at Jackson Lake Dam and Mr. Schlopkhol felt sure [Mac] could get a government job at American Falls but we weren't sure we wanted to go farther west.

In October we were discussing the possibility of going east to New York state [where] Mac's sister and brother-in-law were farming. From there, we could make the trip to visit my mother and sister's family in New Jersey. Reports from New York were not encouraging. There were plenty of houses available but none furnished and work was scarce. So that plan had to be discarded.

The work at the lake ended rather early in the month. Most of the preliminary work had been accomplished and winter was starting. Until the permits were actually in the hands of the Idaho company, they could not do any work on building the dam. Although permits were promised, they had not been received. Nevertheless the company expected work could start as soon as spring weather permitted. The fall work had made it possible for us as well as the workers to have ready cash on hand. Mac was receiving ten dollars a day and as we had five horses working, they brought in more. All were receiving what was considered very good wages in those days.

One day the mail brought us an unexpected treat. Elizabeth sent us eight pounds of luscious Imperial and French prunes. They were quite different from the kind we were purchasing in wooden boxes. Cooking a few of the Imperials, we found them to be almost like the preserve, and no sugar used. I think Smiths had raised them as they had a very lovely estate in California.

By the eighteenth, we had a real storm and the snow was several inches deep. Mac had planned to go down country to do some surveying, which had been promised but awaiting for some time, but the storm delayed the trip. When it cleared we enjoyed some beautiful evenings. With all the snow and a big moon, it was so light we could clearly see the Teton peaks ten miles west. It was wonderful! When Mac got away to do the surveying, Mrs. Grimmesey stayed with me and I enjoyed having her. The worst of it was that with no man available, I had to do the milking. I had been practicing before Mac left and then he could finish up, but [I] knew I could do it all if I had to.

Mac returned in a few days in order to vote on November 4. Joe Markham and Grimmesey came by in Joe's car to take us to Elk where we voted. As we all stayed and had dinner at Brown's, we did not arrive home until after 4:30. Harding had all of our votes and evidently most of the votes of the Jackson Hole people.

Mac had various offers of work if we wanted to stay in [the area] during the winter. The Steingrabers wanted to get away for a couple of months and offered $125 per month plus board and only one extra man there. They were in charge of the Hatchet Ranch. People also wanted him to teach school at Elk at the same salary, but that job did not appeal as he would have grades from one to eight. If the children had been of high school age, he might have been interested. Mrs. Cowles really wanted to teach and we were glad she got the eight grades.

We had still quite determined to get outside for a few months but could seem to find no furnished houses where we would like to go. When we figured that the transportation cost to New York and back would probably amount to $1000, beside a big winter bill for wintering cattle, we decided it was well we had given up that idea. Certainly something nearer could be found so we continued to plan.

After election, we were surprised to learn that Mac had been elected Justice of the Peace. His name was not on the ballot but had been written in. No salary was attached to the job and [there was] probably nothing to do, but when Mother wrote and inquired if he was supposed to perform marriages, we were a little fazed. However, he never did have to nor do anything else either.

Mrs. Grimmesey was with me for some time while Mac was away surveying. Not only did she help with the housework, but [she] sewed and got our clothes in much better shape for possible going outside. She made cute romper suits for Neal, one from a skirt of mine that had been burned down the front and one from an outgrown dress of Jeanne's. [She also made] a pretty brown and tan dress for Jeanne from two shades of brown material and some new material, which happened to be on hand. This was trimmed with a blue blanket stitch around collar and cuffs. She also fixed over some of my clothes and after living on the ranch for five years, they surely needed it.

Mac also made a trip to Idaho Falls as the Idaho friends had suggested we come there. While he was away, the telephone line broke again. Of course it would happen then. I started to ride down the road to find the break and met the Germanns who were coming for a visit. That was unbelievably good luck. I rode on down the road while Mr. Germann followed in his car. Finding the break, he repaired it while I rode on to the highway, checking the wire the rest of the way. All was well and the rest of the day, we enjoyed visiting.

In Idaho Falls, Mac was checking possibilities but no furnished house was available. There, too, there was a money shortage as farmers were not getting enough to move crops and they claimed grocery and other business were down fifty percent and no work available. Mac learned, however, that good milk cows were selling for seventy-five dollars that would bring double that in Jackson Hole, so [he] saw possibilities there. The real estate dealer who was a friend said he would keep checking and keep us informed.

A day or two after Germanns were there, there was a Domestic Science Club meeting down on Spread Creek. Since Mrs. Grimmesey could look after the children, I rode horseback over the hill to Germanns' and went the remaining twelve miles in their car. It was getting dark by the time we were getting back so one of the Germann boys rode over the hill with me to make sure I did not lose the trail. I surely appreciated his company though [I] had no difficulty.

But it proved to be too strenuous a day and I suffered a sore throat, stiff back, and plenty of aches for a few days. As the thermometer had been minus ten a couple of mornings, wrangling two cows and milking was hard. One morning I stayed out too long and one foot was so cold that I was sick with the pain after coming in. I was glad Mac arrived home soon and I'd not have to build fires in a cold, below-zero house or go out to milk.

Our tax bill arrived and it was $53.75. Over twenty dollars was for [the] Elk school, which had not even opened, but we were sure it would soon.

One morning, just about daylight, Mac looked out of the front door and said, "Laddie has a new playmate." About fifty feet from the door were Laddie and a coyote, or what [Mac] thought was a coyote. Laddie had a bone and kept snapping but the coyote just turned her head away, paying no attention. Then there was a sound from the house and she was gone. Mac said he had seen a coyote at the spring the night before and this was probably the same one. I had heard one howling several mornings just before daylight.

A few mornings later, the howling started right by the house. Mac said, "That's not a coyote, but a wolf." Laddie was scared and with his tail between his legs ran for the porch. Evidently it was the same animal we [had] thought was a coyote, but [now we] recognized the howl was that of a wolf. She had not howled so near before, and Mac could hardly believe it could be a wolf as they were almost never seen in that country at that time. There were plenty in the early days.

As there was fresh snow for tracking, Mac decided to go wolf hunting instead of elk hunting as planned. He followed the wolf tracks over the hill around Gregorys' barn, then east to Germanns' barn about a quarter mile east. Then they went up the hill again and Mr. Germann joined the hunt. The wolf evidently knew she was being followed, stayed a little way ahead always out of sight, but did not seem much worried. Then she showed up crossing a clearing and Mr. Germann shot but missed. Then she crossed another clearing and both [men] shot. Although they never knew whose bullet killed her, Walt did not care for the hide so Mac had it tanned and it was beautiful. Evidently she was a young female, one of a litter of four whose tracks had been seen in earlier snow, but no wolves [had been seen]. We thought maybe she had started coming around ranches hunting a dog for her mate, but her howl had been too much for Laddie. It always seemed to me almost a shame to kill her but probably not.

[Mac] continued surveying at ranches on Buffalo Creek. He could go there horseback and return by night. A day or two after the wolf hunt, when Mac was surveying over the hill, I received a telegram from Idaho Falls. This was phoned up from Jackson from the realtor saying a five-room house was available, the owner to retain one room, and to wire if

[we] wanted [the house]. When Mac came, he wired back that if the realtor thought it satisfactory, to hold [the house] and we would plan to arrive about December 1. How we ever could I did not know. Mac had three more days of survey work, livestock would have to be taken to winter head-quarters, elk was still to be gotten, packing was to be done, and all the 101 other things. The saddest part of all our plans was that Laddie and Tip had to be sent to dog heaven. Nobody wanted to take them for the winter and we certainly couldn't leave them to starve and freeze to death. But we did keep one of their puppies.

Those were sure busy days but on December 1 we started. We were to drive to Germanns' as the team was to be wintered there, stay overnight, and they would take us down to Jackson in their auto the next morning. It was 9:30 when we reached their house and they had gone to bed as we were expected much earlier and [they] decided we were not coming. But they had arrangements for us to sleep and finally we all got to bed.

We arrived in Jackson soon after noon, staying in Thompsons' hotel overnight. Next morning we left for Victor on the morning bus. By [passen-gers] paying a little extra, the bus driver agreed to arrive in time for the pas-sengers to meet the afternoon train for Idaho Falls. We sat in the bottom of the mail sleigh or on our trunk, and with horse blankets and wool blankets we had brought, we kept quite comfortable. We could even enjoy the ride. Unfortunately there was a delay at the roadhouse at noon. The upcoming stage had broken a shoe (a steel runner on the bottom) so was late in arriving and our driver had to take that sleigh back to Victor. All the luggage and passengers had to be transferred. We were still hoping to arrive on time. Oth-erwise we would have to stay overnight in Victor. We arrived there just as the train was about to pull out, but the conductor held it over until our trunks and ourselves with luggage were [boarded], but not the elk. As we were about to embark he saw the puppy. Though honestly regretful and apologetic, he [said we] could not take the puppy. He said that interstate commerce rules had become so strict, he did not dare allow the dog without a permit. He had already held the train over so long he could not wait longer as he had to connect with a train from the east farther down the line. A man at the station said he would be glad to take the puppy so we had to give him away.

Arriving at Idaho Falls in the evening of December 3, we checked in at the Eleanor, which was the best and a very modern hotel. The next morning we contacted the realtor; the man in charge was out of town, but the assistant in charge said he would check and get the key and take us out. Then we learned the place was not available after all. It seems the wife had gotten mad, left, but then came back so the man was not renting. Of course he had not notified the realtors.

They could not find another place in town right then but were sure another place would turn up soon. We hoped so as a several-day hotel bill had not been in our budget.

A couple of days later a three-room upstairs apartment had been located.[†] That left only two rooms for our use but we took it and got along pretty well while waiting for something larger. The son, a Dr. Walker, proved to be a young dentist and he surely fared well with the amount of dental work we had him do for us. [The] people in the lower apartment were very pleasant and very accommodating and we surely appreciated having electric lights and an indoor bath even though that had to be shared.

This location was 441 I Street and Milners (Mr. Milner was president of the Idaho Water Project) lived at 445 E. He had already invited us over to spend the day with Mac coming for dinner in the evening. The wives of the project people were very nice to us and invited me to many afternoon affairs.

Mac had already started attending farm sales, purchasing cows about to freshen if available at a suitable price, then selling them for more after they freshened. [The] average purchase price was around fifty-two dollars, and they brought much more after they freshened. Of course feeding [and] care had to be added in, but a farmer near town was caring for them. Mac would pay cash for some but his note was always accepted without question. Mr. Hartert, our real estate friend, who was also interested in the Idaho Wyoming project, usually had charge of the auction sales, which may have been the reason any amount of credit was available. [Mac] then needed a truck to attend sales and haul cows if any were purchased. He purchased one a few days later, a secondhand Ford with a steel body and quite respectable looking. After the cows freshened, he would have to go [back] and forth to the farm to milk them.

We were still looking for larger accommodations but nothing seemed to be found. Before the end of the two weeks, [the time] for which we had rented, we were becoming really concerned. Dr. Walker was to be married Christmas Day and wanted all the apartment so we had to be out. Finally a realtor found a little three-room house and although far from satisfactory, [it] gave us a place to go. This was at 120 W. 14th Street. Only two rooms were really furnished: the kitchen and bedroom, which was sort of a combination living room. The third room was not of much value except for storage and use as a pantry. We had to go to the yard to get water from a pump. Unfortunately that soon froze, or quit, and we had to go to a neighbor's pump. There was an indoor toilet but faucets were available only in the kitchen and they must have been frozen solid or the plumbing not completed.

But it was a place to live and we moved the day before Christmas, that being as early as it was available. In spite of all the confusion, we took the

[†] *Here a sentence or two seem to have been omitted from the typescript.*

children to a children's party that evening at the Presbyterian Church we had been attending. We knew that was something quite new in their experience. The program was quite long and little Neal fell asleep just before Santa Claus arrived, which was the high point of the evening. Jeanne missed nothing [and] enjoyed the big tree and everything that went on. Santa gave each youngster a little stocking of candy and peanuts, also one for Neal, so he had his on Christmas morning.

Our elk from Jackson Hole proved very useful.[†] Mac sold a forequarter for nine dollars, which paid most of the shipping charges. He traded [for] another forequarter of beef [and] gave Mr. Hartert a hindquarter for which he returned lamb. What we did not give away to friends, we used ourselves. Elk was a real treat to people [in Idaho Falls].

We had a nice Christmas in spite of difficulties. Our many friends back east added to it with all their generous gifts for us and the children. Money was included in the gifts from Mother and my sister as they knew the children, especially Jeanne, would like to buy things in the stores. All previous Christmases had been done with the catalog. Mac had new beaver cuffs made for my fur coat, which were needed and appreciated.

Mother also sent a box of gifts and the children could hardly wait to open it. [The box contained] the usual array of just what was wanted—articles and gifts. Neal put on his cute romper suit and cap then went back and forth for us to admire him. Jeanne felt very dressed up with her bracelet and beads.

Just after Christmas, Mac purchased several cows from Ucon, about ten miles out. The rest of this paragraph is mostly taken from Mac's letter to Mother and the difficulty he had the following day to locate them: "One which had made a clean getaway is now here. I hauled her in this afternoon in the truck and put her in the little old barn, which belongs to this palatial shanty. She did not object to the ride in the least and I think we can manage to keep her here or at least until the other cattle are located. She is a good looking cow and I hope will nearly double our money invested as soon as her calf arrives, which should be within a few days."

So 1920 ended. We had not found the pleasant housing we had anticipated but had kept reasonably comfortable. And we felt that this was much preferable to being absolutely snowbound with no neighbors for miles and no way of even reaching the main highway regardless of what emergency might arise. We fully expected to find a comfortable house soon, and in spite of the money and work shortage, Mac was already doing well with his cow venture. We were quite happy anyway.

[†] *Linda earlier notes that all of their belongings except the elk meat (and the puppy) were placed on the train at Victor. The McKinstrys must have had the elk meat shipped to them in Idaho Falls.*

CHAPTER ELEVEN

Settling into Pioneer Life

We sent photographs of the children for Mother's Christmas and folks back east. Neal's was especially good. [The] cost was $45 per dozen.

The children enjoyed their Christmas gifts. We had given Jeanne a subscription to the John Martin children's magazines[†] as advertised in the *Geographic* magazine. Neal had some fine blocks. The woodshop boys at the high school made three different sets according to specifications given in the government bulletin on child care. There were thirty pieces in a set and we purchased two sets. Later Mac had a drawing board made there. It proved to be excellent workmanship and cost only $1.25, material cost.

Jeanne began spending some of the Christmas money Mother sent. After choosing two pads of paper, one-quarter yard of cloth for a doll's dress, a green crawling bug, and a whistle, she still had a dollar left. The doll's dress proved to be for brother's baby, rather unusual generosity.

One day Neal had a bad fall and was feeling miserable the next day. We had planned to take him to the doctor the following day but he was feeling OK then so it was unnecessary. When we could easily reach help if needed instead of being snowbound was a joy.

The water development group was still quite confident they would ultimately receive their permit, but thus far only promises [were] received. As Wyoming now demanded a $50,000 bridge across Pacific Creek, a Mr. Carlisle, who claimed a prior right, reduced his demands for a dollar per acre foot to twenty-five cents, so was mostly out of the deal. The costs were proving too high for him. The company continued to have Mac make maps and applications, which might help the deal to go through. One day he needed some forms an engineer would have so [Mac] went to see him, a Mr. Cotton. He proved to be very cooperative and invited Mac to an engineers'

January–March 1921

[†] John Martin's Book: The Child's Magazine *was published monthly between 1912 and 1933.*

meeting in his office that evening. Later Mac was invited to a Presbyterian church dinner where the engineers had a reserved table in an adjoining room. Although Mac was not an engineer, he enjoyed the meetings.

While in Idaho Falls, I had been taking Jeanne to Sunday school and also to the church movies. For a while she was too timid to stay alone in Sunday school but learned to later, so I attended an adult class. We had a wonderful teacher, a Mrs. Holden, and her classes were most interesting.

One day Jeanne came home and said she had learned two new names in Sunday school, Johnny and Peterkin. Finally she was willing to reduce the former name to John but not the Peterkin. Asked if Peterkin had another name, Simon Peter, she agreed but still insisted on [calling him] Peterkin. She had a much loved Peterkin book.[†] Since being in Idaho Falls, we had continued Jeanne's kindergarten lessons as time and conditions permitted.

About the middle of January we put an ad in the paper for a furnished house. Only one reply was received and that was [for] a four-room house soon available in a nice district. Mac phoned immediately and rented it sight unseen, I think. A week or so later we moved in and was it a joy, after nearly two months of makeshift housing. The rent was fifty dollars a month, a little more than we had hoped to pay, but we appreciated and really enjoyed a comfortable home. We were always glad we did.

We could soon return some of our generous invitations but first had to purchase china plates and cups. The dishes at the house were such a motley collection and cracked, we could not offer them to guests. The Milners were there for dinner on Mac's birthday and we enjoyed the evening and the 500 game. Our meat that evening was a delicious four and one-half pound beef roast, total cost, seventy cents. Beef prices were extremely low but the producers were receiving only six cents to eight cents per pound, live weight. First-class hamburger was fifty-one cents [per pound]. Very inconsistent.

Mrs. Milner had entertained for me at a Kensington. I had no idea what that might be but [it] proved to be just a group of ladies gathered together in the afternoon to sew and talk. Refreshments [were served], of course.

As I was going to more activities, I purchased some additional dresses. One which I purchased either then or earlier was a brown and tan which was always my favorite. That may have cost twenty dollars, but usually clothes were far less expensive. Children's dresses if purchased at sales were very low priced. At one I purchased three dresses for Jeanne and think the highest price for one was one dollar.

In February we visited a sugar factory at Lincoln, a few miles out of town, and [I] had my first smell of beet pulp. On the way home we met a

† The Peterkin Papers *by Lucretia P. Hale first appeared as a series in a magazine. The Peterkins were a large, very silly family who had no common sense and always came up with outrageous solutions for simple problems.*

flock of sheep, the first Neal had ever seen. He loved animals if Dad held him, otherwise he [was] afraid of a cat. Was glad he soon recovered [from this fear].

The cows Mac bought were being cared for at Mr. Wackerly's farm, but Mac had to go out each morning and evening to milk any cows that freshened. Of course the milk was good for the calf only the first few days, but usually we were well supplied with milk and cream without patronizing the dairies.

Mac and Mr. Wackerly made plans for a sale to be held in early March. After that we kept more than well supplied with milk and cream. At times, when we'd had to buy from the dairy, whole milk was fifty cents per gallon.

On our anniversary, March 3, Mac sent me red roses, an impossible gift on the ranch. We also acquired an iron box for keeping papers safely, as it was really needed. We have used it ever since. We celebrated that evening by going to a movie, that being the best entertainment offered. Afterward we went to Howard's parlor ice cream, that being the thing to do at that time. Ice cream was not so common then and people patronized ice cream parlors for treats. Previously we had attended only one movie and that was *Earth Bound*, the outstanding one of the year.

We had had to attend that one separately as we had not gotten a babysitter then.

The sale was held in early March, on the seventh, I believe. Mac went out at 4:30 in the morning, coming back about 9:00 to take me out to help make sandwiches. In those days free sack lunches and coffee were furnished to all who attended. People had to bring their own cups. We made nearly 400 meat roll sandwiches. A sandwich, bun, donut or cookie were put into each sack. With several ladies working it did not take long. The attendance at the sale was not nearly as good as hoped as road conditions were very bad. Early thaws had made all side roads impossible for auto travel and the main highways were only passable. The smaller attendance meant less bidding so the sale was not as successful as hoped but we came out pretty well ahead so were glad of that. [We] received about $1400 for fourteen cows. All the workers had a nice hot dinner in the farmhouse. We had been out in the truck a few days before and gotten stuck. I did not know how mud could be so thick and heavy so understood why people could not attend.

We must have enjoyed our movie the evening of March 3 for later we went to see *Way Down East*. That was also a special and the prices were up fifty cents to $1.50. Usually a movie cost fifteen cents to twenty-five cents.

Although some of the furnishings provided at the house was not very satisfactory, I surely enjoyed the electric iron. Practically everything had to be ironed in those days so it was quite a task every week.

On April 3 we had Jeanne and Neal baptized in the Presbyterian church, but then [Neal] was restless and Mac took him home before the sermon. The church seemed to have quite a bit of entertainment for children and we appreciated that.

Before the middle of April, the water project people wanted Mac to return to the ranch to check on dams [and such]. He knew the snows were probably too deep to do any checking until April 30 or probably May. Nevertheless we made tentative plans to leave April 18, and the children and I would remain in Jackson for a while.

In the meantime I disrupted plans. For years I had had discomfort in my lower right abdomen. Dr. Huff said probably [it was] appendicitis but he did not want to operate because the Jackson hospital was not sufficiently equipped for operations. He had said that if the pain continued to see Dr. Cline [in Idaho Falls] and follow his advice. Dr. Cline said it was not safe to take the rough trip over the hill, and so instead of starting for Jackson, I immediately went into the hospital. This was really a big remodeled house but was the best in town. I had nice a sunny bedroom and it hardly seemed like a hospital.

In those days an appendectomy was considered very serious. Dr. Cline said I'd have to stay in bed for a week, and then remain in the hospital for two or three days after getting up. Also I must stay in Idaho Falls for six or seven days more before it would be safe to take the trip over the pass into Jackson.

Mac and the children remained in town for four days at which time Dr. Cline reported all was well so it would be safe for Mac to leave for Wyoming. After reaching Jackson, the children were left in the care of Mrs. Almer Nelson, as Mac knew the ranch would still be snowed in. While I was in the hospital, the people whom we had met were most thoughtful and I received many flowers and calls. I was happily surprised they all remembered me. The Coys, friends we had made through the church, and the Shattucks, invited me to their homes for my week in town. I spent a few days in each of their homes and thoroughly enjoyed my visits. On May 2 Mrs. Shattuck took me to the railway station in her Willys Knight [automobile]. En route we went by the Coy's to pick up three baby white rabbits, which Mrs. Coy was sending to Jeanne and Neal. Mrs. Coy had them in a small covered grape basket, which was easily carried, having the handle over the top.

It was some time later we received the bill for the hospital interlude—$150 to Dr. Cline for the operation and $60.50 for the nine- to ten-day hospital charge. I surely had good care, too.

The ride to Victor is always a long slow one, but the train finally sped up a bit the last few miles as there were no stops. It surely seemed good to

arrive and find Mac waiting for me [at Victor] late that afternoon. We went to the hotel for overnight as we had to wait till morning for the mail stage. We started fairly early and Mac had made arrangements for a team and buggy to take us up to the snow road as he knew that would be easier riding than the mail wagon for the first eight miles. Reaching there, all passengers and the load had to be transferred to the mail sleigh.

Mac said the road over the hill was much better than it had been, but I'm still wondering how it could have been worse. With the melting snows, the roads "go to pieces" and it was three o'clock before we reached the roadhouse on the west side and had dinner. The higher we got, the worse the road, and the snow road had been forced several feet up the mountainside above its regular road bed. And plenty tippy! Frequently I got out and walked as the men had to ride the upper runners of the sleigh to keep it from going over into the canyon. Then, very occasionally, unexpectedly, and momentarily, the sleigh would tip toward the bank. One never knew what next. Then it happened, and we did tip over, fortunately on the upper side. Mac jumped from the sleigh to catch me if thrown. But there were no casualties and we were soon on our way. Just one more frightening experience but I was more than thankful that we were not hurled into the canyon far below. After some eleven miles of this, we reached the end of the snow road so passengers and load were transferred to the mail wagon.

The trip in and out of the valley was almost always hair raising, but winter and spring conditions made it downright dangerous.
(Harrison R. Crandall)

Mac had expected to have an auto meet us at this point but the Snake River bridge had been taken out the day before as being unsafe, and only big teams and wagons could ford the river. So we had to continue sitting in the bottom of the mail wagon.

Finally we reached the riverbed and it seemed a half mile across that part, but Mac said it was only a few hundred feet. The big wagon bumped and bounced over the cobblestones and boulders as the horses carefully picked their way across. Then we reached the river itself. This was much wider than normal, filled with dirty, rushing water and debris. The driver cheerfully remarked, "I hope the ford hasn't changed since yesterday," and the horses plunged in. How they could possibly keep their footing over those wet, slippery stones and pull the big wagon is still more than I can understand. We were surrounded by roily, swirling water, which lapped the bottom of the wagon box. But what a relief when the team began climbing the opposite bank. I'll never forget it.

Here an auto was waiting for us so we quickly drove the last several miles into Jackson, and it was much more comfortable than riding in the big wagon. Even then it was after nine o'clock when we arrived so we went immediately to see the children. They had been allowed to stay up to greet us and how good it seemed to all be together again. There was so much to say, it was nearly ten o'clock before we started for the hotel where we were happily surprised to find they had kept a hot supper for us.

Mac stayed in Jackson overnight then returned up home, but as the ranch was still somewhat inaccessible, the rest of the family remained in Jackson.

I much enjoyed the week and the chance to rest up, although there were some complications. Shortly after we were settled in our room, Mrs. Markham brought John down as he was suffering from an ear infection and just recovering from whooping cough. As they came to the same rooming house, I was concerned about Jeanne and Neal. Although Dr. Huff said there was probably little danger of any infection, he did say it might be wise to move so we went to the Crabtree Hotel. We were taking some of our meals there anyway so it was really more convenient.

The children were most anxious to get back to the ranch, but I was enjoying a little social life in Jackson. Mrs. Huff gave a delicious luncheon, which she said was in my honor, telling the guests to come early and visit. We did. Mrs. Miller, whose husband was formerly forest supervisor but [was] now retired and was the town mayor, entertained at an afternoon party with fourteen guests present. It happened to be on election day and the town band was out celebrating. They added to our fun when they came and serenaded Mrs. Miller. It was quite a thrill.

On the thirteenth of May the children and I returned to the ranch. We took the early morning mail stage and Neal screamed lustily because he had to get up so early. Fortunately he quit after the stage started so all was peaceful.

During the winter and early spring, the mail was never sure of reaching Moran in a day, and occasionally the mail man would take first class mail and travel the last few miles on skis. But by the thirteenth of May, the main highway was reasonably good and roads really dry around Jackson.

Before noon we stopped at a ranch house to change horses and for lunch, and it was there a half-grown kitten was given to me. The children were delighted and I was glad to have it, too, as a cat was needed on the ranch. With another change of horses en route we made excellent time and arrived at Loziers' place about 3:30 in the afternoon, some thirty-five miles from Jackson. As Loziers had left Jackson Hole, the Elmer Arthurs were living in their house. Luckily Mrs. Arthur was home and could phone to our ranch. I knew Mac would not be expecting us that early, if at all that day, and it was fortunate he happened to be indoors when she phoned to our ranch. He said he would start down immediately but would have to walk the three miles. Slop, the saddle pony, was the only horse yet brought back to our place from winter quarters and he was running out on the wide open range. [It was] easier to just walk than hunt for him. En route through Elmer's pasture, Mac caught two of Elmer's horses so we drove back home

The Snake River proved yet another obstacle for Jackson Hole residents. Here the approach to the bridge near Wilson seems to have washed out and an overhead cable car or hand car has been constructed to cross the high water. (JHHS&M, Bruce Porter Collection)

with a borrowed team and wagon. It surely was good to all be home together again back in our ranch house.

While Mac had been there alone he had done mostly outside work, checking on the Idaho water project and survey work that would keep him away from home overnight. But he had gotten the house cleaned and ready for us.

One interesting surveying job was down country at the home of Mr. Pederson, who was a retired engineer and having made some invention for the Remington Arms Company was now enjoying life on royalties [he] received. His home was a very modern estate and Mac was made welcome as a special guest. Quite a contrast to batching.

While doing survey work [Mac] learned of some of the happenings of the preceding winter and how concerned the Buffalo Creek ranchers had been for a while. A crazy man had suddenly appeared, and then would disappear only to arrive again. Since he had threatened to shoot all the women and the children in school, that was closed for a time as no one knew when he might reappear. He was finally apprehended and taken out of the country. All the ranchers could breathe more easily and the school was reopened.

It was reported that Beavertooth Charlie pretended to go crazy, hoping to avoid his financial difficulties.

As for our affairs, we had to begin bringing our livestock home. The horses were brought up from their winter quarters and a heifer from Germanns. Our good old milk cow had died but as the heifer soon freshened, we had milk in a short time.

Two of the baby rabbits I had brought back from Idaho Falls, which Mac had been taking care of while the children and I were in Jackson, were doing only fairly well and Mac said they needed some green feed. Some of the south slopes were baring up and immediately getting green, and Jeanne was more than happy spending her time gathering extra food for them. It really helped and they were soon thriving.

We [had been] a little surprised when two of the three rabbits brought over survived the cold and ordeal of the trip over the mountains. I still wonder how often they were right side up, if ever, en route.

Of course our two little rabbits were kept in an enclosure and fed. When Jeanne started after greens one morning, she came running back, saying there was moose at our beaver pond. I wondered if she might be mistaken but thought I had best walk back with her. We approached cautiously and sure enough there were two big bulls and a new cow just across the stream. They saw us about the time we saw them but just continued feeding, though watching us. At that time of year they are not looking for trouble, and after a while [they] just ambled off, though always watching

us. That fall there was to be an open season on moose but only one hundred licenses to be issued; $50 for residents and $100 for out of state [hunters]. We never had a moose license but the meat from a young animal is excellent and we have enjoyed the treat given to us.

We were also surprised at the rapidity with which rabbits reproduced. It wasn't too many months before rabbits seemed to be running everywhere, as long since we had had to let them out from their enclosures. There was plenty of feed available. All went well for a while until one night they were discovered by the owls. The next morning we noticed a decrease in rabbits and couldn't imagine what had happened until Mac found several carcasses with the heads eaten off. Then we tried to get the owls but they were hard to find in the daytime. One evening he did succeed in shooting one and it fell from the tree. He thought he had killed it but upon picking it up found it to be still alive so gave it a terrific blow on one side of the head to finish it. Then he tossed it into the woodshed to be disposed of in the morning. It happened to be washday and the girl helping us went into the shed early in the morning to use the washing machine. Immediately she dashed out, wide-eyed and frightened. It seems the owl was not dead but was sitting on top of the machine, one side of his head bashed in, but his other eye wide open, yellow and staring. That was one owl long remembered.

The rabbits continued to decrease but evidently learned caution and being fewer of them [became] less inviting to the owls. But there were always plenty of rabbits for eating and to produce new families. And the owls seemed to search for easier prey.

After being home a short time, I realized I was back in the country where one must expect the unexpected and be prepared. The five members of the Markham family surprised us with a visit one morning, arriving

The ranch began to take on a more settled look with outbuildings, haystacks, and a clothesline.
(McKinstry)

about 11:30. By noon Walt Germann and Jim Cowles had arrived. They were driving cattle from Buffalo Creek to the Pacific Creek range so were near. Mac came about 12:30. With Mrs. Markham's help, dinner was soon on the table for I had put scalloped potatoes in the oven much earlier. Meat was never a problem with the elk available and canned vegetables were quickly prepared. There were eleven of us at the table instead of four, but we were always glad to see our friends.

A couple of days later Dick Ohl, ranger, phoned and said that the next day they were putting in a bridge over Buffalo Creek where the water was so deep during the spring runoff. Help was wanted from the ranchers and there was always good cooperation. Of course Mac went down with the others, and with plenty of help, the wooden bridge was mostly completed that day.

A few days later was the day of the big picnic at the Jim Cowles ranch. Ever since returning, I had been hearing about it and Mrs. Cowles said it was to be an open meeting of the Domestic Science Club and whole families were invited, making it a big community affair. During the morning people arrived in wagons of some kind with baskets and boxes loaded with food. At noon these were unpacked and the food arranged on a big table. It was a huge meal and a delicious one. The crisp fried chicken, ham, and sliced chicken were an appreciated change from the usual elk meat diet, though juicy slices of elk roast were thoroughly enjoyed, too. Without the semblance of a grocery store within forty miles, there was an unbelievable variety of tempting vegetable dishes and salads as delicious as they were attractive. With no shortage of butter, eggs, and cream, an amazing assortment of sponge and butter cakes had been brought, the butter cakes generously frosted. Pies, too. Those cakes with creamy, homemade ice cream were something to be remembered.

Entertainment had been planned for all ages for the afternoon. The men were to play games, have contests, or just talk, and teenagers could dance to the music of a big phonograph. The women first attended a short meeting of the club at which Mrs. Bailey had charge of weighing and measuring the small children according to articles written at the time by Dr. Emerson and published in *Woman's Home Companion*. But most of the afternoon was spent just visiting, exchanging recipes, and supervising the little children if needed or joining in the general fun. Altogether it proved to be a gala day for the whole community.

Mac had to leave a while in the afternoon to go over to the Hatchet Ranch where he arranged to get twelve hens and eggs for setting. Were we surprised the next morning to find those hens laid seven eggs while cooped up in the box. Also we acquired a young dog. He looked so much like

Settling into Pioneer Life

191

Laddie that we named him Lad, but he never did compare with Laddie as a dog. I don't even remember what became of him.

The next day, May 29, we succeeded in getting our garden planted. We always had to wait until very late in the spring as the frost continued. But when garden growth really started, vegetables grew quickly during the long sunny days and they seemed to learn to resist cold nights. Some survived heavy early fall frosts.

Mr. Peterson, a civil engineer from Idaho Falls, arrived the first day of June. The Idaho company wanted further information, which required more surveying at Two Ocean Lake and up Pacific Creek. He had to stay with us as nowhere else was available and Mac was helping with the surveying.

Since they wanted to put in as long days as possible, [it] meant a 6:30 breakfast. That was very early rising for Mac to have the range hot, cow milked, all outside [chores] done, and horses fed and ready for starting. Early for me, too, to have breakfast and then lunches ready at that time in the morning.

With Mac away all day, I had all the responsibility and extra work at home and [was] glad that I no longer had the nagging pain [that] bothered me before the Idaho Falls operation. My room in the temporary hospital there was not exactly sterile, being a large room [with] three windows with lace curtains and a big rug on the floor, but [it] was much pleasanter than the usual hospital rooms. And I seemed to acquire no undesirable germs. It was a joy to be able to wash, mop, and do whatever was needed without discomfort. The children and I often ate our lunches out-of-doors, having whatever was easy to prepare. If a rancher came by, I could quickly scramble some eggs and with bread and butter and fruit sauce that was sufficient.

We were enjoying lots of fresh native trout with our meals. Two Ocean Lake was excellent fishing; many ranchers went for fish and usually gave us all we could use. Mac got some, too, but had little time for fishing.

We were getting lots of milk, too, as our cow gave six to eight quarts twice a day. With the separator, we had all the cream we wanted to use and plenty for butter.

Mr. Snell rode up one day bringing letters and papers. He reported putting fifty pounds of sugar (long awaited), chicken wire for the bunny pen, and several fiber boxes in Loziers' empty house, as all had been left at the roadside mail box. Since it was almost Jeanne's birthday, we were sure one box must be for her, and Mac just had to take time out to go for it. A child's birthday without Mother's box was unthinkable.

The surveying was taking much longer than anticipated. They were nowhere near through in three or four days although we were all tiring of 6:30 breakfast and 7:30 suppers. It was usually at least that late before the men returned and there was so much to be done thereafter. Mac had horses to care for, milking, and all outside chores. I had the children to care for, dishes to do, and general [clean-up] that consumed much time. That was once a day I didn't appreciate the separator. It had to be taken apart and washed every night as well as morning. But finally, after seven or eight days, Mr. Peterson decided to return to Idaho Falls with the information on hand. Some of the surveys had not worked out as well as hoped, so there was some uncertainty about what the company might want to do and he thought it best to report.

In the meantime, Jeanne had celebrated her birthday on the sixth. After Mother's box arrived, she could hardly wait to open it but had to and was not disappointed in the contents when she did. Sewing card, paint, and a manicuring set were especially enjoyed and the latter kept her busy in the following days.

The rest of the family was always remembered in a box from Mother. A box of Rinso was of special interest to me as I had not seen any before. [I] had used Lux, but the Rinso had sounded so good that I planned to use that on the next washday.

After Mr. Peterson left, Mac had more time for ranch work and could do some surveying for ranchers. He put a good floor in the cabin and thought he would take over a cot, also his big desk. This would give additional room in the house and make an extra room for emergency. We had received word from Selma Kause, a Washington friend whom we had met through the church there, that she planned to accept our longstanding invitation and make us a visit late in the summer. Her visit was anticipated.

About the middle of the month, Mac brought the geese home from Loziers' place where Elmer Arthur had cared for them all winter. They seemed happy to be home, remembered and visited the beaver pond, Braman's place, and all their old-time haunts but always returned home again.

About the twenty-fifth of the month, we all went to Elk to vote to become a new county with Jackson [as] the county seat. We were now part of Lincoln County and Evanston was our county seat. That was many (230) miles south of Jackson and very inaccessible for Jackson Hole people. During most of the year, the trip had to be made via stage and train and a week was required for the round trip, so we wanted the northern end of the county separated with Jackson our county seat.

That same day Mr. Peterson returned from Idaho Falls to do further work. The Idaho company wanted more surveying done, especially the meadows several miles up Pacific Creek. The Two Ocean Lake project would require an enormous amount of dirt hauling, which would be expensive. If a reservoir could be built up the creek, it might be less expensive

The geese spent the winter at the neighbor's ranch and returned home to Mc-Kinstrys' homestead in the summer. (JHHS&M)

and Two Ocean Lake would not be spoiled at all. We hoped this would be possible. So Mac, Mr. Peterson, and the two boys who were helping were working several miles up Pacific Creek every day.

A few days later, at the end of the month, the unexpected happened and changed all plans. About 2:30 in the afternoon Dad Snell, who was camped at Two Ocean Lake as caretaker, phoned me that water [was] coming through the dam. He wanted Mac to come up right away, but Mac was several miles up Pacific Creek and I had no way of contacting him. I dashed over to Braman's, hoping he could ride up and find them. The family had just returned home from getting mail but said he would start out immediately. Also I phoned Joe Markham at Moran asking if he could possibly go up to Two Ocean. He could not leave but said he would send up some men right away. There seemed to be nothing more I could do but wait and worry. After a few hours Mr. Braman returned. He said he rode up the creek, found where the horses were tied, but the men of course were not there. Then he went on up the creek for an hour, hollering all the way and finally located the surveyors. The two boys who were helping with the survey had ridden up horseback, so Mac borrowed one of the horses and he and the other boy cut across country to Two Ocean Lake. Mr. Peterson and the second boy drove the team back and then to the lake. The men from Moran arrived first but could not locate the trouble. Mac and Mr. Peterson found the water was coming up from beneath the headgate but couldn't figure why. The men from Moran were sent back up there for sacks to fill with sand but it took hours for them to return. (No one ever did know why.) Before they arrived, the flow increased and the dam caved in. Too late for sacks then. The men thought perhaps they could fell some big trees, put them across the outlet, and at least check the flow but could not get them in place.

When Mr. Braman returned he said he was going up to Two Ocean with his team so I made a big can of sandwiches to send up. It seems Dad Snell had cooked potatoes so the men had some sort of a supper, since he had also made coffee. They worked until long after dark and it was nearing midnight when Mac, Mr. Peterson, and Herb Whiteman got [back to the house] that night.

The men worked all day Tuesday but with no equipment, it was almost impossible to get logs in place, but they finally succeeded in checking the flow to some extent. Elmer Arthur and Snell were at our house for supper that night and then rode home on Slop and Ginger. It was later before Mac got his supper as he had had to hunt for horses. On Wednesday the men continued working. Mac said they'd be home at a reasonable hour but about 6:00 phoned they would not be home until late. He had to come down for some equipment so I made another batch of sandwiches for him to take up. I guess it was 11:30 when they all arrived back but the children and I were asleep.

They never did know what caused the leak and then the break in of the dam. It may have been that the water forced its way through the gravel under the dam, muskrats might have chewed the wood, or something else may have happened. No one will ever know. The part of the headgate that the men had thought might possibly give away was all right until after the leak was undermined so much that the dam caved. Two Ocean Lake lowered some three feet in as many days, which meant a lot of water flowed out somewhere. The swampy land and beaver dams below the dam held it in check but much flowed on down. Where the creek crossed our road below Thompsons', it was some three feet deep for a couple of days, gradually lessening. In spite of all the water that did flow into the Snake River, it made no appreciable increase there.

Thursday morning Mac and Mr. Peterson went up to the lake to check, but since nothing more could be done there, [they] went on up Pacific Creek to continue surveying. They were supposed to be home for a 6:30 supper but of course were later. Mac was so tired from all the extra work and late hours, I hoped he would soon have a chance to rest. As the surveying was practically completed there, Mr. Peterson returned to Idaho Falls.

The fore part of July, Mother sent three mosquitos netting canopies. They were wonderful to have especially during the mosquito season. And Mother's box also came in time for Neal's birthday.

Both youngsters enjoyed the building blocks and Neal loved to give the dog a ride in his cart. On Saturday night the thirteenth of July, the Steingrabers, who were in charge of the Skinner Ranch, gave a big dance for the whole Jackson Hole community. Lena Feutz was helping us at the time and said she would stay with the children, [saying] she did not care about the dance and would not go if she were at home.

Mac and I planned to ride over the hill, meet the Browns at Germanns', and go the next ten miles in their truck. The plans [didn't] work out. We couldn't find any horses so [the] Browns came all the way to the ranch to get us. It was 8:30 when we started, then [we] got stuck temporarily in Two Ocean Creek, but the crowd was still awaiting us when we reached Buffalo Bridge. Then [we] all went on up to the Skinner Ranch.

The dance was held in the loft of a huge barn and a crowd was already there. Forty or fifty people were up from Jackson and ranchers from all along the way between. They had a six- or seven-piece orchestra from Jackson so the music was good. Since the Skinner ranch had [its] own electric light plant, the loft was well lighted; the floor had been planed and cleaned and plenty of wax sprinkled on so it made a nice dance floor. Supper was about 2 A.M. and it was daylight before the dance was over. We left soon afterward and arrived home about 6:30 in the morning. We'd had a good time but strenuous, but [we] were glad to have attended at least one of the big Jackson Hole dances.

A few days later the Domestic Science Club met at Mrs. Stilson's. By request the subject was to be Frostings and Fillings. I [spent] considerable time brushing up but Mac sure enjoyed the resulting product.

We kept expecting to see some of the Idaho Falls people in [to check on the work] but they continued to send checks to pay for any expenses. Of course it was much too wet to do any work at Two Ocean Lake, but some work was done at Emma Matilda in preparation for the dam. We did not know what the status of their permits [was] by then and wondered how the [permits] were progressing. We were hearing more about the probability of the Park extension so [we] knew the Park Service would oppose in every way possible the building of any dams in that area.

It was in August that we learned the move for a new county at our part of Jackson Hole had been approved. We were now Teton County and Jackson the county seat.

Now that Mac had less work to do at the lake, he had more time for ranch work and surveying for other ranchers. It seemed good to have him able to do these other jobs as they needed to be done, too. There were always ranchers who wanted ditches surveyed.

On July 15 the phone rang. [I]t was from Moran and from [our friend] Selma as she had arrived there. From what we had last heard we were not expecting her until the next week. Mac went for horses and we said we would meet her as soon as we could. I hurried around and got a little room ready for her as Jeanne had been using it. Then we all drove to Moran.

It was good to see her and she was the same as ever. Although she was still teaching in elementary grades, she was teaching in college before retirement. She had the ability to make history, or any subject she taught, come alive for her pupils. She always wore her skirts well down toward the ankles and to be our knowledge never changed for she much disapproved of short skirts. Always loyal to her friends, she spent all her money on scholarships for needy students, summer classes, or helping someone else. [She was] always ready to do what others wanted and enjoyed being helpful. We drove up to Two Ocean Lake a day or so after she arrived, and finding so many wild strawberries, we did not arrive home until after one o'clock. Those berries were the sweetest ever and we knew dinner could wait.

That was the day twelve baby chicks hatched from the fourteen eggs under our hen. Mac had to help several out of the shell, which isn't a good thing to do, but [it was] necessary and the little chicks all thrived. The children loved them. [W]e [had] bought feathered out chicks from Lena's father and he brought them up the day he came for Lena. She had to return home to help there and cook for her father and [the] hay hands.

Selma enjoyed just taking ranch life as it came. The children liked her immensely. They would all take little walks and go to the garden to bring back vegetables for dinner.

Jeanne had always had trouble with tonsils and adenoids and Dr. Huff said she should have them removed. We would have preferred to wait until she was older but thought it best not to. So on July 27, Jeanne and I took the mail truck to Jackson. It was a big white truck but far more comfortable than the stage and much quicker. Mac, Selma, Emma, a girl who was helping then, and Neal were left at home to look after things there.

Jeanne and I went to the Crabtree Hotel and Dr. Huff was to operate the next morning. He said we could probably return to the hotel that evening. The next morning we went to the hospital quite early, Jeanne without any breakfast, and then learned that Dr. Huff had not returned that morning from a late call the night before. About nine o'clock, after a very busy day, he had received a call to go to Snake River station, the southern entrance to Yellowstone Park and at least sixty miles from Jackson. It seemed some tourists had arrived there who had the mumps, had caught cold, and were really sick. When it was well after eight o'clock and he had not arrived, Mrs. Huff said to wait until nine o'clock before giving Jeanne breakfast and then the operation would have to be delayed. Not long after Dr. Huff arrived, saying he had been home only a half hour. So the operation was performed and Dr. Huff said they were the worst tonsils and adenoids he had ever seen in so young a child. He did not understand how she could breathe through her nose at all, and [the] tonsils were decayed and flabby. The regular hospital nurse was on vacation and replacing her was one from Idaho Falls General Hospital. She proved to be the one I had when I had my appendix out and we remembered one another. Jeanne stood the operation well, and Dr. Huff said she could return to the hotel in the evening so Mr. Crabtree took us over. Jeanne was pretty tired and lifeless the next day, but after the second day, Dr. [Huff] said we could return home as there was no danger of infection.

The day we arrived in Jackson we happened to meet Mrs. Thompson, our first Jackson Hole neighbor, and had dinner with her. She was en route to the Thompson Hotel and insisted we join her. Although Mr. Thompson ran the hotel, he had nothing to do with the dining room so Mrs. Thompson would go there to eat. The Thompsons were not on speaking terms but he would talk with Pearl.[†] Later that evening we had a nice visit at Mrs. Huff's but after that night neither of us enjoyed Jackson.

[†] *Thompsons had a daughter named Pearl, and Emily Thompson also had a sister named Pearl.*

Jeanne was glad to return home and did not mind the trip in the truck. Although her throat was still pretty sore, she was glad to be home and out-of-doors there, continuing to gain. Dr. Huff's charge for the operation was thirty dollars, which included the ether, which Mrs. Huff gave. The hospital bill was ten dollars.

Some few days after returning from Jackson, I entertained the Domestic Science Club for lunch. There were twelve adults and twelve children but all seemed to enjoy it. In the evening a couple of men who were working for Mac that day at Two Ocean Lake came for supper. All together the week had been somewhat hectic, but Jeanne got along well and her throat was no longer sore.

Although Selma had missed the big dance at the ranch, we were invited there one Sunday when Mrs. Steingraber asked us over for dinner. It proved to be quite an occasion as there were twelve guests. Unfortunately some extra men arrived and there was no place at the table for Mrs. Steingraber. For dessert [she served] all the ice cream we could possibly eat with a luscious chocolate cake, and more of that before we left for home.

About the middle of the month, we had a delightful launch trip on Jackson Lake. Mr. Markham invited us to ride up with the man who read the gauges, a Mr. Elder. Mr. Grimmesey also went and ran the launch. We went some twelve miles up the lake right to the base of the Tetons. The men were gone about two hours checking water reports, but Selma, the children, and I just wandered around, found a few huckleberries, and enjoyed the scenery. Returning, there was wind enough to make the launch roll part of the way, which was fun and enjoyed, although Neal was frightened at first.

Our days were beautiful but the thermometer usually registered twenty-seven or twenty-eight at night. The low temperature did not seem to hurt the garden and we were glad of that.

One Saturday we went to a county demonstration meeting at Elk. We all took lunches and the meeting followed. Mrs. Braman went with us, so she drove our team, which made it easier for me. Mrs. Arthur and baby went with us from her place, but with all the children, the trip was strenuous and tiring, especially since Neal was fussy and wanted to go home all the time. A few days later our little domestic science group met with Mrs. Jack Fee, but as that was some twelve miles down country, [I] felt it was too far down country for us to drive. So that meeting had to be omitted.

During the month that Selma [was] there, we had discussed a possible trip back east for the children and me. Mac could not go but urged us to go so we could visit Mother and other relatives so that they could become acquainted with the children. If we went when Selma was returning east, she could help me with the children en route but I would still be alone with them after reaching New York or Washington. Travel was not so convenient then as it was later and airplanes [were] unheard of, but it was finances that really decided the matter. We felt we did not have the $400, or more, to spend and I worried over the responsibility. I was glad it was settled that way and Selma would make us a longer visit. A couple of days after the Elk meeting, Mac left for a trip to Idaho Falls, evidently to bring back a truck. Bob Coolidge and his wife, who had been camping at Two Ocean Lake, came down and camped at our place while Mac was away.

Mr. Brown was going to Ashton to meet the Chaplines, so Mac rode that far with him and took the train. Returning the following day, he drove back in the truck but was delayed in reaching Ashton that night. Along the way he heard some awful cries for help so he stopped. A touring car had overturned in a ditch carrying some three feet of water. Some people were trying to pry it up as there were some people still in the car. Though all helped they could not raise it.

Mac waded into the three-foot-deep water of the irrigation ditch and went to the other side of the car where he thought the door could be opened. In the back was an elderly woman, a girl, and a young man sitting in water up to their shoulders or higher. As the car was upside down, they were too frightened to move, not knowing what they might get into. The woman said the car was resting on her, but when Mac took hold of her and lifted, [he] found that only her dress was caught, and he lifted her out. The others then scrambled out, unhurt. He was going to take them to the nearest town but some ranchers in the vicinity had arrived by then so the people went to some ranch to dry out. Mac went on to Ashton, arriving there around midnight after he and his brand new pants had had an unexpected bath.

Sunday morning he found [Mr.] Brown and [the] Chapline family still in Ashton as Brown's truck had been in the garage the day before. They started out together in their respective trucks, but unfortunately Mac's did not work well on the hills, and they got only part way home. But the next morning they all arrived safely.

Since Selma was staying a little longer and into September, she said she wanted to take us all to Jackson to the Frontier Days. We never had attended any but had heard much about this annual event ever since we had been in Wyoming. This celebration lasted for several days and came the last of August and early September. We could only go for Thursday and Friday as Mac was to do surveying on Saturday. On Sunday we expected friends from Idaho for the Labor Day weekend.

Selma engaged one of the Crabtree Hotel tents and Jeanne was to sleep with her. We were all going in the truck and were to camp near her. Mac put up a tent over the truck and [we] all went to the Hotel Crabtree for meals.

Leaving home early Thursday morning, [we] ate lunch in Kelly and arrived in Jackson about two o'clock. We immediately went over to the ballpark where the rodeo was being [held] and we wanted to see that as it was the first one for all of us. Interesting of course. In the evening we decided on [attending] a hospital benefit, a play given at the high school. Preceding that was a clever vaudeville program put on by the "Dude Ranchers." This was a little shocking but seemed to worry Selma more than anyone else. Then came the play.

It had been pouring rain but [the rain] occasionally let up and this occurred just after the first act. Since both children were asleep, and we were all tired, we decided to leave and get back to our camp. Arriving there, Jeanne refused to sleep with Selma so the four of us piled into the truck. Although the tent over the truck helped, it could not keep us dry in the downpour that kept on most of the night. We surely appreciated the old quilts Mrs. Thompson had loaned us. It was partly clear in the morning, but still threatening, so by 3:30 we decided to leave for home. It rained almost all of the way, sometimes a downpour, and when we reached the dugway, the truck could not make it up. The ignition had gotten wet and the hill was steep and slippery. We still were about a mile and a half from home and it was pitch dark. Luckily Mac seems to be able to see in the dark for there was nothing to do but walk home. Across Two Ocean Creek, which was overflowing, and across the deep runoffs from the hill, Mac had to carry us across one by one. Neal rode on his shoulders all the way. We started out wet and chilled from riding so far in the truck with only the canvas over us but were well warmed by the time we reached home at ten o'clock. No one suffered any ill effects—all just a part of ranching.

Although showery the next morning, Saturday, Mr. Germann came early to take Mac to do surveying at the Hatchet Ranch. He planned to be home Sunday afternoon before Coys were to arrive, although we hardly expected them because of so much rain.

Selma, the children, and I had a quiet day catching up on things. Carl Roice, wife, and baby came down from Two Ocean Lake in the late afternoon for a visit. We were late with supper and just ready to sit down when Mr. and Mrs. Coy, twelve-year-old Katherine and an eighteen-year-old nephew arrived. The plan was for them to come Saturday, not Sunday, as Mac had understood. We soon had enough supper for all and later got everyone bedded down for the night, thanks to the extra room in the cabin. They had brought extra bedding but it had gotten wet and could not be used that night. I phoned to Mac who said that he would return as early as he could in the morning in a borrowed car. The Labor Day weekend was enjoyed in spite of the wet weather. Katherine rode horseback most of the day, the others riding, hiking, or visiting. They left for Idaho Falls the following day.

On September 7 we had to take Selma to Moran for her trip home. She had made us a long visit but she enjoyed it and we did, too. I really had had no extra work as she helped so much, doing about all the dishes, extra sewing for the children, and whatever was needed that she could do. She was always treating us to candy and gifts [for] the children, who had enjoyed her visit, also. A park bus was going out from Moran to Ashton [Idaho] that afternoon and she could go on that.

That morning we had to take her trunk to the dugway road where Mr. Brown would pick it up and take it to Ashton to the railroad. There would not be room for the trunk on the bus. Just as we got to the dugway we met Mr. and Mrs. Banks and children, Mr. Markham, and a Mr. Black and they were heading for our place. Mr. Black was a civil engineer from New Jersey whose home proved to be about thirty miles from Upper Montclair where Mother and my sister's family lived. The men wanted to go up to the lake but Mrs. Banks and the children stayed at the ranch. She insisted they would not stay for dinner but when it was nearly noon, I got dinner ready anyway and all were persuaded to stay. The four children [had] their dinner in the kitchen and the seven adults ate in the living room. We enjoyed it all and the dishes were done before [it was] time to leave with Selma. In the early afternoon we went to Moran and saw Selma safely started on the bus. Again we met the folks who had been at the house for dinner. They insisted we stay for supper with them at the hotel. Mr. Black had caught a five-pound trout and that would be especially prepared for him and his group that night. Mac could not stay as he had to go to Lava Creek to get a grader to use on the dugway road where they were cutting down the steep hill. The rest of us enjoyed the fish and the dinner, which was served in style.

Two days later, four of the men from the Idaho Falls group who were promoting the irrigation project were in: Mr. Milner, Johannessen, Shane, and a Mr. Martin, a civil engineer whom they had brought. They had arrived at Moran in a big car the night before. [They came to the ranch] in the morning and Mac took them up Pacific Creek to the Dave Ferrin place where surveying had been done, using the team. They had planned to come back here and take the car to Two Ocean but decided to walk across. About 12:45 Mac phoned from Two Ocean and said they were going on [to] Emma Matilda and would probably be back in an hour and a half.

The dinner I had gotten quickly after 11:30, because I expected the men would arrive and be in a hurry, was still waiting. Potatoes, elk meat in milk gravy, string bean salad, canned corn, bread, butter, and coffee. Desert was Del Monte pears with plain cake. I wondered what it would taste like by the time the men arrived but don't remember any complaints.

The Idaho men were quite confident that their permit was now definite and expected to build a big dam next summer. It was too late to start this year but they did want the small dam replaced.

In the middle of the month, Mac had been working on our irrigation ditch, Walt Germann and Carl Roice helping him. He was planning to prove up on the ranch and water that fall, and one requirement was to have the ditch completed and in working order.

A few days after Selma left, we learned about her trip out to the railroad, which had been most unpleasant. We had noticed that most of the people on the bus were not the usual tourist type but thought little of it. They proved to be kitchen help of one of the lodges in Yellowstone, and throughout the trip their remarks tended to be vulgar and coarse. A disappointing farewell from a lovely summer in a beautiful country.

With all the late summer events I had missed the last two Domestic Science [Club] meetings. One was the day Mac left for Idaho Falls but was at Mrs. Jack Fee's ranch, much too long a drive for me.

The second was at Mrs. Smith's over in Buffalo Creek location. Another long distance but due to rain, the roads were slippery especially off the main highway. We doubted if we could get there at all, about fifteen miles round trip.

After Selma left we decided to put Jeanne in the little room and let her have it for her own bedroom. She was very proud of it and though lonesome to be by herself at first, she soon adjusted.

On September 30 I was reckoning up the number of eggs we had gotten from the twelve hens we purchased from the Hatchet Ranch on May 28, the day of the big picnic at Mrs. Cowles. We could hardly believe they had laid 750 eggs. Also we had churned some thirty-five pounds of butter but still had had to buy some butter and eggs the last few weeks. We put five or six dozen in water glass as extra eggs were always needed in wintertime.

We needed more meat, but Mac was busy at Two Ocean Lake all the time, and we didn't like to get fresh meat until we were pretty sure it would stay frozen all winter. Germann, Cowles, and Snell Sr. were all working for the company at Two Ocean Lake and Josephine Roice was cooking for them. Mac usually stayed up at noon if he could get a hot meal. The work would have to stop soon as winter might arrive any time.

Another box from Mother arrived and caused the usual joy and excitement. Jeanne hoped Mother would send Neal a shorter jump rope so he wouldn't take hers by mistake! Neal bit his harmonica when he blew but it seemed to work just as efficiently. He now took his new doll baby to bed instead of the bear and doll he had been taking.

During October we had some stormy weather. The work stopped at Two Ocean Lake and Mac started surveying around Kelly as work could be done down there. He was away several days at a time but Phoebe Gardner was helping me and could do the milking. It was her mother who, in the early spring of 1915, rode over some almost impassable roads, bringing a gunny sack of watercress tied behind her saddle. There were warm springs on their place so that water never froze. That was a gift never forgotten.

When the weather cleared after a stormy week, it was perfectly beautiful out. The sky was a beautiful blue and the peaks were so white. The weather was just perfect and it was indescribably lovely—ideal weather for [the] domestic science meeting, which met the last of October. Mrs. Braman had a bad cold so I had to go alone, but I thoroughly enjoyed the horseback ride over the hill and then on to Mrs. Henry Bailey's place. Instead of the hostess furnishing the luncheon for all, we had decided to each bring a few sandwiches and the club furnished coffee. It was a very successful plan and we were ready to start work on our program much earlier than usual. Pastry had been the subject requested and with all helping, we made many things in a short time. These included a mince pie, a caramel pie, coconut tarts, cheese straws and rings, circle tarts with jam filling and whipped cream, turnovers, frosted pastry sticks, and patty shells. Everyone seemed delighted

Jeanne at age five and Neal at age two with Laddie II. (McKinstry)

with the results and it was completed, as well as more or less eaten, by four o'clock. My ride home was thoroughly enjoyed and I arrived before dark.

Some of the regular attending members were not at the club meeting but some newcomers made the usual number. Mrs. Cowles wasn't speaking to Mrs. Bailey, as I guess their business deal wasn't progressing very well, and the Germanns and the Baileys happened to be at outs. So those two members were absent but Mrs. Fee, Mrs. Hall, and Mrs. Thorndike, the latter were newcomers, were present although it meant a round trip of some twenty-five miles for them, a long trip on horseback. Since people knew we expected to leave our ranch during the winter to avoid being completely snowed in, Mrs. Bailey offered us the use of their cabin if they went out for the winter. Their place [was] more accessible to a main highway and we appreciated the offer, but since that community had the reputation of misunderstanding, disputes, and scraps we'd rather not be there.

[If] the Lozier house [was] available, we would probably go there. It [was] the nearest for us and right on the Jackson-Moran highway.

When Mac arrived home from the Kelly surveying trip, he brought a real load, 600 pounds of potatoes and 950 pounds of wheat.

After he returned, he had to go to Idaho Falls early in November. Phoebe was with me so he could get away. When he went out earlier, he brought in the heavy truck he had used in hauling cattle the preceding winter. If he could sell or trade it for a lighter one, he was going to do so.

Soon after he left, Harold Hammond, who own[ed] a dude ranch near the Bar BC, came over horseback. He needed some surveying done before the first of the year. The land was taken under the old survey, and the lines did not coincide with the new survey and his water application would not be accepted. His time limit had already been extended. Newcomers near Fees' needed ditches surveyed so there was plenty of work awaiting [Mac], weather permitting.

Phoebe and I were having our difficulties. Red, our good milk cow, and on which we were counting on for a plentiful supply of milk for the next several months, was due to have a calf. Mac said she should be milked out as soon as possible after the calf arrived as it would be unable to take all her milk. A night or two later, she didn't come home with the other cattle. Phoebe was ill the next day so I spent most of the day searching for the cow and calf but had no luck. She didn't come home that night either so couldn't be milked and we were worried. About nine o'clock the following morning, she and the calf showed up and Red was in real need of being milked. After we succeeded in getting them into the corral, Phoebe got almost a water pail full of milk. The dog, cat, and chickens had a feast. After that [Red] was milked regularly and our worries over that ended. A few days later, and in another truck, Mac returned from Idaho Falls. I think through Mr. Patterson's help, someone had been found who wanted a heavy truck and had a light one to dispose of, so a deal was soon made.

For nearly a month we had been missing Ginger, the white horse Mac had brought from North Dakota. She never seemed able to adjust to the altitude, had had various difficulties over the years, and we wondered if she had wandered off never to return. Then one night when Mac went to the barn there she was, although he wasn't sure if it was Ginger or her ghost.

Thanksgiving Day arrived and we had a good dinner even with a limited assortment of groceries. Roast chicken and fixings, mashed white and browned sweet potatoes, onions, and scalloped corn. Mint sherbet, frozen by setting out-of-doors, was good with our cabbage salad and first course. Pumpkin pie and plenty of whipped cream for dessert. Phoebe was still with us and enjoyed it, too.

Just before Thanksgiving, Mac had to go to Germanns' for more hay, but it was a long hard trip because of the slush and snow, the hay rack heavy and awkward. In December he had to haul more. Carl Roice was working with him then as Carl needed more hay also. Hay seemed to be scarce but Walt Germann seemed to have plenty and generously seemed to be sharing it with the other homesteaders at a nominal price. Between breakdowns and weather, hauling was difficult, but enough was finally brought.

That fall Mac proved up on our water right. The ditch was never completely finished until Mac and some neighbors completed it and put it in usable condition. Then he went down and proved up.

We were still uncertain about how much we could continue developing the ranch. The bill for the Yellowstone Park extension was revised quite regularly in Congress and each time seemed to receive more favorable consideration. Our ranch would be included if the park was extended. But making our winter plans was more important as we might be snowed in any day. About a week before Christmas, we moved to the Lozier house.

This house was smaller and not so nice as ours but it was well built and the kitchen range was still there. Their fenced pastures, well-built chicken coop, and extra buildings near the house helped for storage. Being only a few hundred feet to the mail box on the highway was a joy, too. Jeanne could run down and check on mail and loved to do it. Later, when there was snow and only a trail to the box and a moose was reported in the vicinity, she was less enthusiastic.

Mac got a tree before Christmas and we all enjoyed that. We had our usual excitement for Christmas being so generously remembered by Mother,

In the 1920s, automobiles and trucks started to be used more frequently in the valley. Mac acquired a heavy truck and then traded for a lighter one. Men soon gerry-rigged snow plows onto the front of trucks.

On the back of this photo is written: "Fellow in white is John Lewis, Jack Teevebaugh was a game warden. Jack Teevebaugh with Buick touring car he made into a truck. Was heavy outfit — He fabricated a wooden plow for fall plowing only."
(JHHS&M)

relatives, and friends. Mother's boxes were Christmases in themselves and the children were always excited by them. We all appreciated the gifts. Neal always called Santa Claus pictures "Gamma Claus." He could not understand who Santa was but knew his grandmother sent most of his gifts.

After the Christmas festivities the snow got deeper but the children surely enjoyed it. Neal was not yet three and at first did not like the cold snow but soon wanted to get in all over and roll in it. It was amazing how efficient he was at getting about. He liked to borrow Jeanne's skis and would walk all around. One day we suddenly discovered him about a quarter mile down the field following ski tracks made by Mac. He surely looked tiny way down there but was traveling right along.

Another day he wanted my snowshoes—webs. I wondered how he could possibly manage those with his little short legs, but in no time at all he was walking all around having a grand time. He was always active and could handle himself well.

In late winter when the snow crusted, both children had great fun sliding downhill. There were plenty of hills just northwest of Loziers' house, and sometimes we and the Snells from over across the highway, all went. We could go as high as we wanted on the hills

Reality Sets In

After Christmas we settled down to routine. Mac continued working part-time for the Idaho project, but we felt they never would be able to obtain government permission to build a large dam with the Yellowstone Park extension receiving more and more backing. The Idaho company remained optimistic so wanted lumber and preparations for next year. But it was the lumber business that caused the unexpected and near tragic.

For some years Mac had had an understanding with Si Ferrin that Mac could take the lumber needed by the Idaho company [from Ferrin's stock] and pay for what was taken. They had already purchased several thousand feet and all were satisfied with the arrangement. Then Ferrin decided to sell all of his lumber and made a special price if Mac would take it all. He checked with Joe at the USRS [U.S. Reclamation Service which became the Bureau of Reclamation] and found that they wanted lumber, the Idaho Company wanted more, Jim Cowles wanted some, and so did we, so we drove to Elk and told Ferrin we would take it all. A few days later, Joe and Mac and Cowles began hauling the lumber and continued taking it for about a week, finishing up then, and putting a check in the mail to pay for it. When they started taking lumber, Ferrin was in Jackson but his foreman came rushing over and accused the men of stealing lumber. They explained the situation to him but he wasn't very well satisfied.

Ferrin came to Elk after the last was taken, called up Mac and Cowles, and told them to meet him at the ranch on Saturday before noon. Neither went, both saying they were too busy and were going to feed Germanns' cattle that morning. Monday [Mac] called up Ferrin and said if he was not satisfied with the way things were going to call the Idaho company as he was working under their orders.

January 1922

In this chapter, Linda writes about the highlights of their lives from 1922–1924, rather than providing a chronological narrative of each year.

Ferrin had calmed down by then and said he would take it up with the judge in Jackson, which Mac said was OK with him. The trouble was, from all reports, Si was in with a bunch of crooks and the judge seemed to be with them but the next development was unexpected. The sheriff at Jackson phoned up [to say] that a warrant had been sworn out by Ferrin against Mac and that he would have to come the next day and furnish bond. So the next day he took the mail stage to Jackson, checking in at the Crabtree Hotel where he knew he would have good accommodations and excellent meals. It was nearly six when the stage reached Jackson and though he tried to reach Judge Fuller that night, he was told it was after hours and he would have to wait until morning. As he stepped out from the hotel a little later in the evening, he was asked by a man if his name was McKinstry. He said, "Yes."

[The man] replied, "My name is Francis and I am the sheriff. You are a gentleman and I hated to give you that warrant but Ferrin had sworn out the warrant and I had to."

He offered to be of any help that he could and said he would go with Mac to see Judge Fuller the next morning.

Mac phoned to Johannessen, the Idaho company attorney, and he said he would be in whenever a trial was set. The next morning Francis succeeded in making an appointment with Judge Fuller, and although Mac doubted if he had to make bond, the sheriff said he had better do so if they insisted and one was made out for $200.

By this time the whole affair was the talk of the town on the telephone, and the town people and they all said they hoped Mac would sue Ferrin afterward, and plenty. No date had been set for any trial and since Mac had to stay in town an extra day he soon learned why. He was told there had been a lot of disturbances in Wilson, and Francis said he thought it was mostly spite work. It seemed that the D.A. at Kemmerer had phoned to Jackson to tell them to set no trial date until March at which time he would come for the trial. That took the matter out of Fuller's hands and evidently Fuller, Ferrin, and their friends were disturbed and realized they had started more than they could handle. Suddenly the atmosphere changed and both put themselves out to be as friendly as possible to Mac.

While Mac was away Mrs. Grimmesey stayed with me. Herb Whiteman brought her down as he was hauling hay from Gregorys' and helped us with feeding and milking and after supper stayed for the evening. Also Sam Richardson, a man working at Ferrins' ranch, was here for dinner. Guess he [was] through there and had no use for Ferrin.

Two days after Mac left, he returned on the mail stage. No date was ever set for a trial and [we] guessed Ferrin and Fuller began backing down

*Budge funeral procession:
Willi Wolff, Joe Markham,
Charlie Hedrick, James
Budge. Mrs. Budge on the
edge of the photograph.*
(JHHS&M, W. C. Lawrence
Collection)

on a lot of things. I have wondered how the warrants for the Wilson people ever came out but never remember any trials for which the D.A. from Kemmerer came in. No liable suit was brought against Ferrin as much as the community people would have enjoyed it.

The one and only funeral we ever attended in Jackson Hole occurred one winter after we moved to the Lozier ranch. No letter seems to remain about it but I shall always have memories even though I never knew the boy who died. The love and concern of the whole community was expressed at that time in never forgotten ways.

It all occurred in the middle of the winter and when a terrific storm was raging. The Budge family, long residents of Jackson Hole, was relatively new to the Buffalo Creek community where they had been living for some months past. One of the teenage boys was stricken with pneumonia, a very fatal disease in those days. Dr. Huff had responded to their call though [he] probably had to travel several miles on skis. After arriving at their ranch, he just stayed, nursing the boy day and night, but it was a losing battle. By then travel between Jackson and Moran was absolutely impossible for nothing could get across the bleak miles of the Antelope Flat country. Neither a coffin nor preacher could come from Jackson but there had to be a funeral.

The men of the Buffalo community made a plain box from lumber available. Some way the ladies found material with which they made a really attractive lining. Just a plain box top for the cover. Flowers were there, some very pretty ones, but all made with paper, though I vaguely remember a half dozen or so badly wilted carnations. I have often wondered how they could possibly be there at all.

Long before, the Allens had started a little cemetery across the road from their ranch, and this was the only place for the Budge boy to be buried. The funeral was held in the old unused dance hall right by the road as that was still standing. Nothing was left in the building but a little old iron stove, which was supposed to give off a little heat at least. Seating arrangements were made by putting planks across cut logs and blankets spread over them. These were around one or two sides of the room.

The morning of the funeral the ranchers who could get there brought their teams and tried to break out a road up the hill to the cemetery. It was impossible with the deep snow; the horses simply could not do it, so that plan had to be abandoned. Since we were living in the Lozier house at the time, the few families who could get there stopped by that morning for coffee, or lunch, or brought their own lunches, glad of a warm place to eat. Early in the afternoon we all went to the Allen ranch to the funeral. It was not like any funeral I had ever attended, but that is one funeral always to be remembered, but the details are hazy. Some woman sang a solo as best she could with only a fiddle to accompany her. Neither participant was trained but they tried. One of the Mormon ranchers said a few words in eulogy although public speaking was not in his line, but he, too, gave all that he had. I think we sang one verse of a well-known hymn to the fiddle accompaniment and the service closed by uniting in the Lord's Prayer.

Then came time for the burial. An opening at the top of the hill cemetery had been dynamited out so the casket could be lowered into it. The casket was covered, carried out, and lashed to a sled made with skis. Some of the men then skied up the hill to the little cemetery, dragging the sled. None of the other people attempted to climb, and after waiting a little while in the cold, we sadly started for our homes. Judging from my own reactions, it was probably the saddest and most meaningful funeral ever attended. Certainly it has been long remembered.

A few days later the storm abated, roads were gradually opened, and travel between Jackson and the upper end of the valley was reestablished. Life again went on as usual.

One night not too long after moving to the Lozier ranch, I was quite badly frightened. Mac had gone up to our ranch and the dog had gone with him. He said he would not return until morning as there were various small jobs to be done.[†]

It was a quiet, beautiful moonlight night. The children and I had been sleeping when I was suddenly awakened by the rattling of the back screen door. Mac could easily unhook the door if he shook it a bit so I decided he had arrived home earlier than expected, and called, "Is that you, Mac? Want me to unlock the door?"

† *Linda's manuscript contained two separate accounts of this anecdote. The two versions have been combined here.*

Mrs. H. C. McKinstry   Graduate. School of Household Arts   Framingham, Massachusetts

The Wild Goose Tea Room was the McKinstrys' effort to supplement their income while relying on Linda's expertise in cooking and their surplus cream, eggs, milk, and butter. This is the top of her letterhead for the enterprise. (JHHS&M)

There was no answer but the door immediately stopped rattling. Then I was worried. Wondering and thinking that we now lived on the main highway, I lay still thinking perhaps I imagined or dreamed it all. Too frightened to get up, I just kept quiet, waiting, and then the shaking and rattling began again. Someone must be trying to get in. I called out again, "Mac is that you?," hoping my voice didn't show my fright. No answer, but again the rattling stopped and all was quiet. By then I was really frightened, but I was glad Jeanne and Neal had not wakened. Knowing I couldn't sleep until I knew who was out there, I slipped into a bathrobe and walked as noiselessly as possible to the bedroom door and far enough out to see the kitchen door. Carefully I peeked around to the kitchen door, and to my relief no one was standing there, only a sort of big, dark lump against the door. Then I had the courage to go all the way to the door. Cautiously approaching the door, I saw a dark, round creature on the porch then noticed a larger round creature waddling toward the woodshed. The creature on the porch seemed unwilling to move. Shutting the inside door, I went back to bed and slept.

Mac said afterward that porcupines often are ravenous for salt and these creatures had evidently found salt embedded in the wood portion of the old screen door.

Early in 1922 we often talked of what we could do with our ranch to produce more income. We hesitated about going too deeply into cattle raising because we felt uncertain about our range if Yellowstone Park was extended. We knew we would be included if it was. It might be possible to fence our pond and obtain a permit to raise beaver and muskrat but again what might happen if we found ourselves in the Park?

Then I suggested the possibility of opening a tea room. I think I had a long, deep down desire to have one though I had never had any training or knew anything about them. We knew the tourist traffic now would not justify such a venture but felt that more and more tourists would be coming every year. The Park busses from the east over Togwotee Pass had to pass the Lozier place to reach Moran. It would be nice to have contact with

Jeanne and Neal McKinstry stand under the sign for the Wild Goose Tea Room. Although hard to read here, the sign offered lunch, tea, and supper. In the photo is a tent which is perhaps the one where Linda's friend Elizabeth Smith stayed. (McKinstry)

people from the "outside" world for I knew I was beginning to miss them. Also, a tea room would be an outlet for our surplus milk, cream, and butter. My idea was to serve only light lunches or sandwiches, ice cream, desserts, cake, cookies and coffee, tea, milk, and lemonade.

Mac agreed with the idea even though it meant a lot of work for him, and he may have had even more doubts than I. We looked at several possible sites but decided on a place about one-quarter mile from the [Lozier] ranch house. Three acres of land on the opposite side of the road belonged to Loziers' place. We hoped he would sell it to us, but [he] did not want to though [he] said we were welcome to use it.

Although still working at home and for the Idaho company, Mac found time to get out logs, peel them ready for constructing a little log building there, having help when needed from some of the neighbors. It was already early spring and we wanted to open that summer, 1922. After deciding to operate a tea room, [and] after the building was ready, all the furnishings had to be decided upon and purchased. Most of this had to be done via catalog and time allowed for delivery. Jim Cowles made nice tables; chairs were purchased and painted. Window curtains and drapes were planned, and Mother and Mary did most of that buying. Marquisette scrim was used for the white curtains with the picture of a wild goose painted on one corner. Since it was so difficult to know actual colors from catalogs, it helped to have Mother and Mary make the selections. I was glad of their interest and help. The predominating color of the drapes was to be yellow with dark blue for an accent.

Dishes, glasses, and silver eating utensils were decided upon and ordered as well as any necessary cooking utensils. I enjoyed making selections and hoped Mac was not too bored with it all. [I] also hoped Mother and Mary enjoyed their part. We planned on serving just light lunches, sandwiches, and dessert, putting up box lunches if asked for. A girl was helping me get ready but it was still well into July before we could open. Our ice cream was made in the second year by the Philadelphia recipe, just milk and cream, sweetened and flavored. Since it had to be frozen by armstrong that was Mac's job. Since we used as much cream as possible [without having it] turn to butter, it was really delicious ice cream. That and a chocolate fudge cake gained quite a reputation and [were] repeatedly ordered.

There really was not enough traffic at that time to make the whole affair very successful but at least it paid running expenses—less baby care, and I enjoyed meeting the people from the outside and getting a little different perspective. The tourist trade lasted but little more than two months but we had not planned to stay open longer.

The winter of 1922–1923 we [again] lived in the Lozier ranch house and Mac taught in the Buffalo school. Mrs. Snell and I would take our children to the Elk school as Jeanne and the Snell boy both needed to go, and the Elk school was nearer than the Buffalo [school]. Mac would go to [the] Buffalo school on horseback so would leave the team harnessed to the spring wagon for my use. Joe Chapline was teaching at Elk. However, we could not continue long as the weather soon became cold and often stormy.

The people at Buffalo Creek were delighted when Mac took the school. And I know he was good for the children. Some of his methods may not have been very authentic but all seemed satisfied. One incident I remember him telling about was the boxing match.

Germanns and Smeikles were at outs with each other, but Garl Germann and Cecelia Smeikles brought their difficulties to school with them. They were about the same age (fifteen or sixteen) and about equal in physical strength. If they were not fighting verbally, quite likely they were using their fists. Mac soon tired of it and said there'd be a boxing match to see who was champion and planned accordingly. He found two pairs of boxing gloves, which had been brought out with our supplies, and took them to school. Tying them onto the hands of children, he told them to go to it. They started out vigorously but it was awkward and tiring and they soon decided they'd had enough. So, calling "time," [Mac] said it was a draw, neither was champion, [and] they'd better call off their fighting and settle down. Whether it was the advice or desire to have no more boxing exhibitions, conditions definitely improved.

I know onion lunch day made him unhappy. The children of one family brought big onions to school to go with their bread and butter sandwiches. They ate the onions like apples and by the time lunch was over, there was no mistaking what lunch had been that day.

Mac taught at the Buffalo (Creek) School in 1922-1923. This photograph is of the 1920-21 students so would include some of his students. The identifications on the back are hard to follow but it says: Hula Smith, Teacher. Front Row (l to r): 1. Lana Gregory, 2. Laura Germann behind Lana, Pearl Germann (now House), Helen Bailey, Ruth Bailey, behind Ruth: Alfred Germann. Next Row - Garl Germann, behind Garl is Myrl Gregory, Cecilia Smykel, Elizabeth Smykel, Ted Lozier, Glenn Smith. Back Row - either Nobe Gregory or Fred Smykel, Faye Gregory, Bill Gardner. (JHHS&M)

I doubt if he found teaching quite so boring as expected. The grades were mixed from the second up, but any teaching [of] the upper grades or high school work was really enjoyed. For the boys especially to have daily contact with a man of Mac's type was invaluable. I know they learned things never found in books. Parents and children, too, regretted when the year was up and wanted him to continue teaching another year.

The summer of 1923 the Tea Room was open with local help. Mrs. Steingraber was especially helpful. The Tea Room was closed early in September as [our] new arrival was expected in October and we planned to spend the winter in Jackson. Having taught Jeanne by the Calvert school method for the first grade, she was more than ready for second grade school work in Jackson.

[At the Tea Room, we] kept potato salad on hand and supplies for sandwiches but made them up as ordered. [The] kinds were salmon, egg, lettuce, and peanut butter. Most of these were ten or fifteen cents as I remember; one or two kinds may have been twenty cents each.

Also on hand [were] White Mountain Nut cake and chocolate fudge cake as well as cookies, so box lunches were quickly prepared.

Beverages served [were] coffee, hot or iced tea, lemonade, and milk. Bottled varieties, if even heard of in those days, were practically unknown.

Meeting people was one of the best things about having the Tea Room. One couple from Massachusetts even wrote back after they returned home, signing it "From your Mass. Cousins."

On October 12, 1923, we had a fine new baby girl. We named her Stella. I had rather hoped she would arrive on the eleventh since that was

Mother's birth date. Since winter was arriving, we had decided to stay in Jackson and had rented a little house there. Jeanne could be in school and there were other children for her to play with. But she hated it all and being away from all out-of-doors. She never was interested in making friends with other children, much preferring her own company.

The following February just about Valentine's Day, we were grief stricken. Early that morning Mary had phoned from New Jersey, not with Valentine's greetings, but to say Mother had passed away the preceding night with a heart attack. Although Mother and all of us had long known that might happen because of a certain heart murmur, she never seemed to let it worry her. I guess the rest of us sort of forgot about it for it was a real shock when it happened. Since it was the middle of winter in Jackson Hole, the road travel conditions of those days made it impossible to even get back east for the funeral. It was another shock to receive a letter from her about a week later, written of course when all was well, and to realize that that would be the last one ever to arrive.

We were all glad when spring arrived and we could get back up country to the Lozier place. It would have been a week or two later before we could have reached our own ranch. When July finally arrived, we opened the Tea Room. Elizabeth Smith, my former college friend, came from California to help with that and a combined summer vacation. She had a big tent by the Tea Room and enjoyed living there. The rest of us lived at the ranch house and we all had meals there.

It was a good summer for all of us and for Stella especially. A little Mormon girl, Alice Feutz, came from Idaho. She knew about housework and meals, loved babies and they loved her. Certainly Stella did. Although she had considerable work taking care of the ranch house, washing, and helping or preparing meals, she always had lots of time to care for Stella and play with her. Often as we would be walking up the road to the ranch house, we would hear Alice singing at the tops of her lungs, "Barney Google, Barney with the great big googley eyes," or some such nonsense. Peals of laughter from Alice and gurgles of delight from Stella. I am sure Stella had a happier and more fun-filled summer with Alice than she would have had with me if I had been only caring for the family and doing all the ranch house duties. As it was, I was enjoying the Tea Room and Elizabeth being there and neither of us was overworked at all.

I can look back on [it] as being a happy summer for all concerned and our last one in Jackson Hole. At the end of the tea room season, we had a grand chicken dinner, inviting all the Jackson friends who had been so nice to me whenever I was in town. The list sounded like the elite of the whole town, which they were, as our 1924 guest list showed:

The McKinstrys said good-bye to their friends from Jackson Hole. Shown are Pearl Germann, Walt Germann, Rose Crabtree, and Nan Budge.
(JHHS&M)

Charles and Edna Huff "May our friendship grow and grow until no better friends we know."

Harry and Beatrice Wagner (Banker)

C.R. and Genevieve Van Vleck "The Merchant and Merchantress"

Grace G. Miller (and Robert?)

Herbert and Joyce Whiteman "To the Wild Goose Tea Room came the Wild Goose parson"

Arthur H. Beaty

Elizabeth Smith "Beneath this roof dwelleth true hospitality."

Harold and Linda McKinstry

The dinner was probably late August. Elizabeth soon returned to California. Alice, our little Mormon girl, who had faithfully tithed all summer, giving three dollars of her thirty dollar monthly income to her church, returned to Idaho. Before she left, we all hurried around frantically so our family could be ready to arrive in Casper about the time school opened. That summer was really the last of our actual homesteading life and [I] am so glad it was a happy one.

We [spent] that school year in Casper. [We] moved to Denver in 1925. With three children to educate, we felt we must be near public schools.

Jeanne remembered and loved Jackson Hole and remembered something of our life there. Neal was too young to remember much of it and Stella too young to remember any of it. This is being written that they all may know something about it.

Epilogues from Linda and Stella

The reports of 1922 to 1924 are so brief that I am enclosing a few more facts, which may be of value.

This Jackson Hole report would have been impossible to write except for the letters written to Mother in those early days, which she saved. My sister brought them to me.

[It would also have been impossible] without Mac's help in remembering and his doing all this huge amount of typing. Thanks to everyone.

In the summer of 1922, the U.S. government must have cancelled all rights of the Idaho company for transporting water from Two Ocean and Emma Matilda Lakes to Idaho. We believe they must have been working under a state permit at the time. Mac received word while working on the small dam at Two Ocean Lake. Since it ended the Idaho project, it also ended the main source of our income. Therefore Mac decided to teach at the Buffalo school the school year of 1922–1923.

Realizing Jeanne was not getting first-grade work during the brief attendance at Elk school, I sent for the first grade courses of Calvert School. She completed that during the winter so was more than ready for the second grade in the Jackson school that fall.

After opening the Tea Room during the summer of 1923, [I went with] the children to Jackson in time for the fall opening of school. We all planned to spend the winter there since the new arrival was due in October. Mac did not go early in September and even taught a few weeks at the Buffalo school until the new teacher could take over. He then quit to do some promised surveying for the ranchers, arriving in Jackson by the time Stella and I arrived home from the hospital. That was probably about October 22.

After spending the winter in Jackson, Mac returned to the Lozier house fairly early in the spring, but the children and I had to wait until Jeanne's

Added by Linda at an unknown date.

school year was over. That summer, 1924, was our final year on a ranch and at the Tea Room. As soon as people learned we were leaving for Casper at the end of summer and were selling our ranch equipment and furniture, there were plenty of buyers and much was sold early. Most of the livestock except needed cows had been sold.

We arrived in Casper in time for school. Neal entered kindergarten, being five years old, and Jeanne went into third grade. Mac worked for the Watts Hardy Dairy Company and the meeting with Fred Watts was the beginning of a long friendship with Fred and Kate.

That summer we returned to Jackson Hole briefly to clear up a few last things. The winter we had left for Idaho Falls, we had packed a trunk with some wedding gifts not usable in Jackson Hole, keepsakes and treasures of former days in Washington and even of our own early days. With the permission of Joe Markham, the trunk had been stored in the USRS [U.S. Reclamation Service] warehouse and, [as we did] not have use for it until permanently settled, had remained stored. Inasmuch as Mac did not want his surveying equipment in Casper before leaving for there, he had stored his transit with tripod and all necessary drafting equipment at the USRS storehouse. When we returned to Moran that summer (1925), we learned that [the] Jackson Hole fire had dealt us a final blow. A devastating fire had swept the storehouse and everything [was] destroyed. We were making not only a final break with homesteading but had also lost most of the tangible mementos of our earlier life. Arriving in Denver, we stayed with the Balls a week or more and then were settled in a home of our own. Neal started in first grade at Edison and Jeanne in fourth grade. We were starting city life again.

Mac says we did not sell our ranch until a year or so after returning to Denver. The deal was handled by Robert Miller of Jackson, [the] former forest supervisor, or Harry Wagner. Of course the Rockefeller interests bought it. We understood they were buying all the deeded land in the reserve, returning it to the government, getting the land back in its primitive state as quickly as possible. They did their work well. Within only a few years, tourists driving over the old road of lower Yellowstone would never [have] dreamed that the land was formerly dotted with many little flourishing homesteads. Each had its warmly built log ranch house with barns and other buildings all of logs. A few years later the exact locations were most difficult to find. The Rockefeller interests succeeded well in their determination to quickly remove all evidence of former habitation.

Looking back from my very advanced age of ninety-one, I am still amazed that a city bred New England girl and a Red River Valley man from [the] North Dakota plains could adjust so quickly to mountain living and the totally new demands of homesteading. But they could and we did. Those years, with all their ups and downs of ranch life, are the never to be forgotten ones and we are glad we had them.

signed: Linda McKinstry

Added by Linda in 1977.

In 2015 Jackson Hole Historical Society and Museum Executive Director Sharon Kahin, interviewed the McKinstrys' youngest daughter Stella to complete some of the family's story.

Stella mentioned that the McKinstry brand in Wyoming was the KIN and the homestead was called the KIN Ranch. They maintained that brand in Colorado.

According to Stella, Linda and Mac McKinstry left Jackson Hole in September 1924 because homesteading in Jackson Hole was a struggle and because uncertainly about the future extension of Yellowstone National Park made further development of their land and water a questionable proposition. They also wanted better schools for their three children.

They moved to Casper, Wyoming, but they "couldn't stand the smell of oil," so after a year they moved to Denver where Mac was in partnership with Max Ball, a friend since his days in Washington, D.C. Together they started the Colorado Fur Farm to raise silver foxes and other fur-bearing animals in the foothills outside of Denver near Rollinsville. The high altitude and cold weather helped produce beautiful furs. The family lived in Denver where the fur farm had an office in the First National Bank building.

Summary of a 2015 interview with Stella McKinstry.

The children attended school in Denver; however, every weekend and in the summer they were at the farm where they had horses and were able to enjoy some of the rural lifestyle they had left behind in Wyoming. Mac managed and then owned the fur business until about 1940.

Linda taught night school in Denver and tested high altitude recipes for a baking company, possibly Betty Crocker. Stella remembered that Linda often rode a street car to work with a bowl of dough on her lap. Linda's recipes appeared in the company's cookbook for high altitude cooking.

Around 1939, they sold the fur farm, retaining the cottage and surrounding land which is still in the family. They then bought a ranch on Buckhorn Creek outside of Fort Collins, Colorado, and moved the family there where they were still able to enjoy riding horses and the outdoors while Mac worked in financial businesses. They lived on the ranch for five years and later moved into Fort Collins.

Stella said that her mother especially loved homesteading and had only fond memories of their time in Jackson Hole near Moran, Wyoming.

❧ INDEX ❧

NOTES ON THE PRODUCTION OF THE BOOK

The text is set in type from the Adobe Garamond family
with Myria Pro by Adobe as a secondary font.
Display type is Skitch from the Yellow Design Studio
and Old Book from the International Type Company

The text is printed on sixty-pound Tessaroni White,
a white, acid-free, recycled paper.
The book is covered with ten-point stock,
printed in four colors, and coated with matte film lamination,
by Versa Book Manufacturing.